拯救我的出国考试写作系列

SAVING
MY WRITING
TEST OF ENGLISH

拯救
我的SAT写作

Essay

SAT

Saving My SAT Essay

姜伟生◎编著

科学出版社
北京

内 容 简 介

  SAT考试分为三个项目：写作、数学和批判性阅读。SAT写作是SAT考试的第一部分。本书介绍SAT写作的结构和话题分类，并提供SAT写作的素材。本书的SAT写作素材分为8个主题，包括"商业与发明""哲学与文学""科学与探索""政治与权力""社会与变革""艺术与流行""音乐与演艺"和"挑战与竞技"，以上每个话题为一个章节，每个章节包括名人事例和他们脍炙人口的名言。本书最后列有人物的索引和重要历史事件表，便于读者查阅。

图书在版编目(CIP)数据

拯救我的SAT写作 / 姜伟生编著. —北京：科学出版社，2013
（拯救我的出国考试写作系列）

ISBN 978-7-03-037361-8

 I. ①拯… II. ①姜… III. ①英语–写作–高等学校–入学考试–美国–自学参考资料 IV. ①H315

中国版本图书馆CIP数据核字（2013）第083736号

责任编辑：阎 莉 常春娥 / 责任校对：胡小洁
责任印制：张 倩 / 封面设计：无极书装

联系电话：010-6401 9007 / 电子邮箱：changchune@mail.sciencep.com

科 学 出 版 社 出版
北京东黄城根北街16号
邮政编码：100717
http://www.sciencep.com
双青印刷厂 印刷
科学出版社发行　各地新华书店经销

*

2013年4月第 一 版　　开本：890×1240　1/16
2015年2月第二次印刷　　印张：17
字数：730 000

定价：40.00元
（如有印装质量问题，我社负责调换）

一本提供
人物和历史素材的
SAT 写作辅导书

SAVING
MY SAT
ESSAY

谨以此书献给我的父亲母亲

To My Parents

前言
PREFACE

  参加 SAT（Scholastic Assessment Test）考试的中国大陆学生在写作部分遇到的最大问题，不是没有思路，而是"有话说不出来"。在教学的过程中，笔者发现在中国以母语汉语完成基础教育的学员，可以深刻地分析思考 SAT 写作部分的话题；但是答题时很难用英语表达自己的想法，特别是陈述一些常用的例证。比如，谈到"竞争与合作"这个话题，学员们几乎都知道"teamwork""cooperation"等关键词，但是想用"达尔文"和他的"适者生存"观点来证明自己的观点时，却发现自己拼写不出来"达尔文（Charles Darwin）"和"适者生存（Survival of the fittest）"的英文。为了帮助考生更便捷地复习 SAT 写作，作者在本书中收录整理近百位常用名人的事例和他们脍炙人口的名言。建议读者在使用本书语料时，用自己的语言改写事例。本书在写作基础讲解方面着墨很少，读者可以参考作者另外一本拙著《拯救我的 TOEFL 写作》，学习选词、造句、语法、谋篇布局等基础写作技巧。感谢加拿大多伦多新东方 SAT 班学员，是你们各种富有启发性的疑问让我更加深入地学习和思考。

  最后，感谢爸爸妈妈的爱和支持。儿子爱你们。

姜伟生

2013 年 2 月

使用本书

USE THIS BOOK

针对 SAT Essay 备考，本书为读者提供：

- ☐ 简明的应试策略及写作指导；
- ☐ 8 大类共 92 个人物的历史素材；
- ☐ 近 90 组名人名言；
- ☐ 历年 SAT Essay 的题目归类。

本书主要内容介绍如下：

- ☐ 第一章（Chapter 1）是有关 SAT 写作方法的简介；
- ☐ 第二章（Chapter 2）到第九章（Chapter 9）提供人物史料。

对于多数中国本土的 SAT 考生，人物史料是一块重要的短板。考生很难在短时间内阅读大量的人物传记并总结出自己需要的写作素材。针对这一问题，本书为读者总结出如下 8 个大类的人物素材。

- ☐ 商业与发明 Business and Invention
- ☐ 哲学与文学 Philosophy and Literature
- ☐ 科学与探索 Science and Exploration
- ☐ 政治与权力 Politics and Power
- ☐ 社会与变革 Society and Reform
- ☐ 艺术与流行 Art and Fashion
- ☐ 音乐与演艺 Music and Performing
- ☐ 挑战与竞技 Challenge and Competition

请读者注意以下几点：

- ☐ 在阅读本书人物史料时，能够将重要内容改写成自己的文字，用铅笔写在 "Paraphrase the Story in Your Own Words" 栏目里，并且背熟；
- ☐ 限于篇幅，对于文章的发展与结构、句子的构建、措辞、语法及常用表达等内容，请读者参考本书作者的一本拙著《拯救我的 TOEFL 写作》（*Saving My TOEFL Writing*）；
- ☐ 有关 "Critical thinking" 和 "Complex thinking" 方面的内容，感兴趣的读者可以参考本书作者的另一本拙著《拯救我的新 GRE 写作》（*Saving My Revised GRE Issue*）；
- ☐ 为避免抄袭嫌疑，使用本书的写作素材时，读者需要对其合理引用或变换措辞。

若想了解更多的人物素材，推荐读者阅读 Britannica Guide 系列中的以下几本图书：

- *The 100 Most Influential Scientists;*
- *The Ideas That Made the Modern World : The People, Philosophy, and History of the Enlightenment;*
- *Inventions That Changed the Modern World;*
- *The 100 Most Influential World Leaders of All Time;*
- *The 100 Most Influential Painters & Sculptors;*
- *Explorers and Explorations That Changed the Modern World;*
- *The 100 Most Influential Women of All Time;*
- *The 100 Most Influential Writers of All Time.*

目录

CONTENTS

Chapter 1

SAT Essay 简介
SAT ESSAY INTRODUCTION

Chapter 2

商业与发明
BUSINESS AND INVENTION

Chapter 3

哲学与文学
PHILOSOPHY AND LITERATURE

Chapter 4

科学与探索
SCIENCE AND EXPLORATION

Chapter 5

政治与权力
POLITICS AND POWER

Chapter 6

社会与变革
SOCIETY AND REFORM

Chapter 7

艺术与流行
ART AND FASHION

Chapter 8

音乐与演艺
MUSIC AND PERFORMING

Chapter 9

挑战与竞技
CHALLENGE AND COMPETITION

Chapter 10

附录
APPENDIX

Chapter 1
SAT Essay 简介
SAT Essay Introduction

本 章 目 录

SAT 写作介绍
SAT Essay Introduction

SAT 考试的全称为 "学术评估测试"（Scholastic Assessment Test），是美国大学入学的重要衡量标准之一。SAT 考试共分三个项目：写作、数学和批判性阅读。每个项目各占 800 分，SAT 考试的总分为 2400 分，考试总时间约 3 小时 45 分钟。

SAT Essay 是 SAT 考试写作中的第一部分，也是整个 SAT 考试的第一部分。写作项目的另外一部分是语法考试。

Essay 题签有一页（图 1.1），主要有两部分内容，如图中所示的 A、B 两部分。A 部分主要涉及考试的基本要求等内容。B 部分为 Essay 命题作文的考试题目。

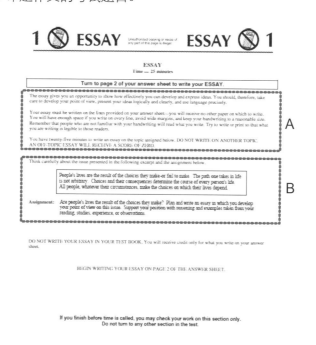

图 1.1　SAT 考试 Essay 部分的题签页

A 部分的英文和下文的出入很小：

> The essay gives you an opportunity to show how effectively you can develop and express ideas. You should, therefore, take care to develop your point of view, present your ideas logically and clearly, and use language precisely.
>
> Your essay must be written on the lines provided on your answer sheet—you will receive no other paper on which to write. You will have enough space if you write on every line, avoid wide margins, and keep your handwriting to a reasonable size. Remember that people who are not familiar with your handwriting will read what you write. Try to write or print so that what you are writing is legible to those readers.
>
> You have twenty-five minutes to write an essay on the topic assigned below. DO NOT WRITE ON ANOTHER TOPIC. AN OFF-TOPIC ESSAY WILL RECEIVE A SCORE OF ZERO.

A 部分的主要内容如下：

- ☐　考生写作时需要展开观点论述；

- ☐　考生写作时需要注意文章要符合逻辑、表达清楚、用语准确；

☐ 考生答题时，必须用铅笔写在指定的两张答题纸上，并且没有多余的作文答题纸；

☐ 书写时，字母间距不要过大，字迹不要潦草；

☐ 考试时间为 25 分钟，用铅笔答题；

☐ 请注意，SAT Essay 为命题作文，跑题的文章将直接被判零分。

考生考试时，不需要花时间阅读这部分内容。

B 部分的形式类似以下方框中的内容。这部分主要有两部分内容：文摘和作文题目。

Think carefully about the issue presented in the following excerpt and assignment below:

Winning does not require people to be against someone else; people can reach their goals through cooperation just as well as they can through competition. Winning is not always the result of selfish individualism. People achieve happiness by cooperating with others to increase the happiness of all, rather than by winning at others' expense. Ours is not a world in which the price of one person's happiness is someone else's unhappiness.

Adapted from Gilbert Brim, *Ambition*

Assignment: When some people win, must others lose, or are there situations in which everyone wins?

Plan and write an essay in which you develop your point of view on this issue. Support your position with reasoning and examples taken from your reading, studies, experience, or observation.

文摘（excerpt）一般是和作文题目相关的一段文章，作用是给考生一定的思路。这里请考生注意，对于大部分在中国接受教育的高中程度的学生来说，想把这部分内容读清楚是有一定难度的，这会浪费宝贵的时间。另外，这部分内容通常会引起先入为主的思维定势，不利于文章写作。考生可以根据自己的能力，决定是否花时间阅读这段内容。

Don't ignore the excerpt. You may find some phrases that you can use in your essay. Referring back to the excerpt by paraphrasing it or using some words from it can be an effective technique.

Winning does not require people to be against someone else; people can reach their goals through cooperation just as well as they can through competition. Winning is not always the result of selfish individualism. People achieve happiness by cooperating with others to increase the happiness of all, rather than by winning at others' expense. Ours is not a world in which the price of one person's happiness is someone else's unhappiness.

作文题目（Assignment），是这部分最重要的信息。前文已经提到，SAT Essay 部分为命题作文，跑题就会被判为零分。因此，考生需要将主要精力放在理解"Assignment"上，并且思考如何对文章展开论述。本书的附录给出了历年 SAT Essay 的主要题目分类，请考生认真研读作文的题目要求。

Assignment: When some people win, must others lose, or are there situations in which everyone wins?

Essay 部分的答题纸有两页（图 1.2），每页答题纸的版面略小于普通的 A4 纸。

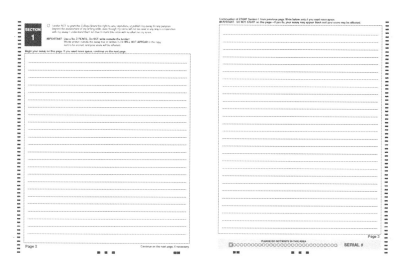

图 1.2　SAT 考试 Essay 部分的答题纸样例

SAT Essay 部分通常由两名教师阅卷，每名教师的打分区间是 0~6 分，最高分是 6 分。两名教师打分之和的区间为 0~12 分，最高分 12 分。当两名阅卷教师的打分差超过 1 分时，第三名阅卷人将会介入打分。

满分（6 分）作文的要求如下：

An essay in this category is outstanding, demonstrating clear and consistent mastery, although it may have a few minor errors. A typical essay

□ effectively and insightfully develops a point of view on the issue and demonstrates outstanding critical thinking, using clearly appropriate examples, reasons, and other evidence to support its position

□ is well organized and clearly focused, demonstrating clear coherence and smooth progression of ideas

□ exhibits skillful use of language, using a varied, accurate, and apt vocabulary

□ demonstrates meaningful variety in sentence structure

□ is free of most errors in grammar, usage, and mechanics

从以上评分标准可以看出 SAT Essay 主要强调四个方面的技能：思考、文章发展、文章组织和语言。

本书主要提供 SAT 的写作素材，想要了解更多有关文章发展、组织和语言等方面的内容，请读者参考本书作者的一本拙著《拯救我的托福写作》（*Saving My TOEFL Writing*）。

有关 "Critical thinking" 和 "Complex thinking" 方面的内容，感兴趣的读者可以参考本书作者的另一本拙著《拯救我的新 GRE 写作》（*Saving My Revised GRE Issue*）。

SAT Essay 结构

SAT ESSAY STRUCTURE

比较常见的 SAT 结构是"1+3+1"，即开头一段，正文三段，结尾一段。参考下图的结构。

Opening Paragraph	Thesis Statement	Summary of Examples (optional)
Body Paragraph A	Topic Sentence A	Supporting Evidence (Development)
Body Paragraph B	Topic Sentence B	Supporting Evidence (Development)
Body Paragraph C	Topic Sentence C	Supporting Evidence (Development)
Concluding Paragraph	Reminder of Thesis Statement	Final Remarks (optional)

开头段落（Opening Paragraph）通常包括两部分内容："Thesis Statement"和"Summary of Examples"。如果考生善于写"引子（Hook）"，在文章最开头加一段"引子"也是可以的。

- ☐　"Thesis Statement"是文章的中心主旨句，是文章开头必不可少的部分。"Thesis Statement"通常为一句话，一般是开头段落的最后一句。"Thesis Statement"平衡观点，对文章内容进行宏观概括。

- ☐　"Summary of Examples"是对文章中所用例子的总结，根据考生的习惯，这部分可以出现在开头段落，也可以出现在结尾段落。

正文段落（Body Paragraph）通常包括两部分内容："Topic Sentence"和"Supporting Evidence"。一篇作文通常有 3 个正文段落。

- ☐　"Topic Sentence"是段落的中心句，SAT Essay 考试的每段"Topic Sentence"通常是对本段采用的人物史料的总结。

- ☐　"Supporting Evidence"是对人物史料的细节展开，用来支撑文章的核心观点。

结尾段落（Concluding Paragraph）包括两部分内容："Reminder of Thesis Statement"和"Final Remarks"。

- ☐　"Reminder of Thesis Statement"重申文章主旨，需要注意的是这句话中的关键词一定要和"Thesis Statement"的关键词有所区分。

- ☐　"Final Remarks"是文末的评论性的结语，可以是"做预测""提出解决办法""提出文章讨论的现实意义"或"号召行动"等内容。当然，也可以总结文章中的人物史料例证。

具体的文章结构请参考以下两篇例文。

- 【文章主旨句】*Learning the lessons taught by failure is a sure route to success.*【总结文章例证】*In the fields of politics, business, and personal struggle, we could find compelling examples that support this thesis.*

- 【段落中心句】*The United States, the first great democracy of the modern world, is also one of the best examples of a success achieved by studying and learning from earlier failures.*【人物史料细节支撑】*After just five years of living under the Articles of Confederation, which established the United States of America as a single country for the first time, the states realized that they needed a new document and a new more powerful government. In 1786, the Annapolis convention was convened. The result, three years later, was the Constitution, which created a more powerful central government while also maintaining the integrity of the states. By learning from the failure of the Articles, the founding fathers created the founding document of a country that has become both the most powerful country in the world and a beacon of democracy.*

- 【段落中心句】*The Internet search engine company, Google Inc., has suffered few setbacks since it went into business in the late 1990s.*【人物史料细节支撑】*Google has succeeded by studying the failures of other companies in order to help it innovate its technology and business model. Google identified and solved the problem of assessing the quality of search results by using the number of links pointing to a page as an indicator of the number of people who find the page valuable. Suddenly, Google's search results became far more accurate and reliable than those from other companies, and now Google's dominance in the field of Internet search is almost absolute.*

- 【段落中心句】*The example of Rod Johnson's success as an entrepreneur in the recruiting field also shows how effective learning from mistakes and failure can be.*【人物史料细节支撑】*Rather than accept his failure after being laid off, Johnson decided to study it. After a month of research, Johnson realized that his failure to find a new job resulted primarily from the inefficiency of the local job placement agencies, not from his own deficiencies. A month later, Johnson created Johnson Staffing to correct this weakness in the job placement sector. Today Johnson Staffing is the largest job placement agency in South Carolina, and is in the process of expanding into a national corporation.*

- *Failure is often seen as embarrassing, something to be denied and hidden.*【总结文章例证，重申文章主旨句】***But as the examples of the U.S. Constitution , Google, and Rod Johnson prove, if an individual, organization, or even a nation is strong enough to face and study its failure, then that failure can become a powerful teacher.***【提供解决方法】*The examples of history and business demonstrate that failure can be the best catalyst of success, but only if people have the courage to face it head on.*

- 【引子】*"Money makes the world go round." Sadly, this famous quotation frequently rings all-too-true.*【首先让步，后阐述文章主旨句】*Though many people, in their personal lives, seem driven by benevolent qualities such as personal satisfaction, altruism, and even love, these same individuals often allow greed and recognition to dominate their professional existence.*

- 【段落中心句】*Ken Lay, the former Chief Executive Officer of Enron, is one individual who was definitely driven by his desire for wealth.* *In order to boost the Enron stock price and, in turn, make millions of dollars for himself, Lay allegedly lied about the company's profits and concealed its debts. Once these fraudulent activities were made public, Enron's stock became virtually worthless and the company had to file for bankruptcy protection. Unfortunately, Enron employees were the chief casualty of the scandal. As a result of Ken Lay's greed, most Enron employees lost their jobs, while others lost almost all of their savings.*

- 【段落中心句】*Christopher Columbus is a second person whose unyielding craving for riches and recognition dominated his life.* *In 1492, after adopting the title "admiral of the ocean seas," Columbus set sail for China and India in search of silver and gold. Upon his arrival in the "New World", Columbus treated the native populations not as humans to be respected but as slaves to further his wealth and power. In his defense, Columbus was acting similarly to many other explorers of his time. However, this does not alter the fact that he was a man for whom wealth and power were paramount.*

- 【段落中心句】*The doctor in John Steinbeck's novel The Pearl is a final example of a person driven by* monetary gain. In *The Pearl*, a small child named Coyotito is bitten by a scorpion. However, the doctor refuses to treat Coyotito because Kino, Coyotito's father, has no money. Later, however, after Kino finds a beautiful pearl, the doctor is more than happy to treat Coyotito, thinking that Kino will pay for the medical services with the pearl.

■ 【重申文章主旨句】***The drive for wealth and recognition is a significant component of human nature.*** 【总结文章例证】*As the examples of Ken Lay, Christopher Columbus, and the doctor from The Pearl demonstrate, financial gain as a motivator often trumps personal satisfaction.* 【预测未来】*We can only hope that, as people continue to evolve, love, happiness, and a sense of personal fulfillment will replace individual riches as humanity's ultimate goal.*

SAT 写作话题分类

SAT ESSAY TOP TOPICS

SAT Essay Topic 1. 成功与失败

【2009.06】Think carefully about the issue presented in the following excerpt and assignment below:

Winning does not require people to be against someone else; people can reach their goals through cooperation just as well as they can through competition. Winning is not always the result of selfish individualism. People achieve happiness by cooperating with others to increase the happiness of all, rather than by winning at others' expense. Ours is not a world in which the price of one person's happiness is someone else's unhappiness.

Adapted from Gilbert Brim, *Ambition*

Assignment: When some people win, must others lose, or are there situations in which everyone wins?

Plan and write an essay in which you develop your point of view on this issue. Support your position with reasoning and examples taken from your reading, studies, experience, or observations.

【2009.11】Think carefully about the issue presented in the following excerpt and assignment below:

No matter how much people try and how much they believe in themselves, everyone encounters situations in which it is impossible to succeed. People are often advised, "Never give up," but sometimes, when it seems as though success will not be achieved, they should stop trying, learn from the experience, and move on.

Adapted from Phyllis George, *Never Say Never*

Assignment: Is it better for people to stop trying when they feel certain they will not succeed?

Plan and write an essay in which you develop your point of view on this issue. Support your position with reasoning and examples taken from your reading, studies, experience, or observations.

【2008.12】Think carefully about the issue presented in the following excerpt and assignment below:

The biggest difference between people who succeed at any difficult undertaking and those who do not is not ability but persistence. Many extremely talented people give up when obstacles arise. After all, who wants to face failure? It is often said about highly successful people that they are just ordinary individuals who kept on trying, who did not give up.

Adapted from Tom Morris, *True Success: A New Philosophy of Excellence*

Assignment: Is persistence more important than ability in determining a person's success?

Plan and write an essay in which you develop your point of view on this issue. Support your position with reasoning and examples taken from your reading, studies, experience, or observations.

【2008.5】Think carefully about the issue presented in the following excerpt and assignment below:

From talent contests to the Olympics to the Nobel and Pulitzer prizes, we constantly seek to reward those who are "number one." This emphasis on recognizing the winner creates the impression that other competitors, despite working hard and well, have lost. In many cases, however, the difference between the winner and the losers is slight. The wrong person may even be selected as the winner. Awards and prizes merely distract us from valuable qualities possessed by others besides the winners.

Assignment: Do people place too much emphasis on winning?

Plan and write an essay in which you develop your point of view on this issue. Support your position with reasoning and examples taken from your reading, studies, experience, or observations.

【2006.10】Think carefully about the issue presented in the following excerpt and assignment below:

While some people promote competition as the only way to achieve success, others emphasize the power of cooperation. Intense rivalry at work or play or engaging in competition involving ideas or skills may indeed drive people either to avoid failure or to achieve important victories. In a complex world, however, cooperation is much more likely to produce significant, lasting accomplishments.

Assignment: Do people achieve more success by cooperation than by competition?

Plan and write an essay in which you develop your point of view on this issue. Support your position with reasoning and examples taken from your reading, studies, experience, or observation.

【2010.05】Think carefully about the issue presented in the following excerpt and assignment below:

In business, the term "personal brand" describes how companies define themselves and differentiate their products from those of other companies. People, too, are often advised to develop a kind of personal brand or style—to make themselves stand out from other people by developing unique characteristics. Nowadays, people who want to be successful in school, at work, or in their personal relationships must emphasize their differences from their peers in the same way that companies emphasize their differences from their competitors.

Assignment: Do people succeed by emphasizing their differences from other people?

Plan and write an essay in which you develop your point of view on this issue. Support your position with reasoning and examples taken from your reading, studies, experience, or observations.

SAT Essay
Topic 2. 个体与集体

【2008.11】 Think carefully about the issue presented in the following excerpt and assignment below:

Independent people—those who rely on themselves rather than on others—get what they want through their own efforts. Interdependent people combine their efforts with the efforts of others to achieve their goals. To be most effective, people need to be interdependent. People who do not think and act interdependently may achieve individual success, but they will not be good leaders or team players.

Adapted from Stephen R. Covey, *The Seven Habits of Highly Effective People*

Assignment: Is it necessary for people to combine their efforts with those of others in order to be most effective?

Plan and write an essay in which you develop your point of view on this issue. Support your position with reasoning and examples taken from your reading, studies, experience, or observations.

【2011.05】Think carefully about the issue presented in the following excerpt and the assignment below.

Many people think that success is impossible without help and support from others. They believe that even the strongest and most successful leaders need advisers to define their goals, and followers to carry out their plans. Real success, however, cannot be claimed by those who need others to solve their problems and help them confront obstacles. Only those whose accomplishments are truly their own can claim to be successful.

Assignment: Is real success achieved only by people who accomplish goals and solve problems on their own?

Plan and write an essay in which you develop your point of view on this issue. Support your position with reasoning and examples taken from your reading, studies, experience, or observations.

【2008.6】Think carefully about the issue presented in the following excerpt and assignment below:

Much of what we do has become so complex that most activities require groups or teams of people to perform them. However, although groups are useful for some purposes, for other purposes they can be worse than useless. It is important to focus on what individuals can be and do, since focusing exclusively on groups and teams becomes counterproductive.

Adapted from Stanley M. Herman, *A Force of Ones*

Assignment: Are the actions of individuals more valuable than the actions of groups or teams?

Plan and write an essay in which you develop your point of view on this issue. Support your position with reasoning and examples taken from your reading, studies, experience, or observations.

【2009.10】Think carefully about the issue presented in the following excerpt and assignment below:

Call it a clan, call it a network, call it a family. Whatever you call it, whoever you are, you need one. You need one because you are human. You didn't come from nowhere. Before you, around you, and, presumably, after you, there are others. Even if you live alone and even if your solitude is by your own choice, you still cannot do without a network or a family.

Adapted from Jane Howard, *All Happy Clans Are Alike: In Search of the Good Family*

Assignment: Does everyone, even people who choose to live alone, need a network or family?

Plan and write an essay in which you develop your point of view on this issue. Support your position with reasoning and examples taken from your reading, studies, experience, or observations.

SAT Essay
Topic 3. 独立思考

【2009.12】Think carefully about the issue presented in the following excerpt and assignment below:

People are often criticized for working out their own ideas before learning all that others have discovered about a problem or subject. But those people are right; it is possible to know too much, especially at first. The time for thorough inquiry and extensive research is later, after you have made your own discoveries and come to your own conclusions.

Adapted from Charles Horton Cooley, *Life and the Student*

Assignment: Is it better for people to work out their own ideas on a problem or issue before learning how others have approached it?

Plan and write an essay in which you develop your point of view on this issue. Support your position with reasoning and examples taken from your reading, studies, experience, or observations.

【2007. 05】 Think carefully about the issue presented in the following excerpt and assignment below:

We do not take the time to determine right from wrong. Reflecting on the difference between right and wrong is hard work. It is so much easier to follow the crowd, going along with what is popular rather than risking the disapproval of others by voicing an objection of any kind.

Adapted from Stephen J. Carter, *Integrity*

Assignment: Is it always best to determine one's own views of right and wrong, or can we benefit from following the crowd?

Plan and write an essay in which you develop your point of view on this issue. Support your position with reasoning and examples taken from your reading, studies, experience, or observations.

【2006.12】 Think carefully about the issue presented in the following excerpt and assignment below:

In order to be the most productive and successful people that we are capable of being, we must be willing to ignore the opinions of others. It is only when we are completely indifferent to others' opinions of us—when we are not concerned about how others think of us—that we can achieve our most important goals.

Assignment: Are people more likely to be productive and successful when they ignore the opinions of others?

Plan and write an essay in which you develop your point of view on this issue. Support your position with reasoning and examples taken from your reading, studies, experience, or observations.

SAT Essay
Topic 4. 科技与社会

【2008.05】 Think carefully about the issue presented in the following excerpt and assignment below:

Technological advances have freed society from tiresome labor, such as washing clothes by hand, hauling heavy loads, and walking long distances, and have given people increased access to information and entertainment. Yet, when given a choice, many people still resist using modern conveniences. There must be something to be gained from not using technology.

Assignment: Are there benefits to be gained from avoiding the use of modern technology, even when using it would make life easier?

Plan and write an essay in which you develop your point of view on this issue. Support your position with reasoning and examples taken from your reading, studies, experience, or observations.

【2009.05】 Think carefully about the issue presented in the following excerpt and assignment below:

Thanks to great advancements in technology, we live today in a world in which knowledge is more readily available to greater numbers of people than ever before in history. Having more and better technology, however, has not made people wiser or more understanding. Indeed, people are so overloaded with information today that they have become less, rather than more, able to make sense of the world around them than our ancestors ever were.

Assignment: Has today's abundance of information only made it more difficult for us to understand the world around us?

Plan and write an essay in which you develop your point of view on this issue. Support your position with reasoning and examples taken from your reading, studies, experience, or observations.

【2009.12】 Think carefully about the issue presented in the following excerpt and assignment below:

An Internet phone service is offering unlimited free telephone calls for anyone who signs up. There is only one catch: the company will use software to listen to customers' phone conversations and then send customers advertisements based on what they have been talking about. For example, if they talk about movies with their friends, advertisements for movies will appear on their computer screens. Commentators have voiced concern about customers' giving up their privacy in exchange for phone service.

Assignment: Should people give up their privacy in exchange for convenience or free services?

Plan and write an essay in which you develop your point of view on this issue. Support your position with reasoning and examples taken from your reading, studies, experience, or observations.

【2007.06】 Think carefully about the issue presented in the following excerpt and assignment below:

The advancements that have been made over the past hundred years or more are too numerous to count. But has there been progress? Some people would say that the vast number of advancements tells us we have made progress. Others, however, disagree, saying that more is not necessarily better and that real progress—in politics, literature, the arts, science and technology, or any other field—can be achieved only when an advancement truly improves the quality of our lives.

Assignment: Have modern advancements truly improved the quality of people's lives?

Plan and write an essay in which you develop your point of view on this issue. Support your position with reasoning and examples taken from your reading, studies, experience, or observations.

SAT Essay Topic 5. 目标

【2009.01】 Think carefully about the issue presented in the following excerpt and assignment below:

The history of human achievement is filled with stories of people who persevere, refusing to give up in the struggle to meet their goals. Artists and scientists, for instance, may struggle for years without any apparent progress or reward before they finally succeed. However, it is important to recognize that perseverance does not always yield beneficial results.

Adapted from Robert H. Lauer and Jeanette C. Lauer, *Watersheds*

Assignment: Is striving to achieve a goal always the best course of action, or should people give up if they are not making progress?

Plan and write an essay in which you develop your point of view on this issue. Support your position with reasoning and examples taken from your reading, studies, experience, or observations.

【2009.11】 Think carefully about the issue presented in the following excerpt and assignment below:

Some people ruin their chances of achieving success or refrain from attaining a goal because they have learned that success is selfish. But they should not feel guilty about trying to achieve their own goals. People who act on their inner desires—their greatest wishes and ambitions—only make their own and other people's lives better and are more likely to benefit society. Imagine how much better the world would be if everyone could be happy and fulfilled.

Adapted from Sheri O. Zampelli, *From Sabotage to Success*

Assignment: Do society and other people benefit when individuals pursue their own goals?

Plan and write an essay in which you develop your point of view on this issue. Support your position with reasoning and examples taken from your reading, studies, experience, or observations.

【2008.01】 Think carefully about the issue presented in the following excerpt and assignment below:

Often we see people who persist in trying to achieve a particular goal, even when all the evidence indicates that they will be unlikely to achieve it. When they succeed, we consider them courageous for having overcome impossible obstacles. But when they fail, we think of them as headstrong, foolhardy, and bent on self-destruction. To many people, great effort is only worthwhile when it results in success.

Adapted from Gilbert Brim, *"Ambition"*

Assignment: Is the effort involved in pursuing any goal valuable, even if the goal is not reached?

Plan and write an essay in which you develop your point of view on this issue. Support your position with reasoning and examples taken from your reading, studies, experience, or observations.

【2007.03】 Think carefully about the issue presented in the following excerpt and assignment below:

It is easy to imagine that events and experiences in our lives will be perfect, but no matter how good something turns out to be, it can never live up to our expectations. Reality never matches our imaginations. For that reason, we should make sure our plans and goals are modest and attainable. We are much better off when reality surpasses our expectations and something turns out better than we thought it would.

Assignment: Is it best to have low expectations and to set goals we are sure of achieving?

Plan and write an essay in which you develop your point of view on this issue. Support your position with reasoning and examples taken from your reading, studies, experience, or observations.

SAT Essay Topic 6. 创新与守旧

【2008.06】 Think carefully about the issue presented in the following excerpt and assignment below:

A society composed of men and women who are not bound by convention—in other words, they do not act according to what others say or do—is far more lively than one in which all people behave alike. When each person's character is developed individually and differences of opinion are acceptable, it is beneficial to interact with new people because they are not mere replicas of those whom one has already met.

Adapted from Bertrand Russell, *The Conquest of Happiness*

Assignment: Is it better for society when people act as individuals rather than copy the ideas and opinions of others?

Plan and write an essay in which you develop your point of view on this issue. Support your position with reasoning and examples taken from your reading, studies, experience, or observations.

【2007.10】 Think carefully about the issue presented in the following excerpt and assignment below:

We value uniqueness and originality, but it seems that everywhere we turn, we are surrounded by ideas and things that are copies or even copies of copies. Writers, artists, and musicians seek new ideas for paintings, books, songs, and movies, but many sadly realize, "It's been done." The same is true for scientists, scholars, and businesspeople. Everyone wants to create something new, but at best we can hope only to repeat or imitate what has already been done.

Assignment: Can people ever be truly original?

Plan and write an essay in which you develop your point of view on this issue. Support your position with reasoning and examples taken from your reading, studies, experience, or observations.

 SAT Essay Topic 7. 选择与决定

【2009.01】 Think carefully about the issue presented in the following excerpt and assignment below:

People are taught that they should not go back on their decisions. In fact, our society supports the notion that to change your mind is evidence of weakness and unreliability, leading many people to say, "Once I decide, I decide!" But why do people make such a statement? If factors, feelings, and ideas change, isn't the ability to make a new decision evidence of flexibility, adaptability, and strength?

Adapted from Theodore I. Rubin, *Compassion and Self-Hate*

Assignment: Should people change their decisions when circumstances change, or is it best for them to stick with their original decisions?

Plan and write an essay in which you develop your point of view on this issue. Support your position with reasoning and examples taken from your reading, studies, experience, or observations.

【2009.05】 Think carefully about the issue presented in the following excerpt and assignment below:

Good decision making generally requires people to think carefully and logically and to pay attention to practical details. However, people who depend on their feelings and emotions to make important decisions are not likely to spend hours gathering information, making lists, considering all possible outcomes, and so forth. When comparing the advantages or disadvantages of one course of action to another, these people ask themselves, "What do my feelings tell me?"

Assignment: Should people let their feelings guide them when they make important decisions?

Plan and write an essay in which you develop your point of view on this issue. Support your position with reasoning and examples taken from your reading, studies, experience, or observations.

【2008.10】 Think carefully about the issue presented in the following excerpt and assignment below:

People usually assume that the quality of a decision is directly related to the time and effort that went into making it. We believe that we are always better off gathering as much information as possible and then spending as much time as possible analyzing that information. But there are times when making a quick judgment is the best thing to do. Decisions made quickly can be as good as decisions made slowly and cautiously.

Adapted from Malcolm Gladwell, Blink: *The Power of Thinking Without Thinking*

Assignment: Are decisions made quickly just as good as decisions made slowly and carefully?

Plan and write an essay in which you develop your point of view on this issue. Support your position with reasoning and examples taken from your reading, studies, experience, or observations.

SAT Essay
Topic 8. 历史与现在

【2008.05】 Think carefully about the issue presented in the following excerpt and assignment below:

Common sense suggests an obvious division between the past and present, between history and current events. In many cases, however, this boundary is not clear cut because earlier events are not locked away in the past. Events from history remain alive through people's memories and through books, films, and other media. For both individuals and groups, incidents from the past continue to influence the present—sometimes positively and sometimes negatively.

Assignment: Do incidents from the past continue to influence the present?

Plan and write an essay in which you develop your point of view on this issue. Support your position with reasoning and examples taken from your reading, studies, experience, or observations.

【2008.02】 Think carefully about the issue presented in the following excerpt and assignment below:

Newness has become our obsession. Novelty is more interesting to us than continuing with whatever is "tried and true." We discard the old so we can acquire the most recent model, the latest version, the newest and most improved formula. Often, we replace what is useful just because it is no longer new. Not only with material goods but also with cultural values, we prefer whatever is the latest trend.

Adapted from Gilbert Brim, *"Ambition"*

Assignment: Should people always prefer new things, ideas, or values to those of the past?

Plan and write an essay in which you develop your point of view on this issue. Support your position with reasoning and examples taken from your reading, studies, experience, or observations.

【2005.12】 Think carefully about the issue presented in the following excerpt and assignment below:

How valuable is history for our generation? On the surface this question is not as easy as it once might have been, for there is a widespread belief that history may no longer be relevant to modern life. We live, after all, in an age that appears very different from the world that came before us.

Adapted from Stephen Vaughn, *"History: Is it Relevant?"*

Assignment: Is knowledge of the past no longer useful for us today?

Plan and write an essay in which you develop your point of view on this issue. Support your position with reasoning and examples taken from your reading, studies, experience, or observations.

SAT Essay Topic 9. 名人与英雄

【2008.06】 Think carefully about the issue presented in the following excerpt and assignment below:

Most of us are convinced that fame brings happiness. Fame, it seems, is among the things people most desire. We believe that to be famous, for whatever reason, is to prove oneself and confirm that one matters in the world. And yet those who are already famous often complain of the terrible burden of fame. In fact, making the achievement of fame one's life goal involves commitments of time and effort that are usually wasted.

Adapted from Leszek Kolakowski, *Freedom, Fame, Lying and Betrayal: Essays on Everyday Life*

Assignment: Does fame bring happiness, or are people who are not famous more likely to be happy?

Plan and write an essay in which you develop your point of view on this issue. Support your position with reasoning and examples taken from your reading, studies, experience, or observations.

【2007.06】 Think carefully about the issue presented in the following excerpt and assignment below:

Heroes may seem old-fashioned today. Many people are cynical and seem to enjoy discrediting role models more than creating new ones or cherishing those they already have. Some people, moreover, object to the very idea of heroes, arguing that we should not exalt individuals who, after all, are only flesh and blood, just like the rest of us. But we desperately need heroes—to teach us, to captivate us through their words and deeds, to inspire us to greatness.

Adapted from Psychology Today, *"How To Be Great! What Does It Take To Be A Hero?"*

Assignment: Is there a value in celebrating certain individuals as heroes?

Plan and write an essay in which you develop your point of view on this issue. Support your position with reasoning and examples taken from your reading, studies, experience, or observations.

【2007.10】 Think carefully about the issue presented in the following excerpt and assignment below:

Having many admirers is one way to become a celerity, but it is not the way to become a hero. Heroes are self-made. Yet in our daily lives we see no difference between "celebrities" and "heroes". For this reason, we deprive ourselves of real role models. We should admire heroes—people who are famous because they are great—but not celebrities—people who simply seem great because they are famous.

Adapted from Daniel Boorstin, *The Image: A Guide to Pseudo-Events in America*

Assignment: Should we admire heroes but not celebrities?

Plan and write an essay in which you develop your point of view on this issue. Support your position with reasoning and examples taken from your reading, studies, experience, or observations.

SAT Essay Topic 10. 权威与质疑

【2009.06】 Think carefully about the issue presented in the following excerpt and assignment below:

So-called common sense determines what people should wear, whom they should respect, which rules they should follow, and what kind of life they should lead. Common sense is considered obvious and natural, too sensible to question. But people's common sense decisions may turn out to be wrong, even if they are thought to be correct according to the judgment of vast majorities of people.

Adapted from Alain de Botton, *The Consolations of Philosophy*

Assignment: Can common sense be trusted and accepted, or should it be questioned?

Plan and write an essay in which you develop your point of view on this issue. Support your position with reasoning and examples taken from your reading, studies, experience, or observations.

【2007.11】 Think carefully about the issue presented in the following excerpt and assignment below:

All people judge or criticize the ideas and actions of others. At times, these criticisms hurt or embarrass the people receiving them. Other criticisms seem to be intended to make the critics appear superior. And yet criticism is essential to our success as individuals and as a society.

Adapted from Ken Petress, *"Constructive Criticism: A Tool for Improvement"*

Assignment: Is criticism—judging or finding fault with the ideas and actions of others—essential for personal well-being and social progress?

Plan and write an essay in which you develop your point of view on this issue. Support your position with reasoning and examples taken from your reading, studies, experience, or observations.

【2007.11】 Think carefully about the issue presented in the following excerpt and assignment below:

Many people believe in the truth of certain "facts" or ideas merely because someone with authority has told them that these things are true. However, many facts and ideas once upheld by experts or authority figures have turned out to be false, including some that have been generally believed and accepted. Thus, people should have never assumed the truth of anything that they have not carefully examined or tested for themselves.

Assignment: Is it a mistake to believe something simply because an authority claims that it is true?

Plan and write an essay in which you develop your point of view on this issue. Support your position with reasoning and examples taken from your reading, studies, experience, or observations.

【2009.11】 Think carefully about the issue presented in the following excerpt and assignment below:

The philosopher John Locke once said that new ideas are usually opposed for no other reason than that people are unfamiliar with them. Locke thought people should not be suspicious of new ideas. He may have been right. After all, people once opposed the idea that the Earth is round. Still, people should not accept new ideas simply because they are new. It is foolish not to question new ideas.

Assignment: Should new ideas always be questioned?

Plan and write an essay in which you develop your point of view on this issue. Support your position with reasoning and examples taken from your reading, studies, experience, or observations.

SAT Essay Topic 11. 探索与发现

【2010.01】Think carefully about the issue presented in the following excerpt and assignment below:

Great discoveries often occur when a person explore the unknown, venturing far from what is familiar. But important breakthroughs—innovative solutions to difficult problems, for example—can also result when people take the time to look closely at their daily surroundings. In fact, the greatest discoveries often occur when people recognize in their familiar surroundings certain opportunities that others have overlooked or when people recognize that the way things have always been done is unjust or ineffective or unnecessary.

Assignment: Do people make the greatest discoveries by exploring what is unfamiliar to them or by paying close attention to what seems familiar?

Plan and write an essay in which you develop your point of view on this issue. Support your position with reasoning and examples taken from your reading, studies, experience, or observations.

【2006.01】Think carefully about the issue presented in the following excerpt and assignment below:

Every important discovery results from patience, perseverance, and concentration—sometimes continuing for months or years—on one specific subject. A person who wants to discover a new truth must remain absorbed by that one subject, must pay no attention to any thought that is unrelated to the problem.

Adapted from Santiago Ramon Cajal, *Advice for a Young Investigator*

Assignment: Are all important discoveries the result of focusing on one subject?

Plan and write an essay in which you develop your point of view on this issue. Support your position with reasoning and examples taken from your reading, studies, experience, or observations.

【2005.03】Think carefully about the issue presented in the following excerpt and assignment below:

Even scientists know that absolute objectivity has yet to be attained. It is the same for absolute truth. But, as many news reporters have observed, the idea of objectivity as a guiding principle is too valuable to be abandoned. Without it, the pursuit of knowledge is hopelessly lost.

Adapted from "Focusing Our Values", *Nieman Report*

Assignment: Are people better at making observations, discoveries, and decisions if they remain neutral and impartial?

Plan and write an essay in which you develop your point of view on this issue. Support your position with reasoning and examples taken from your reading, studies, experience, or observations.

SAT Essay Topic 12. 成就与挑战

【2011.06】 Think carefully about the issue presented in the following excerpt and the assignment below.

People assume that every accomplishment—each step in what we call progress—will lead to the solution to a problem and will help them reach the goal of understanding themselves and the world around them. In reality, however, each new answer provokes additional questions and each fresh discovery uncovers further complications. Every accomplishment leads to further problems, added responsibilities, more complications, and new challenges.

Assignment: Does every achievement bring with it new challenges?

Plan and write an essay in which you develop your point of view on this issue. Support your position with reasoning and examples taken from your reading, studies, experience, or observations.

【2009.01】 Think carefully about the issue presented in the following excerpt and assignment below:

Most people underestimate their own abilities. They tend to remember their failures more vividly than their successes, and for this reason they have unrealistically low expectations about what they are capable of. Those individuals who distinguish themselves through great accomplishments are usually no more talented than the average person: they simply set higher standards for themselves, since they have higher expectations about what they can do.

Assignment: Do highly accomplished people achieve more than others mainly because they expect more of themselves?

Plan and write an essay in which you develop your point of view on this issue. Support your position with reasoning and examples taken from your reading, studies, experience, or observations.

【2006.01】 Think carefully about the issue presented in the following excerpt and assignment below:

A colleague of the great scientist James Watson remarked that Watson was always "lounging around, arguing about problems instead of doing experiments." He concluded that "there is more than one way of doing good science." It was Watson's form of idleness, the scientist went on to say, that allowed him to solve "the greatest of all biological problems: the discovery of the structure of DNA." It is a point worth remembering in a society overly concerned with efficiency.

Adapted from John C. Polanyi, *"Understanding Discovery"*

Assignment: Do people accomplish more when they are allowed to do things in their own way?

Plan and write an essay in which you develop your point of view on this issue. Support your position with reasoning and examples taken from your reading, studies, experience, or observations.

SAT Essay Topic 13. 快乐

【2011.05】 Think carefully about the issue presented in the following excerpt and the assignment below.

Most of us tend to find rules, limits, and restraints irritating. We want to be free of anything that limits our choices. But limitations protect us. Without limitations on our behavior, too many of us will act without regard to the consequences for ourselves, for others, and for the future. Limitations contribute to, rather than take away from, our overall happiness.

Assignment: Do rules and limitations contribute to a person's happiness?

Plan and write an essay in which you develop your point of view on this issue. Support your position with reasoning and examples taken from your reading, studies, experience, or observations.

【2007.11】 Think carefully about the issue presented in the following excerpt and assignment below:

People today have so many choices. For instance, thirty years ago most television viewers could choose from only a few channels; today there are more than a hundred channels available. And choices do not just abound when it comes to the media. People have more options in almost every area of life. With so much to choose from, how can we not be happy?

Assignment: Does having a large number of options to choose from make people happy?

Plan and write an essay in which you develop your point of view on this issue. Support your position with reasoning and examples taken from your reading, studies, experience, or observations.

【2006.12】 Think carefully about the issue presented in the following excerpt and assignment below:

Abraham Lincoln said, "Most people are about as happy as they make up their minds to be." In other words, our personal level of satisfaction is entirely within our control. Otherwise, why would the same experience disappoint one person but delight another? Happiness is not an accident but a choice.

Assignment: Is happiness something over which people have no control, or can people choose to be happy?

Plan and write an essay in which you develop your point of view on this issue. Support your position with reasoning and examples taken from your reading, studies, experience, or observations.

【2007.06】 Think carefully about the issue presented in the following excerpt and assignment below:

People are happy only when they have their minds fixed on some goal other than their own happiness. Happiness comes when people focus instead on the happiness of others, on the improvement of humanity, on some course of action that is followed not as a means to anything else but as an end in itself. Aiming at something other than their own happiness, they find happiness along the way. The only way to be happy is to pursue some goal external to your own happiness.

Adapted from John Stuart Mill, *Autobiography*

Assignment: Are people more likely to be happy if they focus on goals other than their own happiness?

Plan and write an essay in which you develop your point of view on this issue. Support your position with reasoning and examples taken from your reading, studies, experience, or observations.

Notes

Chapter 2

商业与发明

BUSINESS AND INVENTION

本 章 目 录

诺贝尔

ALFRED BERNHARD NOBEL[1] (1833–1896)

Although he was recognized during his own lifetime as the ***inventor of dynamite*** [炸药的发明者], Alfred Bernhard Nobel is known today for the trust he established to award **an eponymous prize** [同名奖项] each year to the finest minds in several fields.

In addition to inventing dynamite and creating the Nobel Prize, Nobel patented his discoveries of ***blasting gelatin***[2] [硝酸甘油炸药] (a more powerful form of dynamite) and ***smokeless blasting powder*** [无烟炸药粉末]. Nobel also perfected various forms of ***detonating cap*** [起爆帽] technologies.

In 1866 Nobel produced what he believed was **a safe and manageable form of nitroglycerin** [操作安全的硝酸甘油] called dynamite. He established his own factory to produce it but in 1864 an explosion at the plant killed Nobel's younger brother and four other workers. ***Deeply shocked by this event*** [因此事深感震惊], he now worked on a safer explosive and in 1875 came up with gelignite.

These inventions ***drastically reduced the cost*** [极大地减少成本] of blasting rock, ***drilling tunnels*** [钻隧道], building canals and many other forms of construction work. The market for dynamite and detonating caps grew rapidly and Alfred Nobel also proved himself to be a very skillful ***entrepreneur*** [企业家] and ***businessman*** [商人].

Although he lived in Paris much of his life he was constantly traveling. Victor Hugo[3] at one time described him as "***Europe's richest vagabond*** [欧洲最富有的流浪汉]".

By the time Alfred Nobel died on December 10th, 1896, he had ***accumulated a massive fortune*** [积累大量财富]. He never married and was a ***committed pacifist*** [坚定的和平主义者] throughout much of his life.

When he died on December 10, 1896, he ***left almost his entire estate to a foundation*** [几乎把整个产业赠给基金会] dedicated to rewarding, as he put it, "those who, during the preceding year, shall have ***conferred the greatest benefit on mankind*** [给人类带来最大福祉]." The very first awards were made in 1901 on the ***fifth anniversary of Nobel's death*** [诺贝尔逝世五周年].

Nobel himself, however, ***remains a figure of contradictions*** [充满矛盾的人物]: a brilliant, lonely man, part ***pessimist*** [悲观主义者] and part ***idealist*** [理想主义者], who invented the powerful explosives used in ***modern warfare*** [现代战争] but also established the world's ***most prestigious prizes*** [最有声望的奖项] for intellectual services rendered to humanity.

---

1 Swedish chemist, engineer, and industrialist, who invented dynamite and other, more powerful explosives and who also founded the Nobel Prizes.

2 gelatin，硝酸甘油，是一种清油状液体，可以由震动引发爆炸。

3 Victor Hugo，雨果(1802–1885)，法国浪漫主义作家，代表作有《巴黎圣母院》(*Notre-Dame de Paris*)、《悲惨世界》(*Les Misérables*)。

 **Nobel**

If I have a thousand ideas and only one turns out to be good, I am satisfied.

I intend to leave after my death a large fund for the promotion of the peace idea, but I am skeptical as to its results.

Nobel Prize

The Nobel Prize is an international award administered by the Nobel Foundation in Stockholm, Sweden. The Nobel Prizes are widely regarded as the most prestigious awards given for intellectual achievement in the world.

Beginning in 1901, the Nobel Prize was awarded annually in five categories: peace, literature, physiology or medicine, chemistry, and physics. In 1968 the Bank of Sweden funded the addition of a sixth prize category, economics.

The Royal Swedish Academy of Sciences [瑞典皇家科学院] chooses the winner each year in physics and chemistry.

The Royal Caroline Medical Institute [卡洛琳皇家医学院] selects the medicine or physiology Nobel Prize recipient.

The Swedish Academy [瑞典文学院] determines the literature winner.
The Norwegian parliament [挪威议会] chooses the peace prize recipient.

改写 | **Rewrite the Story** | **in Your Own Words**

卡内基

ANDREW CARNEGIE[1] (1835–1919)

Andrew Carnegie, one of the wealthiest men in American history, known as ***the King of Steel*** [钢铁大王], convinced people that individuals should progress and ***succeed through hard work*** [通过努力工作取得成功].

He was the first son of William Carnegie, a ***linen weaver*** [亚麻纺织工]. William Carnegie's ***handloom business dwindled*** [手工纺织业倾颓] ***in the wake of industrialization*** [随着工业革命到来], and in 1848 the family emigrated to the United States.

There, at the age of 13, Andrew ***began his career as a bobbin boy*** [从做纺织工开始他的职业生涯] in a cotton factory. ***A voracious*** [如饥似渴的] reader, he ***took advantage of*** [利用] the ***generosity*** [慷慨] of an Allegheny[2] citizen who opened his library to local working boys.

Books provided most of his education as he moved from being a Western Union[3] messenger boy to ***telegraph operator*** [电报接线员] and then to ***a series of positions*** [一系列职位] leading to the ***superintendent*** [主管] of the Western Division of the Pennsylvania Railroad.

While still employed by the Railroad, Carnegie ***invested in a new company to manufacture railway sleeping cars*** [投资新公司生产铁路卧铺车]. From there, he ***expanded his business ventures*** [拓展经营业务] to encompass the building of bridges, ***locomotives*** [火车头] and rails. Then In 1864, Andrew Carnegie ***devoted his full energies to the iron business*** [将全部精力投入到钢铁生意].

Carnegie's growing wealth enabled him to ***profit from the depression*** [从萧条期获益] of the 1890s. When others ***faced bankruptcy*** [面临破产], he ***managed to gobble up steel production facilities*** [得以吞并钢铁生产设施]. By 1900, he controlled about one quarter of the nation's steel output. In 1901, J. P. Morgan[4] offered to buy all of Carnegie's steel ***holdings*** [股份] for the price of $500 million. Carnegie's acceptance made him the world's richest man.

In 1889, he wrote "The Gospel of Wealth" in which he ***boldly articulated his view*** [大胆表达自己的观点] that ***the rich are merely "trustees" of their wealth*** [富人仅仅是财富的托管人] and ***are under a moral obligation*** [负有道德义务] to distribute it in ways that ***promote the welfare and happiness of the common man*** [改善百姓的幸福安乐].

Carnegie was ***a prolific writer*** [多产的作家], but the quotation for which he is most famous comes from "The Gospel of Wealth": "The man who dies thus rich dies disgraced." ***He took his admonishment to others to heart*** [他身先士卒，践行自己对别人的训诫] and spent the last two decades of his life distributing the ***great bulk of his fortune*** [他的大量财富].

---

1 Scottish-born American industrialist who led the enormous expansion of the American steel industry in the late 19th century. He was also one of the most important philanthropists of his era.

2 Allegheny, 阿勒格尼, 美国宾夕法尼亚州一地名。

3 西联汇款, 1851 年于纽约成立, 以前主要业务为收发电报, 现在主要业务为国际汇款。

4 JP 摩根公司。1935 年, 摩根财团将 JP 摩根银行拆分成两部分。一部分为 JP 摩根, 从事传统的商业银行业务; 另一部分取名摩根士丹利(Morgan Stanley), 从事投资银行业务。2000 年, JP 摩根与大通银行及富林明集团合并, 成立摩根大通(JP Morgan Chase)。

Opposing charity [反对施舍] instead, Carnegie has **provided educational opportunities** [提供教育机会] for thousands of people by establishing more than 2,500 libraries in small communities and **founding schools** [设立学校].

By the time of his death in 1919, Andrew Carnegie had given away about $350 million, but the **legacy of his generosity continues to unfold** [他慷慨的馈赠仍然继续着] in the work of the trusts and institutions that he endowed.

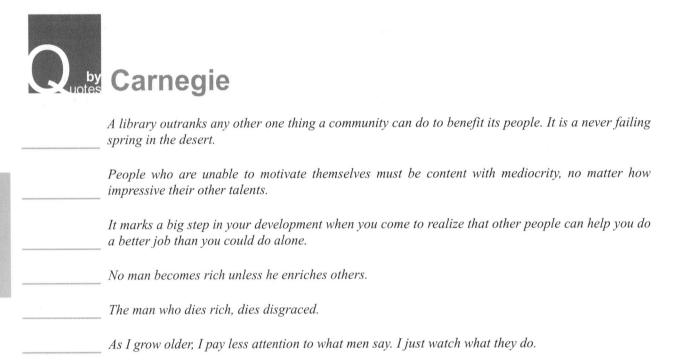

Q by Quotes | Carnegie

A library outranks any other one thing a community can do to benefit its people. It is a never failing spring in the desert.

People who are unable to motivate themselves must be content with mediocrity, no matter how impressive their other talents.

It marks a big step in your development when you come to realize that other people can help you do a better job than you could do alone.

No man becomes rich unless he enriches others.

The man who dies rich, dies disgraced.

As I grow older, I pay less attention to what men say. I just watch what they do.

改写 | Rewrite the Story | in Your Own Words

洛克菲勒

JOHN DAVISON ROCKEFELLER[1] （1839–1937）

Determined to work for himself [决心为自己打工], Rockefeller saved all the money he could and in 1850 ***went into business*** [经商] with a young Englishman, Maurice Clark. The company, Clark & Rockefeller Produce and Commission, sold ***farm implements*** [农具], ***fertilizers*** [化肥] and ***household goods*** [家庭用品].

Rockefeller's company was fairly successful but ***did not bring him the wealth he desired*** [没能带给他渴望的财富]. In 1862 Rockefeller heard that Samuel Andrews had developed a better and cheaper way of ***refining crude petroleum*** [精炼石油]. Rockefeller sold his original business and invested it in a new company he set up with Andrews called Standard Oil[2].

One of the business problems that Rockefeller encountered was the high cost of transporting his oil to his ***Cleveland refineries*** [克利夫兰炼油厂] （40 cents a ***barrel*** [桶]） and the ***refined oil*** [成品油] to New York （$2 a barrel）. Rockefeller ***negotiated an exclusive deal*** [谈判达成独家交易] with the railway company where he guaranteed sixty car-loads a day. ***In return*** [作为回报], the transport prices were reduced to 35 cents and $1.30. The cost of his oil was reduced and ***his sales increased dramatically*** [销量猛增].

Within a year, four of his thirty competitors ***were out of business*** [关门大吉]. Eventually Standard Oil ***monopolized oil refining*** [垄断石油精炼业] in Cleveland. Rockefeller now ***bought out*** [买断] Samuel Andrews for a million dollars and ***turned his attentions to*** [将其注意力] controlling the oil industry throughout the United States.

His competitors were given the choice of ***being swallowed up*** [被吞并] by Standard Oil or being crushed. By 1890 Rockefeller's had swollen into ***an immense monopoly*** [巨大的垄断企业] which could ***fix its own prices*** [自由定价] and terms of business because it had no competitors. In 1896 Rockefeller was worth about $200 million.

After various press campaigns against Rockefeller had turned him into one of America's most hated men, Rockefeller began giving his money away. He ***set up the Rockefeller Foundation***[3] [设立洛克菲勒基金会] to "***promote the well-being of mankind*** [提高人类福祉]".

Over the next few years Rockefeller gave over $500 million ***in aid of medical research*** [资助医学研究], universities and ***Baptist churches***[4] [浸信会]. By the time that he died on 23rd May, 1937, John Davidson Rockefeller had become a popular national figure.

---

1 American industrialist and philanthropist, founder of the Standard Oil Company, which dominated the oil industry and was the first great U.S. business trust.

2 标准石油公司。1911 年，美国联邦最高法院裁定标准石油违法垄断，将其支解成 30 多家新公司。其中包括：纽约标准石油，后更名为现在的美孚石油（Mobil）；纽泽西标准石油，后更名为现在的艾克森石油（Exxon）。

3 洛克菲勒基金会，1913 年在纽约注册。

4 浸信会（又称浸礼会），基督教主要宗派之一。

Rockefeller

A friendship founded on business is better than a business founded on friendship.

The most important thing for a young man is to establish a credit... a reputation, character.

I believe in the supreme worth of the individual and in his right to life, liberty and the pursuit of happiness.
I believe that every right implies a responsibility; every opportunity, an obligation; every possession, a duty.
I believe that the law was made for man and not man for the law; that government is the servant of the people and not their master.
I believe in the dignity of labor, whether with head or hand; that the world owes no man a living but that it owes every man an opportunity to make a living.
I believe that thrift is essential to well-ordered living and that economy is a prime requisite of a sound financial structure, whether in government, business or personal affairs.
I believe that truth and justice are fundamental to an enduring social order.

改写 | Rewrite the Story | in Your Own Words |

贝尔
ALEXANDER GRAHAM BELL[1] (1847–1922)

What would life be like without the telephone [没有电话的生活会怎样]? It's hard to imagine. Yet up until 1876 the ***transmission of the human voice over a wire*** [通过电线传输声音] to a listener who could respond immediately seemed ***a utopian dream*** [乌托邦般的幻境].

In 1876, on the rented top floor of a ***boardinghouse*** [出租公寓], it became a reality. The voice was that of Alexander Graham Bell calling to his assistant in another room, "Mr. Watson, come here. I want you." ***Probably the most important revolution in the history of human communication had occurred*** [可能人类史上最重要的通讯革命就这样发生了].

Bell had long ***been fascinated by*** [着迷于] the idea of transmitting speech, and by 1875 he had come up with a simple receiver that could ***turn electricity into sound*** [将电转化为声音].

Others were working along the same lines, including an Italian-American Antonio Meucci[2], and debate continues as to ***who should be credited with inventing the telephone*** [电话发明该归功于谁]. However, Bell ***was granted a patent*** [被授予专利权] for the telephone on 7 March 1876 and it developed quickly.

Within a year the first telephone exchange was built in Connecticut and the Bell Telephone Company was created in 1877, with Bell the ***owner of a third of the shares*** [三分之一股份的拥有者], quickly making him a wealthy man.

Alexander Graham Bell might easily have ***been content with the success*** [满足于成功] of his telephone invention. His many laboratory notebooks demonstrate, however, that he ***was driven by a genuine and rare intellectual curiosity*** [被诚挚而又罕有的好奇心驱动着] that kept him regularly searching, striving, and wanting always to learn and to create.

He would continue to test out new ideas through a long and productive life. He would ***explore the realm of communications*** [探索通讯领域] as well as ***engage in a great variety of scientific activities*** [参与一系列科学活动] involving kites, airplanes, sheep-breeding, ***artificial respiration*** [人工呼吸], and ***water distillation*** [净化水].

 Bell

When one door closes, another door opens; but we so often look so long and regretfully upon the closed-door, that we do not see the ones which open for us.

---

1 Scottish-born American audiologist best known as the inventor of the telephone (1876).

2 安东尼奥·穆齐 (Antonio Meucci, 1808–1889)。2002 年, 美国国会 269 议案中, 安东尼奥·穆齐被正式确认为电话的发明者。

God has strewn our paths with wonders and we certainly should not go through life with our eyes shut.

爱迪生

THOMAS EDISON[1] (1847–1931)

Today, ***Edison's name still stands for inventive creativity*** [爱迪生的名字仍然是发明创造的代名词], and his ***electric light bulb*** [电灯泡] is a **well-known** [众所周知的] ***symbol for a bright idea*** [是优秀创意的象征].

The period from 1879 to 1900, when Edison produced and perfected most of his devices, has been called ***the Age of Edison*** [爱迪生时代].

Dubbed "***The Wizard of Menlo Park*** "[2] [被戏称为 "门洛帕克的奇才"], Edison developed many devices which ***greatly influenced life in the 20th century*** [极大地影响了二十世纪的人类生活].

During his career, Edison ***patented more than 1,000 inventions*** [注册超过 1000 项专利], including the ***electric light*** [电灯], the ***phonograph*** [留声机], and the ***motion-picture camera*** [电影]. These three inventions ***gave rise to*** [引起] giant industries—***electric utilities*** [电力工业], ***phonograph*** [唱片] and record companies, and the ***film industry*** [电影工业].

"Mary had a little lamb" were the first words laid down on a revolutionary machine—phonograph by Edison in 1877. ***Speech was too fast to be written down*** [讲话过快而不能被记录下来], so Edison ***devised a way to record the vibrations of the receiving sound*** [发明了一种记录接收到的声音震动的方法], allowing them to be ***played back*** [回放] more slowly and the words written down.

Today most phonographs and ***vinyl records*** [乙烯基制成的唱片] ***gather dust on people's desk*** [尘封在人们的书桌上] or ***have become museum relics*** [成为博物馆中的古董]. But **no one can deny the fact** [没有人能否认这个事实] that phonographs had ***changed the world*** [改变世界] by ***bringing music as well as great oratory into millions of ordinary homes*** [让音乐和演讲进入成千上万的普通家庭].

Edison was largely taught at home by his mother. "My mother taught me how to read good books quickly and correctly," he later said, "and as this ***opened up a great world in literature*** [为我揭开了一个充满文字的世界], I have always ***been very thankful for*** [非常感激] this early training."

A ***hyperactive*** [极度活跃的] child, ***prone to distraction*** [很容易走神], he was deemed "difficult" by his teacher. His mother quickly pulled him from school and taught him at home. At age 11, he ***showed a voracious appetite for knowledge*** [展现出极强的求知欲], ***reading books on a wide range of subjects*** [广泛阅读各种图书]. In this wide-open curriculum Edison developed a process for ***self-education*** [自学] and ***learning independently*** [独立学习] that would serve him throughout his life [受益终生].

Edison ***continued his education*** [继续学习] while working on the train. He ***performed***

---

1 American inventor who, singly or jointly, held a world record 1,093 patents. In addition, he created the world's first industrial research laboratory.

2 这个名字的由来是，爱迪生的主要发明诞生在新泽西州的门洛帕克实验室（Menlo Park Lab）。

chemistry experiments in a baggage car [在行李车厢内进行各种化学实验]. During one of his experiments, a chemical fire started and the car caught fire [车厢着火]. The conductor [售票员] rushed in and struck Thomas on the side of the head, probably furthering some of his hearing loss [使他进一步失聪]. He was kicked off the train [被踢下火车] and forced to sell his newspapers at various stations along the route.

After Edison saved a three-year-old from being run over by an errant train [脱轨列车], the child's grateful father rewarded him by teaching him to operate a telegraph [教他发电报]. By age 15, he had learned enough to be employed as a telegraph operator.

Before starting an experiment, Edison tried to read all the literature on the subject [阅读有关这一问题的所有文献] to avoid repeating experiments that other people had already conducted [避免做其他人已经完成的实验]. Perhaps the best illustration of Edison's working methods [工作方法最好的写照] is his own famous statement: "Genius is one percent inspiration and 99 percent perspiration."

Edison worked on his experiments with extraordinary intensity [实验工作强度大]. He lived in his laboratory [住在实验室中], getting along on four hours of sleep a day [习惯一天只睡四个小时] and eating meals brought to him by an assistant. He often kept vigils [守夜] of 48 and even 72 hours when an experiment neared completion.

In order to find some suitable material that would carry current and glow [导电和发光], he studied and experimented with 1,600 materials.

Edison began to work at an early age and continued to work right up until his death [坚持工作到生命的最后时刻]. On Edison's death in 1931, the president asked the nation to dim its lights in his honor [总统要求调暗整个国家的灯光来纪念爱迪生].

Some of the inventions attributed to him were not completely original [一些爱迪生名下的发明并非原创] but amounted to improvements of earlier inventions [对先前发明的改进] or were actually created by numerous employees working under his direction [在爱迪生的指导下，由大量的雇员完成的]. Nevertheless [然而], Edison is considered one of the most prolific inventors in history [史上最多产的发明家之一].

Honors were heaped upon him [各种荣誉涌向他] by governments. His name a household word [他的名字家喻户晓], he became the ideal of aspiring inventors [成为有抱负追求的发明者的楷模]. Thomas Edison's light continues to shine.

Quotes by Edison

I have not failed. I've just found 10,000 ways that won't work.

Genius is 1 percent inspiration and 99 percent perspiration.

Many of life's failures are people who did not realize how close they were to success when they gave up.

Opportunity is missed by most people because it is dressed in overalls and looks like work.

Discontent is the first necessity of progress.

Five percent of the people think;
ten percent of the people think they think;
and the other eighty-five percent would rather die than think.

If we all did the things we are capable of, we would astound ourselves.

Our greatest weakness lies in giving up. The most certain way to succeed is to try just one more time.

改写 | Rewrite the Story | in Your Own Words

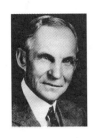

福特

HENRY FORD[1] (1863–1947)

In his own sphere as a maker of machines, Ford _**effected the greatest revolution of his day**_ [促成他那个时代最伟大的革命]. It was due largely to him [主要归功于他] that the motor-car, instead of continuing for years to be _**a luxury for the rich**_ [富人的奢侈品], _**was brought speedily within the reach of comparatively humble folk**_ [迅速地走入寻常百姓家].

Henry Ford did not invent the car; he produced an automobile that _**was within the economic reach of the average American**_ [让普通美国人负担得起]. While other manufacturers _**were content to target a market of the well-to-do**_ [满足于瞄准富人市场], Ford developed a design and a method of manufacture that _**steadily reduced the cost of the Model T**_[2] [稳步地降低了 T 型车的成本].

Instead of _**pocketing the profits**_ [中饱私囊]; Ford _**lowered the price of his car**_ [降低汽车价格]. As a result, Ford Motors sold more cars and _**steadily increased its earnings**_ [稳步地增加收入]—_**transforming the automobile from a luxury toy to a mainstay of American society**_ [把汽车从奢侈玩具转化成美国社会的生活必需品].

Central to Ford's ability to produce an affordable car was the development of the _**assembly line**_ [流水线] that _**increased the efficiency of manufacture**_ [提高生产效率] and decreased its cost. Ford did not _**conceive the concept**_ [创造了这个概念], he _**perfected it**_ [使之完美].

**Prior to the introduction of the assembly line** [引入流水线之前], _**cars were individually crafted by teams of skilled workmen**_ [汽车由成组的技工手工打造]—a slow and expensive procedure.

The assembly line _**reversed the process of automobile manufacture**_ [颠倒了汽车生产过程]. Instead of workers going to the car, the car came to the worker who _**performed the same task of assembly over and over again**_ [不断从事同一个装配任务]. With the introduction and perfection of the process, Ford was able to reduce the assembly time of a Model T from twelve and a half hours to less than six hours.

**The industrial empire which Ford's imagination and drive established** [福特的想象力和驱动力缔造的工业帝国] was in due course to _**yield him an immense fortune**_ [给他带来巨大财富]; but _**wealth was not his ultimate goal**_ [财富并非他的终极目标].

Henry Ford is famous for starting the Ford Motor Company. However, _**he left his mark as a philanthropist**_ [留下了他作为慈善家的印记]. His philanthropist work is still thriving today as the Ford Foundation he created still thrives today. Henry Ford had a vision and belief in education and health. He wanted every man, woman, and child to have extraordinary health care. He _**assembled a not-for-profit organization**_ [组织非营利机构] with teams of doctors to _**serve the common person**_ [服务百姓].

---

1 American industrialist, the founder of the Ford Motor Company, and sponsor of the development of the assembly line technique of mass production.

2 福特 T 型车，福特汽车公司于 1908 年至 1927 年推出。T 型车以其低廉的价格使汽车作为一种实用工具走入了寻常百姓之家，美国亦自此成为了"车轮上的国度"。

Ford

_____ A market is never saturated with a good product, but it is very quickly saturated with a bad one.

_____ Anyone who stops learning is old, whether at twenty or eighty. Anyone who keeps learning stays young. The greatest thing in life is to keep your mind young.

_____ As we advance in life we learn the limits of our abilities.

_____ Before everything else, getting ready is the secret of success.

_____ Coming together is a beginning; keeping together is progress; working together is success

改写 | **Rewrite the Story** | in Your Own Words

迪士尼
WALT DISNEY[1] (1901–1966)

迪士尼王国缔造者
Creator of Disney Empire

The present-day Disney Empire [现如今的迪士尼王国] ***bears little resemblance to*** [今非昔比] the small garage studio in Kansas City where it all began.

Entertainment was more than child's play [娱乐不只是小孩子的玩耍] to Walt Disney. A gifted animator and ***motion picture producer*** [动画片制作人], he ***created a stable of unforgettable cartoon characters*** [创造了一系列让人难忘的卡通角色], starting with Mickey Mouse, that ***provided comic relief*** [提供欢快的慰藉] to men, women and children alike during the Depression, and later ***charmed audiences all over the world*** [让全世界的观众为之着迷].

His father was always ***seeking success in many occupations*** [在众多行业寻找成功] but always finding failure, and the Disney family was always poor. Walt found that he could ***escape his father's harsh discipline by drawing*** [通过绘画逃脱父亲严厉的惩罚].

In 1917, when he was 16 years old, he ***lied about his age*** [虚报自己的年龄] to join the American Red Cross Ambulance Corps. When he ***was mustered out*** [退伍] at the end of World War I, he set up shop as a commercial artist in Kansas City, Missouri. There he discovered the world of animation, and Walt devoted himself to it.

Moving to Los Angeles in 1923 to be with his more successful brother, Roy, Walt began drawing commercially, ***making a modest living*** [清贫度日] by drawing for the ***Alice series of cartoons*** [爱丽丝系列卡通片], about a live action girl who travels to the world of animated cartoon animals.

A multimedia visionary [一位跨媒体的梦想家], Disney ***produced the first feature-length animated film*** [制作了第一部电影长度的动画电影], *Snow White*, opened ***a theme park*** [主题公园] in 1955, ***adapted popular children's books into movies*** [将童话故事改编成电影] and ***produced a weekly TV series in color*** [制作每周播出的彩色电视剧], all with the Disney moniker. Today his name ***is synonymous with*** [同义] family fun. Prior to his death in 1966 in Los Angeles, California, of lung cancer, he began work on his latest theme park in ***Orlando*** [奥兰多市], ***Florida*** [佛罗里达州]: Walt Disney's World.

A ferociously hard worker [工作狂人], he demanded much from his employees. His own tastes remained simple. ***His sole relaxation was his interest in electrical toy railroads*** [唯一的休闲就是摆弄下玩具火车].

---

1 American motion-picture and television producer and showman, famous as a pioneer of animated cartoon films and as the creator of such cartoon characters as Mickey Mouse and Donald Duck. He also planned and built Disneyland.

Quotes by Disney

The flower that blooms in adversity is the rarest and most beautiful of all.

All the adversity I've had in my life, all my troubles and obstacles, have strengthened me... You may not realize it when it happens, but a kick in the teeth may be the best thing in the world for you.

All cartoon characters and fables must be exaggeration, caricatures. It is the very nature of fantasy and fable.

Laughter is timeless. Imagination has no age. And dreams are forever.

No matter how your heart is grieving, if you keep on believing, the dreams that you wish will come true.

All our dreams can come true, if we have the courage to pursue them.

The way to get started is to quit talking and begin doing.

改写 | Rewrite the Story | in Your Own Words |

雷蒙德·克罗克

RAYMOND ALBERT KROC[1] （1902–1984）

How do you create a restaurant empire and ***become an overnight success*** [一夜成名] at the age of 52? As Ray Kroc said, "I was an overnight success all right, but 30 years is a long, long night."

In 1917, 15-year-old Ray Kroc ***lied about his age to join the Red Cross*** [虚报年龄加入红十字会] as an ambulance driver, but the war ended before his training finished. He then worked as a piano player, a paper cup salesman and a ***multi-mixer salesman*** [多用搅拌器销售员].

In 1954 he was surprised by a huge order for 8 multi-mixers from a restaurant in San Bernardino, California. There he found a small but successful restaurant run by brothers Dick and Mac McDonald, and ***was stunned by the effectiveness of their operation*** [惊讶于他们的工作效率]. They ***produced a limited menu*** [提供有限的菜式], concentrating on just a few items—burgers, fries and beverages—which allowed them to focus on quality at every step.

Kroc pitched his vision of creating McDonald's restaurants all over the U.S. to the brothers. In 1955 he founded the McDonald's Corporation, and 5 years later ***bought the exclusive rights*** [买下专有权] to the McDonald's name. By 1958, McDonald's had sold its 100 millionth hamburger.

Ray Kroc wanted to build a restaurant system that would be famous for food of ***consistently high quality*** [一贯的高质量] and uniform methods of preparation. He wanted to serve burgers, buns, fries and beverages that tasted just the same in ***Alaska*** [阿拉斯加州] as they did in ***Alabama*** [亚拉巴马州].

To achieve this, he chose a unique path: persuading both ***franchisees*** [连锁加盟人] and ***suppliers*** [供应商] to ***buy into his vision*** [采纳他的想法], working not for McDonald's, but for themselves, together with McDonald's.

He promoted the slogan, "In business for yourself, but not by yourself." His philosophy was based on the simple principle of a ***3-legged stool*** [三条腿的凳子]: one leg was McDonald's, the second, the franchisees, and the third, McDonald's suppliers. The stool was only as strong as the 3 legs.

McDonald's passion for quality meant that every single ingredient was tested, tasted and perfected to fit the operating system. As restaurants boomed, the ***massive volume of orders*** [大宗订单] ***caught the attention of suppliers*** [吸引了供销商的眼球], who began taking McDonald's standards as seriously as McDonald's did. As other quick service restaurants began to follow, McDonald's high standards rippled through the meat, produce and dairy industries.

Right up until he died on January 14, 1984, Ray Kroc never stopped working for McDonald's. Even when he ***was confined to a wheelchair*** [受轮椅的束缚], he still went to work in the office in San Diego nearly every day. He would ***keep a hawk's eye over*** [像鹰一样注视着] the McDonald's restaurant near his office, phoning the manager to remind him to pick up the trash, clean his lot, and turn on the lights at night.

---

1 American restaurateur and a pioneer of the fast-food industry with his worldwide McDonald's enterprise.

From his passion for innovation and efficiency, to his ***relentless pursuit of quality*** [对质量苛刻的追求], and his many charitable contributions, Ray Kroc's legacy continues to be an inspirational, integral part of McDonald's today.

Q by Quotes Kroc

All money means to me is a pride in accomplishment.

When you're green, you're growing. When you're ripe, you rot.

The quality of a leader is reflected in the standards they set for themselves.

改写 Rewrite the Story | in Your Own Words

山姆·沃尔顿
SAM WALTON[1]（1918–1992）

Sam Walton worked in his father's store while attending school. This was his first ***retailing experience*** [零售经验] and he really enjoyed it. After graduating from the University of Missouri in 1940, he ***began his own career as a retail merchant*** [作零售批发商开始自己的职业生涯] when he opened the first of several franchises of the Ben Franklin ***five-and-dime*** [廉价品商店] ***franchises*** [特许经营] in Arkansas.

This would lead to bigger and better things and he soon opened his first Wal-Mart store in 1962 in Rogers, Arkansas. Wal-Mart ***specialized in name-brands at low prices*** [主营低价品牌商品] and Sam Walton ***was surprised at the success*** [惊异于其成功]. Soon a chain of Wal-Mart stores ***sprang up*** [雨后春笋般出现] across rural America.

Walton's ***management style was popular with employees*** [管理风格受到雇员欢迎] and he founded some of the basic concepts of management that are still in use today. After ***taking the company public*** [公司上市后] in 1970, Walton introduced his "profit sharing plan". The profit sharing plan was a plan for Wal-Mart employees to ***improve their income dependent on the profitability of the store*** [根据商店的收益情况提高收入]. Sam Walton believed that "individuals don't win, teams do".

Employees at Wal-Mart stores ***were offered stock options*** [提供股权] and store discounts. ***These benefits are commonplace today*** [这些福利今日司空见惯], but Walton was among the first to implement them.

Walton believed that a happy employee meant happy customers and more sales. Walton believed that by giving employees a part of the company and ***making their success dependent on the company's success*** [将公司和雇员两者的成功联系在一起], they would care about the company.

By 1991, Wal-Mart was the largest U.S. retailer with 1,700 stores. Walton remained active in managing the company, as president and CEO until 1988 and chairman until his death. He ***was awarded the Presidential Medal of Freedom***[2] [被授予总统自由勋章] shortly before his death.

Walton died in 1992, being the world's second richest man, behind Bill Gates. Wal-Mart stores now operate in Mexico, Canada, ***Argentina*** [阿根廷], Brazil, South Korea, China and ***Puerto Rico*** [波多黎各]. Sam Walton's visions were indeed successful.

 Walton

Outstanding leaders go out of their way to boost the self esteem of their personnel. If people believe in themselves, it's amazing what they can accomplish.

---

1 American retail magnate who founded Wal-Mart Stores, Inc., and developed it, by 1990, into the largest retail sales chain in the United States
2 总统自由勋章，由美国总统一年一度颁发，与国会金质奖章并列为美国最高的平民荣誉。受奖者不需要是美国公民。

_____ *Capital isn't scarce; vision is.*

_____ *High expectations are the key to everything.*

改写 Rewrite the Story | in Your Own Words

巴菲特
WARREN BUFFETT[1] (1930–)

For someone who is such an extraordinarily successful investor, Warren Buffett comes off as a pretty ordinary guy. ***Born and bred*** [生长在] in Omaha, Nebraska, for more than 40 years Buffett has lived in the same **gray stucco house** [灰色粉刷房子] on Farnam Street that he bought for $31,500. He ***wears rumpled, nondescript suits*** [穿着皱巴巴的普通西装], drives his own car, drinks Cherry Coke, and is more likely to be found in a Dairy Queen than a four-star restaurant.

Warren Edward Buffett was born on August 30, 1930, the middle child of three. His father, Howard Buffett, came from a family of grocers but himself became a ***stockbroker*** [股票经纪人] and later a ***U.S. congressman*** [美国国会议员].

Even as a young child, Buffett was pretty serious about making money. He ***used to go door-to-door and sell soda pop*** [曾经挨门挨户贩卖苏打汽水]. When his family moved to Washington, D. C., Buffett ***became a paperboy for The Washington Post*** [成为《华盛顿邮报》的报童] and its rival the *Times-Herald*. Buffett ran his five paper routes like an assembly line and even added magazines to ***round out his product offerings*** [丰富自己的商品种类].

While still in school, he was making $175 a month, ***a full-time wage*** [全职工资] for many young men. When he was 14, Buffett spent $1,200 on 40 acres of farmland in Nebraska and soon began ***collecting rent from a tenant farmer*** [从佃农手里收租].

Buffett ***wasn't keen on going to college*** [不太热衷于读大学] but ***ended up at Wharton at the University of Pennsylvania*** [最终入读宾大沃顿商学院]—his father encouraged him to go. After two years at Wharton, Buffett transferred to the University of Nebraska in Lincoln, for his final year of college. There Buffett took a job with the Lincoln Journal supervising 50 paper boys in six rural counties.

Buffett a***pplied to Harvard Business School*** [申请哈佛商学院] but ***was turned down*** [被拒绝] in what had to be one of the worst admissions decisions in Harvard history. The outcome ended up ***profoundly affecting*** [深刻地影响] Buffett's life, for he ended up attending Columbia Business School, where he ***studied under reverend mentor*** [师从受人敬仰的导师] Benjamin Graham[2], the ***father of securities analysis*** [证券分析之父] who provided the foundation for Buffett's investment strategy.

From the beginning, Buffett ***made his fortune from investing*** [通过投资赚钱]. He started with all the money he had made from selling pop, delivering papers, and operating pinball machines. Between 1950 and 1956, he grew his $9,800 ***kitty*** [全副家当] to $14,000. From there, he organized investment partnerships with his family and friends, and then gradually ***drew in other investors through word of mouth and very attractive terms*** [通过口碑和诱人的条件吸引更多投资者入伙].

---

1 American businessman and philanthropist, widely considered the most successful investor of the 20th century, having defied prevailing investment trends to amass a personal fortune of more than $60 billion.

2 本杰明·格雷厄姆（1894—1976），美国投资家，《有价证券分析》（*Security Analysis*）一书作者。

Buffett's goal was to top the Dow Jones Industrial Average[1] by an average of 10% a year. Over the length of the Buffett partnership between 1957 and 1969, Buffett's investments grew **_at a compound annual rate_** [年复合增长率] of 29.5%, crushing the Dow's return of 7.4% over the same period.

Buffett's **_investment strategy mirrors his lifestyle and overall philosophy_** [投资策略反映其生活方式和人生哲学]. He doesn't collect houses or cars or works of art [艺术品], and he **_disdains companies that waste money on such extravagances_** [鄙弃在奢侈品上大肆挥霍的公司] as **_limousines_** [豪华轿车], private dining rooms, and **_high-priced real estate_** [高价房地产]. He is a creature of habit—same house, same office, same city, same soda—and dislikes change.

In 2006, Buffett announced that he would **_give his entire fortune away to charity_** [将所有财富用于慈善事业], the largest act of charitable giving in United States history. He has established the Buffett Foundation, designed to accumulate money and give it away after his and his wife's death—though the foundation has given millions to organizations involved with **_population control_** [人口控制], **_abortion_** [堕胎], and **_birth control_** [计划生育].

Quotes by Buffett

Someone's sitting in the shade today because someone planted a tree a long time ago.

Price is what you pay. Value is what you get.

It takes 20 years to build a reputation and five minutes to ruin it. If you think about that you'll do things differently.

Should you find yourself in a chronically leaking boat, energy devoted to changing vessels is likely to be more productive than energy devoted to patching leaks.

改写 | Rewrite the Story | in Your Own Words

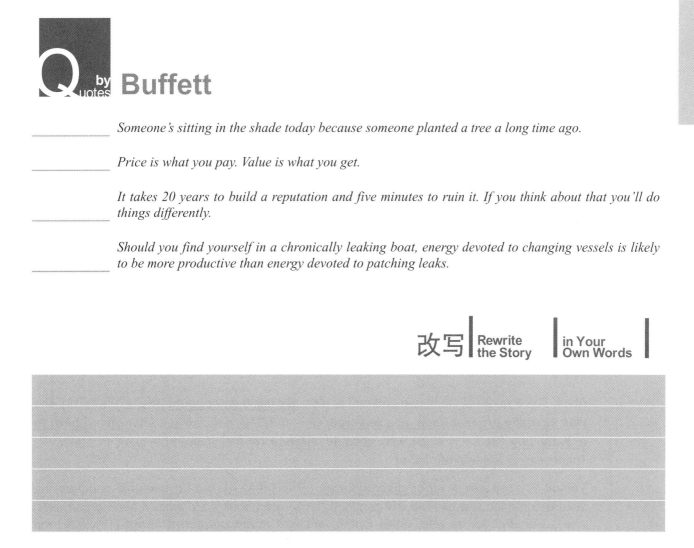

---

1 道琼斯工业平均指数，1896 年公布时包含美国工业最重要的 12 种股票的均数，现在包括美国 30 间最大、最知名的上市公司。

奥普拉

OPRAH WINFREY[1]（1954–）

Through the power of media [通过媒体的力量], Oprah Winfrey ***has created an unparalleled connection with people around the world*** [和全世界的人们建立了空前未有的联系]. As ***supervising producer and host*** [制片人和主播] of the ***top-rated*** [深受欢迎的], ***award-winning*** [备受赞誉的] *The Oprah Winfrey Show*, she has entertained, enlightened and uplifted millions of viewers for the past two decades. Her accomplishments as a global media leader and ***philanthropist*** [慈善家] have established her as ***one of the most respected and admired public figures today*** [当今最受尊敬和敬佩的公众人物之一].

Oprah Winfrey's own story is inspirational [鼓舞人心的] because she ***overcame almost every obstacle*** [克服几乎所有困难] that an individual person might or might not face. She is an icon to people all over the world because of her commitment to help those who have ***been faced with similar obstacles*** [面对相似的障碍].

Born to an unwed teenage mother [诞生于一个未婚先孕的少女妈妈], Oprah Winfrey spent her first years on her grandmother's farm in Kosciusko, Mississippi, while her mother looked for work in the North.

Life on the farm was primitive [农场生活原始], but her grandmother taught her to read at an early age, and at age 3, Oprah was ***reciting poems and Bible verses*** [背诵诗歌和圣经] in local churches. ***Despite the hardships of her physical environment*** [尽管生活艰辛], she enjoyed the church community and the loving support of her grandmother, who ***cherished her as a gifted child*** [把她当作有天赋的孩子加以珍视].

Her world changed for the worse at age 6, when she was sent to Milwaukee to live with her mother, who had found work as a ***housemaid*** [女佣]. In the long days when her mother ***was absent from their inner city apartment*** [不在城区的公寓], young Oprah ***was repeatedly molested by male relatives*** [不断地被男性亲戚性骚扰] and another visitor.

The abuse, which lasted from the ages of 9 to 13, was ***emotionally devastating*** [对于精神是毁灭性的]. When she tried to run away, she ***was sent to a juvenile detention home*** [被送到青少年拘留所], only to be denied admission because ***all the beds were filled*** [床铺都住满了].

At 14, she was out of the house and on her own. ***By her own account*** [据她自己的记述], she ***was sexually promiscuous as a teenager*** [青少年时期的性生活混乱]. After ***giving birth to a baby boy*** [诞下一个男婴] who ***died in infancy*** [死在婴儿期], she went to Nashville, Tennessee to live with her father.

Vernon Winfrey was a ***strict disciplinarian*** [纪律严格的人], but he gave his daughter the secure home life she needed. He required her to read books and write a book report each week. "As strict as he was," says Oprah, "he ***had some concerns about*** [有些顾虑] me making the best of my life, and would not accept anything less than what he thought was my best." ***In this structured environment*** [有秩序的环境], Oprah flourished, and ***became an***

---

1 American television personality, actress, and entrepreneur whose syndicated daily talk show was among the most popular of the genre. She became one of the richest and most influential women in the United States.

honor student [成为一名优等生], ***winning prizes for oratory and dramatic recitation*** [因朗诵和戏剧而获奖].

At age 17, Oprah Winfrey won the Miss Black Tennessee ***beauty pageant*** [选美比赛] and was offered an on-air job at WVOL, a local radio station ***serving the African American community*** [服务黑人社区的当地广播台] in Nashville.

She won an oratory contest, which ***secured her a full scholarship*** [为她带来一份全额奖学金] to Tennessee State University, where she majored in Speech Communications and Performing Arts. Oprah continued to work at WVOL in her first years of college, but ***her broadcasting career was already taking off*** [她的广播生涯已经开始起飞]. She left school and ***signed on with a local television station*** [签约一家当地电视台] as a ***reporter*** [记者] and ***anchor*** [主播].

In 1984, Oprah moved to Chicago to host WLS-TV's morning talk show, *AM Chicago*, which became the number one local talk show. In less than a year, the show ***expanded to one hour*** [时间延长到一小时] and ***was renamed*** [更名为] *The Oprah Winfrey Show*.

It ***entered national syndication*** [进入全国联播节目] in 1986, becoming the ***highest-rated talk show*** [最受好评的脱口秀节目] in television history. In 1988, she established Harpo Studios, making her the third woman in the American entertainment industry（after Mary Pickford[1] and Lucille Ball[2]）to own her own studio.

In April 2000, Oprah and Hearst Magazines introduced *O, The Oprah Magazine*, a monthly magazine that has become one of today's ***leading women's lifestyle publications*** [引领女性生活方式的出版物]. ***It is credited as*** [被赞誉为] being the most successful magazine launch in recent history and currently has a ***circulation*** [发行量] of 2.35 million readers each month.

Quotes by Oprah

Turn your wounds into wisdom.

The biggest adventure you can ever take is to live the life of your dreams.

Be thankful for what you have; you'll end up having more. If you concentrate on what you don't have, you will never, ever have enough.

The more you praise and celebrate your life, the more there is in life to celebrate.

One of the hardest things in life to learn are which bridges to cross and which bridges to burn.

Challenges are gifts that force us to search for a new center of gravity. Don't fight them. Just find a new way to stand.

Every day brings a chance for you to draw in a breath, kick off your shoes, and dance.

---

1 玛丽•璧克馥（Mary Pickford，1892–1979），加拿大电影演员，曾获得过奥斯卡最佳女主角奖和奥斯卡终身成就奖。
2 露西尔•鲍尔（1911–1989），美国一代电视女王。

比尔·盖茨
BILL GATES[1] (1955–)

As founder of Microsoft, Bill Gates is one of the most influential and richest people on the planet. In recent years he has ***retired from working full time*** [从全职工作上退休] at Microsoft, instead he has concentrated on working with his charitable foundation "The Bill and Melinda Gates Foundation[2]".

Gates wrote his first software program at the age of 13. In high school he helped form a group of programmers who ***computerized their school's payroll system*** [使学校工资管理系统计算机化].

In 1975 Gates, then a sophomore at Harvard University, joined his hometown friend Paul G. Allen to ***develop software*** [开发软件] for the first micro-computers. They began by adapting BASIC[3], a popular programming language used on large computers, for use on microcomputers. With the success of this project, Gates left Harvard during his junior year and, with Allen, formed Microsoft in 1876.

The big break for Microsoft came in 1980 when IBM approached them for a new BASIC operating system for its new computers. In the early 1980s IBM was by far ***the leading PC (personal computer) manufacture*** [主要的个人电脑生产商]. However ***increasingly there developed many IBM PC clones*** [出现越来越多的IBM仿制品]. Microsoft worked hard to sell its operating system to these other companies.

Thus Microsoft was able to ***gain the dominant position*** [获得主导地位] of software manufacture just as the ***personal computer market started to boom*** [个人电脑市场开始兴旺]. Since its early dominance no other company has come close to displacing Microsoft as the dominant provider of computer operating software.

In 1990 Microsoft ***released its first version*** [发布第一版本] of Windows. This was a ***breakthrough in operating software*** [操作系统的一次革命] as it ***replaced text interfaces with graphical interfaces*** [用图像界面取代文字界面]. It soon became a best seller and was able to ***capture the majority of the operating system market share*** [获得大多数的操作系统市场份额].

In 1995 Windows 95 was released, ***setting new standards*** [设定新标准] and features for operating systems. This version of windows has been the ***backbone*** [骨干] of all future releases from Windows 2000 to the latest XP, Vista and Windows 7.

With his wife Bill Gates formed the Bill & Melinda Gates Foundation. Bill Gates says ***much of the inspiration came from the example of David Rockefeller*** [大部分灵感来自于洛克菲勒]. Like Rockefeller, Gates has sought to focus on global issues ignored by the government; he also ***expressed an interest in*** [展现出兴趣] ***improving the standards of public school education*** [提高公立学校教学水平] in the US.

---

1 American computer programmer and entrepreneur who cofounded Microsoft Corporation, the world's largest personal-computer software company

2 比尔与美琳达·盖茨基金会，由比尔·盖茨与美琳达·盖茨夫妇资助的，全球最大的慈善基金会。

3 全称为：Beginner's All-purpose Symbolic Instruction Code，是一种初学者使用的程序设计语言。

Gates

Before you were born, your parents weren't as boring as they are now. They got that way from paying your bills, cleaning your clothes and listening to you talk about how cool you thought you were. So before you save the rain forest from the parasites of your parent's generation, try delousing the closet in your own room.

Don't compare yourself with anyone in this world...if you do so, you are insulting yourself.

The world won't care about your self-esteem. The world will expect you to accomplish something BEFORE you feel good about yourself.

Your most unhappy customers are your greatest source of learning.

改写 Rewrite the Story | in Your Own Words

乔布斯
STEVE JOBS[1] (1955–2011)

Steve Jobs, **_the visionary in the black turtleneck_** [身着高领毛衫的梦想家] who co-founded Apple in a Silicon Valley garage, built it into the world's leading tech company and **_led a mobile-computing revolution_** [引领移动计算革命] with wildly popular devices such as the iPhone, died on October 5, 2011. He was 56.

Steve Jobs is great at **_playing the countercultural icon_** [扮演反主流文化的偶像]. He's a **_college dropout_** [大学退学] who once **_backpacked around India_** [背包游印度] **_looking for spiritual enlightenment_** [寻求精神的启迪], and he takes only $1 a year in salary.

But don't let the black mock turtleneck and **_denim trousers_** [牛仔裤] fool you. More than anything else, Jobs is **_a canny CEO_** [精明的首席执行官] （Chief Executive Officer）who knows how to sell product. Steve Wozniak[2] was the **_technical genius_** [技术天才] behind the first Apple computer; Jobs **_saw the marketability_** [看到商机].

The **_hard-driving executive_** [精力充沛的管理者] **_pioneered the concept of the personal computer_** [开创个人电脑新概念] and of navigating them by **_clicking onscreen images with a mouse_** [用鼠标点击屏幕图标]. In more recent years, he introduced the iPod **_portable music player_** [随身音乐播放器], the iPhone and the iPad tablet—all of which **_changed how we live in the digital age_** [改变了我们在数字时代的生活].

It's long been **_Silicon Valley legend_** [硅谷的传奇]: Jobs and Wozniak built their first commercial product, the Apple 1, in Jobs' parents' **_garage_** [车库] in 1976. Jobs **_sold his Volkswagen van to help finance the venture_** [变卖自己的大众车来资助]. The primitive computer, priced at $666.66, had no keyboard or display, and **_customers had to assemble it themselves_** [顾客需要自己组装].

The following year, Apple unveiled the Apple II computer at the **_inaugural West Coast Computer Faire_** [西岸电脑展开幕式]. The machine **_was a hit_** [一炮走红], and the **_personal computing revolution was under way_** [个人电脑革命已经掀起].

Jobs was among the first computer engineers to **_recognize the appeal of the mouse and the graphical interface_** [认识到鼠标和图形界面的魅力], which let users operate computers by **_clicking on images_** [点击图像] instead of writing text.

Apple's pioneering Macintosh computer **_launched_** [面世] in early 1984. Macintosh sold well, but the demanding Jobs **_clashed frequently with colleagues_** [经常和同事产生摩擦], and in 1986, **_he was ousted from Apple after a power struggle_** [权利斗争后，他被赶出苹果公司].

Jobs had more success when he bought Pixar Animation Studios[3] from George Lucas before the company made it big with "*Toy Story*[4]." Jobs brought the same marketing skill to Pixar that

---

1 Cofounder of Apple Computer, Inc. （now Apple Inc.）, and a charismatic pioneer of the personal computer era.

2 斯蒂芬•盖瑞•沃兹尼亚克（Stephen Gary Wozniak, 1950–），曾与斯蒂夫•乔布斯合伙创立苹果电脑。

3 皮克斯动画工作室，是一家专门制作电脑动画的公司。1986 年，史蒂夫•乔布斯以 1000 万美元收购乔治•卢卡斯（George Lucas）的电脑动画部，成立了皮克斯动画工作室。2006 年，皮克斯被迪士尼以 74 亿美元收购，成为华特迪士尼公司的一部分。

4 《玩具总动员》，首部完全以 3D 电脑动画摄制而成的长篇剧情动画片。

he became known for at Apple. In 1996, Apple bought NeXT, **_returning Jobs to the then-struggling company_** [将 Jobs 请回当时苦苦挣扎的 Apple] he had co-founded. Within a year, he was running Apple again—older and perhaps wiser but no less of a **_perfectionist_** [完美主义者].

And in 2001, he **_took the stage_** [登台] to introduce the original iPod, the little white device that transformed portable music and **_kick-started Apple's furious comeback_** [揭开苹果绚烂复出的序幕].

Thus **_began one of the most remarkable second acts in the history of business_** [上演商界史诗般波澜壮阔的王子复仇记]. Over the next decade, Jobs **_wowed launch-event audiences, and consumers_** [让新品发布会现场的观众和消费者为之轰动], with **_one game-changing hit after another_** [一个个打破游戏规则、深受追捧的产品]: iTunes（2003）, the iPhone（2007）, the App Store（2008）, and the iPad（2010）.

Jobs

Stay hungry. Stay foolish.

Your time is limited, so don't waste it living someone else's life.

Don't be trapped by dogma, which is living with the results of other people's thinking.

Don't let the noise of other's opinions drown out your own inner voice. And most important, have the courage to follow your heart and intuition.

If you haven't found it yet, keep looking. Don't settle. As with all matters of the heart, you'll know when you find it. And, like any great relationship, it just gets better and better as the years roll on.

"Stay Hungry. Stay Foolish."
Excerpts of Steve Jobs Stanford Speech[1]

Steve Jobs on a college education

"...I naively chose a college that was almost as expensive as **_Stanford_**[2], and all of my working-class parents savings were being spent on my college tuition. After six months, I couldn't see the value in it. I had no idea what I wanted to do with my life and no idea how college was going to help me figure it out. And here I was spending all of the money my parents had saved their entire life. So I decided to drop out and trust that it would all work out OK. It was pretty scary at the time, but looking back it was one of the best decisions I ever made..."

---

1 2005 年，时任美国苹果公司首席执行官的乔布斯在斯坦福大学毕业典礼应邀发表演讲，本文节选其中部分内容。

2 斯坦福大学（Stanford University），位于美国加利福尼亚，是世界著名大学之一。

Steve Jobs on "connecting the dots" in life

"...you can't connect the dots looking forward; you can only connect them looking backwards. So you have to trust that the dots will somehow connect in your future. You have to trust in something—your **_gut_**[1], destiny, life, **_karma_**[2], whatever. This approach has never let me down, and it has made all the difference in my life..."

Steve Jobs on being fired from Apple

"...We had just released our finest creation—the **_Macintosh_**[3] —a year earlier, and I had just turned 30. And then I got fired. How can you get fired from a company you started?...So at 30 I was out. And very publicly out. What had been the focus of my entire adult life was gone, and it was devastating...I felt that I had let the previous generation of entrepreneurs down—that I had dropped the baton as it was being passed to me...I was a very public failure, and I even thought about running away from the valley. But something slowly began to dawn on me—I still loved what I did. The turn of events at Apple had not changed that one bit. I had been rejected, but I was still in love. And so I decided to start over. I didn't see it then, but it turned out that getting fired from Apple was the best thing that could have ever happened to me. The heaviness of being successful was replaced by the lightness of being a beginner again, less sure about everything. It freed me to enter one of the most creative periods of my life..."

Steve Jobs on faith and starting over

"... (being fired from Apple) was awful tasting medicine, but I guess the patient needed it. Sometimes life hits you in the head with a brick. Don't lose faith. I'm convinced that the only thing that kept me going was that I loved what I did. You've got to find what you love. And that is as true for your work as it is for your lovers. Your work is going to fill a large part of your life, and the only way to be truly satisfied is to do what you believe is great work. And the only way to do great work is to love what you do. If you haven't found it yet, keep looking. Don't settle. As with all matters of the heart, you'll know when you find it. And, like any great relationship, it just gets better and better as the years roll on. So keep looking until you find it. Don't settle..."

Steve Jobs on death and dying

"...When I was 17, I read a quote that went something like: 'If you live each day as if it was your last, someday you'll most certainly be right.' It made an impression on me, and since then, for the past 33 years, I have looked in the mirror every morning and asked myself: 'If today were the last day of my life, would I want to do what I am about to do today? ' And whenever the answer has been 'No' for too many days in a row, I know I need to change something. Remembering that I'll be dead soon is the most important tool I've ever encountered to help me make the big choices in life. Because almost everything—all external expectations, all pride, all fear of embarrassment or failure— these things just fall away in the face of death, leaving only what is truly important. Remembering that you are going to die is the best way I know to avoid the trap of thinking you have something to lose. You are already naked. There is no reason not to follow your heart...No one wants to die. Even people who want to go to heaven don't want to die to get there. And yet death is the destination we all share. No one has ever escaped it. And that is as it should be, because Death is very likely the single best invention of Life. It is Life's change agent. It clears out the old to make way for the new. Right now the new is you, but someday not too long from now, you will gradually

---

1 勇气。

2 轮回转世。

3 苹果机（Macintosh，简称 "Mac"），美国苹果公司生产的个人电脑。

become the old and be cleared away. Sorry to be so dramatic, but it is quite true. Your time is limited, so don't waste it living someone else's life. Don't be trapped by dogma—which is living with the results of other people's thinking. Don't let the noise of other's opinions drown out your own inner voice. And most important, have the courage to follow your heart and intuition. They somehow already know what you truly want to become. Everything else is secondary..."

Steve Jobs on cancer

"...About a year ago I was diagnosed with cancer. I had a scan at 7:30 in the morning, and it clearly showed a tumor on my **_pancreas_**[1]. I didn't even know what a pancreas was. The doctors told me this was almost certainly a type of cancer that is incurable, and that I should expect to live no longer than three to six months. My doctor advised me to go home and get my affairs in order, which is doctor's code for preparing to die...I lived with that diagnosis all day. Later that evening I had a **_biopsy_**[2], where they stuck an **_endoscope_**[3] down my throat, through my stomach and into my **_intestines_**[4], put a needle into my pancreas and got a few cells from the tumor. I was sedated, but my wife, who was there, told me that when they viewed the cells under a microscope the doctors started crying because it turned out to be a very rare form of pancreatic cancer that is curable with surgery. I had the surgery and I'm fine now..."

Steve Jobs: "Stay Hungry. Stay Foolish."

"...When I was young, there was an amazing publication called **_The Whole Earth Catalog_**[5], which was one of the bibles of my generation...It was sort of like Google in paperback form, 35 years before Google came along: it was idealistic, and overflowing with neat tools and great notions...(publisher) **_Stewart (Brand)_**[6] and his team put out several issues of _The Whole Earth Catalog_, and then when it had run its course, they put out a final issue. It was the mid-1970s, and I was your age. On the back cover of their final issue was a photograph of an early morning country road, the kind you might find yourself **_hitchhiking_**[7] on if you were so adventurous. Beneath it were the words: 'Stay Hungry. Stay Foolish.' It was their farewell message as they signed off...And I have always wished that for myself. And now, as you graduate to begin anew, I wish that for you. Stay Hungry. Stay Foolish."

---

1 胰腺。

2 活组织检查，指的是从患者身上某些器官直接摘取细胞或组织，用来检测肿瘤是否良性。

3 内窥镜。

4 肠。

5 《全球目录》是一系列在 20 世纪六七十年代风靡美国的杂志。这本杂志每期都会刊登各种商家提供的有益于自我教育的商品，它是当时年轻人反正统文化（counterculture）的一种体现。

6 Stewart Brand 是《全球目录》的创始人兼编辑。

7 搭便车。

Chapter 3

哲学与文学

PHILOSOPHY AND LITERATURE

SAVING
MY SAT
ESSAY

本 章 目 录

孔子 CONFUCIUS (551–479BC)

苏格拉底 SOCRATES (469–399 BC)

柏拉图 PLATO (428?–347 BC)

亚里士多德 ARISTOTLE (384–322 BC)

马基雅维利 NICCOLÒ MACHIAVELLI (1469–1527)

培根 FRANCIS BACON (1561–1626)

莎士比亚 WILLIAM SHAKESPEARE (1564–1616)

笛卡儿 RENÉ DESCARTES (1596–1650)

伏尔泰 VOLTAIRE (1694–1778)

狄更斯 CHARLES DICKENS (1812–1870)

列夫·托尔斯泰 LEO TOLSTOY (1828–1910)

尼采 FRIEDRICH NIETZSCHE (1844–1900)

萧伯纳 GEORGE BERNARD SHAW (1856–1950)

海明威 ERNEST HEMINGWAY (1899–1961)

孔子

CONFUCIUS[1] (551–479 BC)

Confucius ***was born in Qufu in the feudal state of Lu*** [出生在鲁国曲阜] in what ***is now Shandong Province*** [今在山东省境内].

The wise words and doctrines attributed to Confucius and his followers [孔子及其弟子的言论及学说] ***affected the moral, social and political structures of Chinese life*** [影响中国人的道德、社会及政治生活的方方面面] for two and a half thousand years.

The Confucian writings known as the ***Four Books***[2] [四书] were required reading for the ***ancient Chinese civil service examinations*** [中国古代科举考试] restored in 1313 and not ***abolished*** [废除] until 1905.

The ***Sishu collection*** [四书] (***Four Books*** [四书]) consists of, Daxue ("***Great Learning***[3] [《大学》]"), Zhongyong ("***Doctrine of the Mean***[4] [《中庸》]"), Lunyu ("***Conversations***," or "***Analects***[5] [《论语》]"), and ***Mencius***[6] [《孟子》].

His ***Analects*** [《论语》] contain a collection of his sayings and ***dialogues*** [学说] compiled by disciples after his death [死后由其门徒编纂].

The Wujing[7] [《五经》] collection consists of the Yijing ("***Classic of Changes***[8] [《易经》]"; known to many as the I-Ching), Shujing ("***Classic of History***[9] [《书经》]"), Shijing ("***Classic of Poetry***[10] [《诗经》]"), Liji ("***Collection of Rituals***[11] [《礼记》]"), and Chunqiu ("***Spring and Autumn Annals***[12] [《春秋》]").

Confucius is known as the first teacher in China who wanted to ***make education available to all men*** [让所有人能够接受教育].

Confucius was a wise man. His teachings focused on the ***proper relationships between people*** [人与人之间和谐的关系], including ***respect for one's parents and ancestors*** [尊敬父母及祖宗], and the ***creation of a harmonious society*** [构建和谐的社会] based on virtue.

The faith in the ***possibility of ordinary human beings to become awe-inspiring sages*** [普通人能够成为众人景仰的圣人] ***is deeply rooted in the Confucian heritage*** [深深根植在儒家信仰中], and the ***insistence that human beings are teachable, improvable, and***

---

1 China's most famous teacher, philosopher, and political theorist, whose ideas have influenced the civilization of East Asia.

2 四书，是指《论语》、《孟子》、《大学》和《中庸》。

3 《大学》，本书哲学思想主要在于传授做人做事最根本的道理。

4 《中庸》，本书主旨在于修养人性、学习的方式等，中庸所追求的修养的最高境界是"至诚"。

5 《论语》，孔子门生及再传弟子集录整理孔子和他的弟子等言行为主的汇编。

6 《孟子》，本书主要记述孟子思想。

7 五经，是指《诗经》、《尚书》、《礼记》、《周易》和《春秋》。

8 《易经》，并被儒家尊为"五经"之首，和《黄帝内经》、《山海经》并称为上古三大奇书。

9 《书经》，又称《尚书》，是中国最早的一部史书，也是散文之祖。

10 《诗经》是中国最早的诗歌总集。

11 《礼记》，本书所收文章是孔子的学生及战国时期儒学学者的作品。

12 《春秋》，记载各诸侯国重大历史事件，宣扬王道思想。

perfectible through personal and communal endeavor [通过个人及社会的努力，人是可以被教化、进步及完善的] *is typically Confucian* [是典型的儒家思想].

Confucius thought that kings were able to **govern primarily through the power of setting a good ethical example** [树立道德模范来治理国家], rather than through **military force** [武力] or **criminal penalties** [法律惩罚].

According to Confucius, a good person has **ren** [仁], **translated as** [译作] "**humaneness** [慈悲]" or "**benevolence** [善行]," which is **the summation of all other virtues** [所有美德的总和].

Confucius thought that **there was great joy to** [莫大的愉快] be found in everyday **family life** [家庭生活], **participating in communal activities** [参加公共活动], enjoying music, and spending time with one's friends.

During **China's Cultural Revolution** ["文化大革命"]（1966–1976），Confucius **was condemned** [被责难] as an element of China's "**feudal** [封建制度]" past. However, **economic and social changes** [社会经济发展] in China since the 1980s have **led to renewed interest in** [产生新的兴趣] and **respect for Confucius and Confucianism** [推崇孔子和儒家学说].

From a modern perspective [从现代角度], Confucius's **worldview** [世界观] **has certain limitations** [具有局限性]. He **was ignorant of** [无视] **cultural diversity** [文化多样性]; he accepted the **sexism** [男性至上主义] of his society; He **showed no interest in** [不感兴趣] **natural science or technology** [自然科学技术].

However, Confucius will **no doubt** [无疑地] continue to **inspire people across the world** [鼓舞全世界人民] with **his vision of social harmony** [社会和谐的愿景], his **insight into human virtue** [人类美德的洞察], and his **techniques for cultivating ethical individuals** [培育个人道德的方法].

 by Quotes **Confucius**

By three methods we may learn wisdom: First, by reflection, which is noblest; Second, by imitation, which is easiest; and third by experience, which is the bitterest.

Choose a job you love, and you will never have to work a day in your life.

If you make a mistake and do not correct it, this is called a mistake.

Everything has beauty, but not everyone sees it.

Our greatest glory is not in never falling, but in rising every time we fall.

No matter how busy you may think you are, you must find time for reading, or surrender yourself to self-chosen ignorance.

You cannot open a book without learning something.

Time flows away like the water in the river.

苏格拉底

SOCRATES[1] （469–399 BC）

Of all the famous names of ancient Greece [纵观古希腊所有名流], Socrates is surely the most widely known. ***His fame does not derive from his writings*** [其声望并非来自其著述], for he left none.

Socrates spent much of his time in the streets and ***marketplace of Athens*** [雅典的街道集市], ***querying every man he met*** [质问他所遇到的每一个人] about whether that man knew anything. Socrates said that, if there was an ***afterlife*** [来世], he would ***pose the same questions to the shades in Hades*** [在阴间问同样的问题].

Socrates himself wrote no books, but ***his conversations were remembered by his disciple Plato and later published by him as dialogues*** [他的谈话被其弟子柏拉图以对话体的方式记录下来]. Very often these ***Socratic dialogues*** [柏拉图式的对话] will ***emphasize a specific philosophical question*** [强调某一具体的哲学问题], such as "what is piety?", "what is justice?", "what is virtue", and "what is love?"

Socrates' ***discourse moved in two directions*** [谈话分为两个方向]—outward, to objective definitions, and inward, to discovering the inner person, the soul, which for Socrates, was the ***source of all Truth*** [真理的来源]. Such a search is not to be conducted at a weekend lecture but is the ***quest of a lifetime*** [一生的追寻].

Unlike the Greek philosophers before him [和之前的希腊哲人不同的是], Socrates ***was less concerned with abstract metaphysical ponderings*** [不太关心形而上学抽象的思考] than with practical questions of how we ought to live, and what the good life for man might be.

Socrates ***lived through times of great political upheaval in his birthplace of Athens*** [经历雅典政局的剧变], a city which would eventually ***make him a scapegoat for its troubles*** [成为社会动荡的替罪羊] and ultimately cost his life.

In his quest for truth [追求真理], Socrates managed to ***offend many of the powerful figures of the Athens*** [冒犯雅典的权势]. At the age of 70, after Athens had ***gone through several changes of leadership*** [政权几经更迭], Socrates ***was accused of*** [被控告] not worshipping the gods of the state, of ***introducing unfamiliar religious practices*** [引入异教], and of ***corrupting the young*** [腐化青年]. Socrates' enemies brought him to trial hoping to ***humiliate*** [羞辱] him by forcing him to ***grovel and beg for mercy*** [屈膝求饶].

Far from groveling [非但没有屈节], at his trial, Socrates ***angered the jury*** [激怒陪审团] of 500 by lecturing to them about their ***ignorance*** [无知]. The ***enraged*** [愤怒的] jury ***condemned him to death*** [宣判苏格拉底死罪].

Despite the pleas of his friends [尽管朋友乞求], Socrates refused to ***escape from the prison*** [越狱], saying that if he broke the law by escaping, he would be declaring himself an enemy of all laws. So he ***drank the hemlock*** [喝了毒药] and ***philosophized with his friends to the last moment*** [仍然和朋友探讨哲学直到生命的最后一刻].

---

1 Greek philosopher whose way of life, character, and thought exerted a profound influence on ancient and modern philosophy.

In death, Socrates became the **_universal symbol of martyrdom for the truth_** [为真理殉难的恒久标志].

Quotes by Socrates

The only true wisdom is in knowing you know nothing.

The unexamined life is not worth living.

Wonder is the beginning of wisdom.

I cannot teach anybody anything. I can only make them think.

The only good is knowledge and the only evil is ignorance.

Death may be the greatest of all human blessings.

改写 Rewrite the Story | in Your Own Words

柏拉图

PLATO[1]（428?–347 BC）

拯救我的 SAT 写作

Saving My SAT Essay

Plato **_became a pupil of_** [师从] Greek philosopher Socrates. Then he **_set up a school_** [设立学校]—the first university in 387 BC, called the **_Academy_** [学院]. **_Pupils_** [学生] studied **_astronomy_** [天文学], **_biology_** [生物学], mathematics, politics, and philosophy at the Academy.

Much of Plato's own philosophy is **_a development of Socratic themes_** [苏格拉底哲学体系的发展]. In particular, he extended Socrates' search for the definitions of concepts such as justice, courage, and **_piety_** [虔诚] into a **_full-blown theory_** [成熟的理论] about the nature of reality.

The **_essence_** [精髓] of Plato's philosophy **_is depicted_** [描述] in the Myth of the Cave ["洞穴"比喻], which appears in his most important work, **_the Republic_**[2] [《理想国》].

The myth of the cave describes prisoners chained in such a way that they **_face the back wall of a cave_** [面对着洞穴里侧的一面墙]. They can **_see nothing of_** [不能看见] themselves or of each other.

People walk carrying vases, statues, and other artifacts on their heads [人们用头顶起瓶子、雕像等器物走动] **_before a brightly burning fire_** [在一堆火前] and cast **_shadows on the wall_** [在墙上投下影子].

Prisoners **_can only see the shadows on the wall of the cave_** [只能看到墙上的影子]. They can only hear the echoes. They **_mistake these echoes and shadows for reality_** [他们错以为这些回声和影子是真的].

Then, one of the prisoners **_breaks out of the chains_** [挣脱枷锁] and **_escapes from the cave into the light of day_** [逃出山洞，获得自由]. The **_light blinds him_** [日光让他头昏眼花] so that he would try to **_turn back to the cave_** [返回山洞].

However, the prisoner overcomes all the difficulties and **_gradually accustoms himself to_** [让自己逐渐习惯于] looking at everything by first **_observing objects at night by the light of the moon and stars_** [夜晚趁着月光星光观察物体], and then looking at the shadows of the trees, then at the trees and mountains. Finally he is able to see the sun itself.

Plato suggests that if this enlightened man were to return to the cave and **_liberate his fellow prisoners_** [解放其他囚犯], he would **_be beaten to death_** [被打死]. This is **_a clear allusion to the death of Socrates_** [暗示苏格拉底之死].

The shadowy environment of the cave **_symbolizes the physical world of appearances_** [代表真实世界的表象]. Escape into the sun-filled setting outside the cave **_symbolizes the transition to the real world_** [转换到真实世界], the world of full and perfect being, which is the proper object of knowledge.

---

1 Ancient Greek philosopher, student of Socrates, teacher of Aristotle, and founder of the Academy, best known as the author of philosophical works of unparalleled influence.

2 常译作《理想国》，古希腊哲学家柏拉图的作品。以苏格拉底为主角，采用对话体的形式，主要探讨政治科学。

 **Plato**

Be kind, for everyone you meet is fighting a harder battle.

Every heart sings a song, incomplete, until another heart whispers back. Those who wish to sing always find a song. At the touch of a lover, everyone becomes a poet.

Music gives a soul to the universe, wings to the mind, flight to the imagination and life to everything.

Wise men speak because they have something to say; fools because they have to say something.

We can easily forgive a child who is afraid of the dark; the real tragedy of life is when men are afraid of the light.

The price good men pay for indifference to public affairs is to be ruled by evil men.

改写 Rewrite the Story | in Your Own Words

亚里士多德

ARISTOTLE[1]（384–322 BC）

Aristotle ***received his education from age seventeen in Plato's 'Academy'***[2] [十七岁开始在柏拉图学院接受教育], where he stayed for some 20 years until Plato's death. Later he founded his own institution—'the ***Lyceum*** [学园]', which came to be known as the ***Peripatetic school***[3] [逍遥学派].

In 345 BC, Aristotle became the tutor of the king's young son Alexander（356–323 BC）, later known as ***Alexander the Great*** [亚历山大大帝].

Although Aristotle lived and worked nearly two and a half thousand years ago, his thought ***is still a vital and constitutive part of Western culture*** [是西方文明重要的组成部分].

He was ***Plato's pupil*** [柏拉图的学生], but ***not his uncritical disciple*** [并不是不加批评的那种徒弟]. In Aristotle's school, Platonic philosophy was taught, but it was also criticized.

More than just a philosopher, Aristotle was a scientist, ***astronomer*** [天文学家], ***political theorist*** [政治理论家] and the inventor of what is now called ***formal logic*** [形式逻辑学].

More than any other philosopher before him, Aristotle ***made much of observation*** [做了大量观察] and ***strict classification of data in his studies*** [对研究数据进行严格分类].

The scope of Aristotle's work is immense. It ranges from the ***charting of planets*** [绘制星象图] to the ***classification of fishes*** [鱼类分类]; from study of the winds, the seas and the weather to the analysis of dramatic tragedy; from morals and politics to geometry and number. His influence has been ***immeasurable*** [不可估量的].

In ***astronomy*** [天文学], Aristotle proposed ***a finite, spherical universe*** [有限圆球状的宇宙], with ***the earth at its center*** [地球居于中心]. The central region is made up of four elements: earth, air, fire, and water.

He held that heavier bodies of a given material fall faster than lighter ones when their shapes are the same, a mistaken view that was accepted as fact until the Italian physicist and astronomer ***Galileo*** [伽利略]（1564–1642）***conducted his experiment with weights dropped from the Leaning Tower of Pisa*** [在比萨斜塔完成各种重物的落体实验].

---

1 Ancient Greek philosopher and scientist, one of the greatest intellectual figures of western history. He was the author of a philosophical and scientific system that became the framework and vehicle for both Christian Scholasticism and medieval Islamic philosophy. Even after the intellectual revolutions of the Renaissance（指文艺复兴）, the Reformation（指宗教改革）, and the Enlightenment（指启蒙运动）, Aristotelian concepts remained embedded in western thinking.

2 汉译做"学园"，公元前 385 年，由柏拉图于雅典创立，此后学园（Academy）一词就代表了高等教育机构。

3 汉译做"逍遥学派"，公元前 335 年，由亚里士多德创立，又称亚里士多德学派。亚里士多德在雅典的吕克昂建立了一所学院，该处有一小树林和许多可供散步的林荫道，亚里士多德喜欢在这林荫道上和学生散步、讲课和讨论学问，所以被称为逍遥学派。

Aristotle

Plato is dear to me, but dearer still is truth.

What is a friend? A single soul dwelling in two bodies.

It is the mark of an educated mind to be able to entertain a thought without accepting it.

We are what we repeatedly do. Excellence, then, is not an act, but a habit.

Hope is a waking dream.

Happiness is the meaning and the purpose of life, the whole aim and end of human existence.

The educated differ from the uneducated as much as the living differ from the dead.

The aim of art is to represent not the outward appearance of things, but their inward significance.

改写 | **Rewrite the Story** | **in Your Own Words**

马基雅维利

NICCOLÒ MACHIAVELLI[1] （1469–1527）

Machiavelli's influential writings on **statecraft** [君王之术] have **turned his name into a synonym for cunning and duplicity** [让他的名字成为"狡猾诡辩"的同义词] and **brutal and deceptive means of grasping and retaining power** [用残忍和欺骗的方法夺取和巩固政权].

The Prince[2] [《君主论》], implies that he favored a **monarchy** [君主政体] rather than a **republic** [共和政体], remarking that 'the condition of Italy makes a republic **impracticable** [走不通的]'.

In *The Prince*, Machiavelli's great manual of power, he wrote, "since men love as they themselves determine but fear as their ruler determines, **a wise prince must rely upon what he and not others can control** [聪明的君主应该依赖只有自己能够控制的一切]".

He also advised, "**One must be a fox in order to recognize traps** [君主要像狐狸一般狡猾，才能识别陷阱], and **a lion to frighten off wolves** [像狮子般勇猛，才能击退狼群]. Those who simply act like lions are stupid. So it follows that **a prudent ruler** [精明的统治者] cannot, and must not, honor his word **when it places him at a disadvantage** [让自己处于劣势]".

Machiavellianism [马基雅维利主义] means using **clever trickery** [诡诈], and **amoral**[3] **methods** [不讲道德的方法] to **achieve a desired goal** [达成目的], especially in politics.

Machiavelli believed that **a ruler is not bound by traditional ethical norms** [统治者不应该被传统的道德规范所限制]. **In his view** [在他看来], a prince **should be concerned only with power** [只应该关心权力] and be bound only by rules that would lead to success in political actions.

Machiavelli insists that the **generality of people are simple and are easily deceived** [普通大众头脑简单，容易被欺骗]. The prince should **make sure he is seen as a man of compassion** [被看起来是个充满怜悯之心的人], **good faith** [真诚], integrity, kindness, and religion: '**everyone sees what you appear to be** [大众看到的是戴着面具的你], **few experience what you really are** [几乎没有人了解真实的你]...the **common people are always impressed by appearances and results** [大众通常被表象和结果所影响]'.

---

1 Italian Renaissance political philosopher and statesman, secretary of the Florentine republic, whose most famous work, *The Prince* （Italian: Il Principe), brought him a reputation as an atheist and an immoral cynic.

2 译作《君主论》，是意大利文艺复兴时期马基雅维利的政治科学作品。本书重要的观点是君主该不受任何道德准则的束缚，可以不择手段去实现自己的目的。

3 这里需要区分两个形容词："immoral"和"amoral"。"immoral"是指"不道德的，道德败坏的"，"amoral"是指"与道德分离的、无关的"。有些哲学家认为，政治科学的本身特点就是"amoral"，强调"政治"和"道德"分家。

Machiavelli

I'm not interested in preserving the status quo; I want to overthrow it.

Men are driven by two principal impulses, either by love or by fear.

As a prince must be able to act just like a beast, he should learn from the fox and the lion; because the lion does not defend himself against traps, and the fox does not defend himself against wolves. So one has to be a fox in order to recognize traps, and a lion to frighten off wolves.

Men in general judge more from appearances than from reality. All men have eyes, but few have the gift of penetration.

改写 Rewrite the Story in Your Own Words

培根

FRANCIS BACON[1] （1561–1626）

拯救我的 SAT 写作

Saving My SAT
Essay

Attributed as the originator of the saying '***knowledge is power*** [知识就是力量]', his importance as a philosopher ***is most notable with regard to his concern for scientific method*** [因其对科学方法的关注而著称].

Bacon's ***real interests lay in science*** [真正兴趣在科学]. Much of the science of the period was based on the work of the ancient Greek philosopher Aristotle. While many ***Aristotelian ideas*** [亚里士多德学派的观点], such ***as the position of the earth at the centre of the universe*** [地心说], had ***been overturned*** [被推翻], his ***methodology*** [方法论] was still being used.

This held that ***scientific truth could be reached by way of authoritative argument*** [科学真理可以通过权威的论证获得]: ***if sufficiently clever men discussed a subject long enough*** [足够智慧的人长时间探讨一个问题], the truth would eventually be discovered. Bacon ***challenged this*** [挑战这一观点], arguing that truth ***required evidence from the real world*** [从现实世界获得证据]. He published his ideas, initially in '***Novum Organum***'2 (1620), ***an account of the correct method of acquiring natural knowledge*** [论述获得自然知识的正确方法].

Bacon's ***political ascent also continued*** [政途坦荡]. In 1618 he ***was appointed lord chancellor*** [被任命为大法官], the most powerful position in England, and in 1621 he ***was created viscount St. Albans*** [被封为圣奥尔本斯子爵]. Shortly afterwards, he ***was charged by parliament with accepting bribes*** [被国会指控受贿], which he admitted. He ***was fined and imprisoned*** [被罚款入狱] and then ***banished from court*** [被法院驱逐]. Although the king later ***pardoned*** [赦免] him, this was the ***end of Bacon's public life*** [公众生涯结束].

Bacon's ***personality has usually been regarded as unattractive*** [培根的人格并不具魅力]: he was ***cold-hearted*** [冷漠的], ***cringed to the powerful*** [趋炎附势], and ***took bribes*** [接受贿赂], and then had ***the impudence to say he had not been influenced by them*** [厚颜地说自己没有受到这些行为的影响].

In 1626, he ***died of a bronchitis*** [死于支气管炎] ***brought on by the chill he suffered*** [受寒] when he ***filled a chicken's body with snow*** [将鸡腹填满雪] to ***see if the flesh could be preserved by the cold*** [研究在寒冷条件下肉能否被保存].

---

1 A lawyer, statesman, philosopher, and master of the English tongue.

2 译作《新工具论》，1620 年出版，是英国哲学家培根未完成的巨著《伟大的复兴》（*The Great Instauration*）六个部分中的第二部分，主要探讨科学方法，本书有力地推动了近代实验科学。

 **Bacon**

Some books are to be tasted, others to be swallowed, and some few to be chewed and digested: that is, some books are to be read only in parts, others to be read, but not curiously, and some few to be read wholly, and with diligence and attention.

Knowledge itself is power.

In order for the light to shine so brightly, the darkness must be present.

改写 | Rewrite the Story | in Your Own Words |

莎士比亚
WILLIAM SHAKESPEARE[1] (1564–1616)

Shakespeare's reputation as dramatist and poet actor is unique. Nearly 400 years after Shakespeare's death, he ***remains the most influential writer who ever lived*** [至今最具影响力的作家], although many of the facts of his life remain mysterious. The writings of Shakespeare have been justly termed "the richest, the purest, the fairest, that ***genius uninspired ever penned*** [平凡天才所写过的]."

Aside for the Bible [除《圣经》外], the ***Bard of Avon***[2] [埃文河畔的吟游诗人] (he ***was born and brought up in*** [生长于] Stratford-on-Avon) ***is undoubtedly the most quoted author*** [无疑是被引述最多的作家] in the English language and ***has been translated into almost every written language*** [被翻译成几乎每一种语言]. His plays have been performed over the world for some centuries, and his poetic achievements ***remain the standard of comparison for poets writing in the English language*** [作为其他英诗的评价标准].

It's a wonder that [令人称奇的是] the works of Shakespeare, next to the Bible, ***are the most highly esteemed of all the classics of English literature*** [所有英国古典文学中最受尊崇的]. "So extensively have the characters of Shakespeare been drawn upon by artist, poets, and writers of fiction," says an American author.

His language, ***characters*** [人物性格], ***plots*** [故事情节], and wit ***are all consistently brilliant*** [一如既往地才华横溢]. ***Tragedies*** [悲剧] such as ***Romeo and Juliet***[3] [《罗密欧与朱丽叶》], ***Hamlet***[4] [《哈姆雷特》], and ***King Lear***[5] [《李尔王》] have survived the centuries with their beauty and power and remain some of the most popular and ***oft-produced plays*** [常常被搬上舞台]. His comedies [喜剧], including ***A Midsummer Night's Dream***[6] [《仲夏夜之梦》] and ***Twelfth Night***[7] [《第十二夜》], still charm and entertain.

Shakespeare handled ***drama*** [舞台喜剧], ***romance*** [浪漫] and ***slapstick*** [闹剧] comedy with equal ease. He is also known for his poetry, especially his ***sonnets*** [十四行诗]. Today, around the entire planet, even in countries where English is rarely heard, the name of the most famous writer in history continues to be William Shakespeare.

---

1 English poet, dramatist, and actor, often called the English national poet and considered by many to be the greatest dramatist of all time.

2 "埃文河畔的吟游诗人"，或"吟游诗人"，得名于莎士比亚生长于埃文河畔斯特拉特福地区。

3 译作《罗密欧与朱丽叶》，讲述一对一见钟情的情侣凄美的感情故事。

4 译作《哈姆雷特》，莎士比亚四大悲剧之一，另外三部为《麦克白》(*Macbeth*)、《奥赛罗》(*Othello: The Moor of Venice*) 及《李尔王》(*King Lear*)。
第三幕第一场的经典独白"生存还是毁灭，这是个问题"(To be, or not to be; that's the question) 是戏剧史上流传最广的台词之一。

5 译作《李尔王》(*King Lear*)，故事基于一位传说中不列颠国王李尔（罗马人时代之前），主要线索围绕李尔王和他的三个女儿展开。

6 译作《仲夏夜之梦》(*A Midsummer Night's Dream*)，莎翁的一部浪漫喜剧。

7 又名《随心所欲》(*What you will*)，莎翁的一部浪漫喜剧，得名于基督教圣诞假期中的最后一夜，即第十二夜——主显节 (Epiphany)。

Shakespeare

To be, or not to be, that is the question.

All the world's a stage
And all the men and women merely players.
They have their exits and their entrances;
And one man in his time plays many parts...

The fool doth think he is wise, but the wise man knows himself to be a fool.

Words are easy, like the wind; Faithful friends are hard to find.

改写 | Rewrite the Story | in Your Own Words

笛卡儿

RENÉ DESCARTES[1] (1596–1650)

Descartes may not have been very good looking, but he was smart [笛卡尔称不上美貌，但是他绝顶聪明].

Having made his contribution to math, in1633 Descartes was about to ***publish his manuscript on physics*** [发表其物理学研究手稿], but when ***it dawned on him*** [使他恍然大悟] that 17 years earlier Galileo had ***been arrested by the Inquisition*** [被宗教审判所拘捕] for teaching views about the physical world that were very close to Descartes' views, Descartes ran, did not walk, to his publisher to ***withdraw his manuscript*** [撤回手稿].

Descartes was a good but modern Catholic [笛卡尔是一位虔诚但有现代思想的天主教徒]. He believed that ***Church had made a big mistake in the Galileo episode*** [在伽利略事件上犯下了严重错误]. He correctly saw that if ***religion tried to stem the tide of science*** [宗教试图阻挡科学发展潮流], ***religion would be swept away*** [宗教终将被扫除]. But Descartes did not want to ***go to jail*** [牢狱之灾] to prove it.

He decided to ***ease his ideas about physics onto an unsuspecting religious establishment by smuggling them into a book of philosophy*** [将其物理学观点夹带在哲学书中，这样宗教组织便不会生疑] called ***Meditations on First Philosophy, in Which Is Proved the Existence of God and the Immortality of the Soul***[2] [《第一哲学沉思集，其中论证上帝的存在和灵魂的不灭》].

In his book *Meditations on First Philosophy*, Descartes announced ***a massive intellectual project*** [宏伟的思想工程]. He related his intention to ***tear down the edifice of knowledge*** [拆除知识大厦] and ***rebuild it from the foundations up*** [从地基开始重建].

To discover a firm foundation of absolute certainty upon which to ***build his objective system of knowledge*** [用绝对可靠的事实去构建客观知识系统], Descartes chose a method of "***radical doubt*** [绝对怀疑]," whose motto was "De omnibus dubitandum"—***everything is to be doubted*** [任何事情都是值得怀疑的].

Descartes concluded that ***there was one and only one thing that was absolutely certain*** [只有一件事是肯定的]—that he existed! His assertion "I think, therefore I am" was true whether he was dreaming, and ***whether the senses deceived*** [不论感官是否受到欺骗].

Rene Descartes is often called the father of modern philosophy because he ***rejected Aristotle's idea*** [反对亚里士多德的观点] that ***knowledge is derived from the senses*** [知识源自感官] and ***promoted a 'new science' grounded in reason, observation and experiment*** [倡导新科学应根植于推理、观察和实验].

---

1 French mathematician, scientist, and philosopher. Because he was one of the first to abandon scholastic Aristotelianism, because he formulated the first modern version of mind-body dualism, from which stems the mind-body problem, and because he promoted the development of a new science grounded in observation and experiment, he has been called the father of modern philosophy.

2 法国哲学家笛卡儿所著的一本哲学论文选集，以拉丁语首次出版于 1641 年。

Descartes

Cogito ergo sum. (*I think, therefore I am.*)

If you would be a real seeker after truth, it is necessary that at least once in your life you doubt, as far as possible, all things.

The reading of all good books is like conversation with the finest men of past centuries.

Doubt is the origin of wisdom.

改写 | Rewrite the Story | in Your Own Words

伏尔泰
VOLTAIRE[1] (1694–1778)

Plays, pamphlets, poetry, prose, much of a satirical nature [讽刺性意味], ***flowed from his pen*** [从他的笔下流出]. Voltaire, as much as any individual, ***prepared the ground for the French Revolution***[2] [为法国大革命孕育了土壤], though he himself did not live to see it.

Voltaire is one of the greatest French writers, known especially as a ***courageous crusader against tyranny, bigotry, and cruelty*** [反对暴政、偏执和残忍的勇猛圣斗士].

Voltaire studied law but abandoned it to become a writer. He was ***a prolific writer*** [多产的作家], and ***produced works in almost every literary form*** [创作的文学作品包涵各种文学形式], authoring plays, poetry, novels, essays, historical and scientific works, over 20,000 letters and over two thousand books and pamphlets.

In France, in the 1700's, he was the most ***outspoken writer*** [直言不讳的作家] who ***supported political and social reform*** [支持政治和社会改革]. Because his writing criticized the King and the Church, he ***lived most of his life in constant fear of being jailed*** [一生恐遭牢狱之灾]. Thus, he spent comparatively few years of his life in Paris, where his stay was either forbidden or too dangerous.

Voltaire ***was twice imprisoned in the Bastille*** [两度被收押在巴士底狱] for his remarks and in 1726 ***was exiled to England*** [被流放到英国], where his philosophical interests deepened. ***Voltaire greatly admired the degree of individual liberty he had found in England*** [英国个人自由让伏尔泰大为羡慕].

His advocacy of a free parliament and of religious freedom [支持开放的议会和宗教自由], as well as the theories of Isaac Newton and John Locke[3], soon ***landed him in hot water*** [置身于水深火热之中] again. He was forced to leave Paris and ***took refuge with*** [避难于] an intelligent, cultured woman, La Marquise du Chatelet[4], with whom he ***formed an intimate and enduring relationship*** [亲密而持久的情谊].

History, philosophy, poetry, plays and ***satirical broadsides*** [讽刺抨击] continued to ***pour from his pen*** [从他的笔下流出]. He was now such a dominant figure that even the ***ecclesiastical authorities*** [宗教权威], ***bitterly hostile to his unending criticism*** [憎恶他无休止的批判], ***were reluctant to*** [不情愿] move against him. Voltaire was celebrated throughout Europe and the ***British Isles*** [不列颠诸岛].

The French revolution had recognized its debt to the man [法国大革命一定程度上归功于伏尔泰] whose ***pen had, indeed, proved mightier than the sword*** [文章的威力胜过刀枪].

---

1 One of the greatest French writers. Although only a few of his works are still read, he continues to be held in worldwide repute as a courageous crusader against tyranny, bigotry, and cruelty.

2 法国大革命(1789–1799)，统治法国多个世纪的绝对君主制封建制度土崩瓦解，传统观念逐渐被全新的天赋人权(Natural Rights)、三权分立(Separation of Powers)等的民主思想所取代。

3 约翰•洛克(1632–1704)，英国的哲学家，在社会契约理论(Social Contract)方面做出了重要贡献，他主张政府只有在取得人民同意，并且保障人民拥有生命、自由、和财产的自然权利时，其统治才有正当性。

4 夏特莱(1706–1749)，法国数学家、物理学家、作家，伏尔泰情人之一。

Quotes by Voltaire

Let us read, and let us dance; these two amusements will never do any harm to the world.

Love truth, but pardon error.

Dare to think for yourself.

I don't know where I am going, but I am on my way.

Know more

Age of Enlightenment

The Age of Enlightenment[1] [启蒙运动] covers about a century and a half in Europe, beginning **with the publication of Francis Bacon's Novum Organum** [培根《新工具》的出版] (1620) and ending **with Immanuel Kant's Critique of Pure Reason** [康德《纯粹理性批判》] (1781) or ending with the French Revolution (1789).

Emboldened by the revolution in physics commenced by Newtonian kinematics [发端于牛顿力学体系革命], Enlightenment thinkers argued that **reason could free humankind from superstition and religious authoritarianism** [理性应该把人类从迷信和宗教的独裁中解放出来] that had brought suffering and death to millions in religious wars.

Montesquieu[2] [孟德斯鸠], French political thinker who lived during the Enlightenment, is famous for his articulation of the theory of **separation of powers**[3] [三权分立].

Jean-Jacques Rousseau[4] [让-雅克•卢梭], whose political philosophy influenced the French Revolution as well as the **overall development of modern political, sociological and educational thought** [现代政治、社会、教育思想], is known for his work—**On the Social Contract**[5] [《社会契约论》].

This movement also **provided a framework for the American and French Revolutions** [为美国和法国革命提供框架], the **Latin American independence movement** [拉美独立运动], and also **led to the rise of capitalism** [导致资本主义兴起] and **the birth of socialism** [社会主义的诞生].

1 启蒙运动，通常是指在 18 世纪初至 1789 年法国大革命间的一个新思维不断涌现的时代。本时期的发展特色为不受束缚地、但常常也是不加批判地使用理性，勇于质疑权威与传统教条，朝个人主义方向发展，强调普世人类进步的观念。启蒙运动同时为美国独立战争与法国大革命提供了框架，并且导致了资本主义和社会主义的兴起。

2 孟德斯鸠(1689–1775)，法国启蒙时期思想家、社会学家。

3 "三权分立"即立法权、行政权和司法权分属于三个不同的国家机关，三者相互制约、权力均衡，"三权分立"对 1787 年的《美国宪法》产生了重要影响。

4 让•雅克•卢梭(1712–1778)，法国思想家、哲学家。他流传最广的名言为其著作《社会契约论》(*The Social Contract*)的开篇"人生而自由，但却无往不在枷锁之中"(Man was born free, and he is everywhere in chains)。

5 译作《社会契约论》(*The Social Contract*)，法国思想家卢梭于 1762 年完成，其中"主权在民"的思想是现代民主制度的基石。

哲学与文学 PHILOSOPHY AND LITERATURE

Chapter 3

Adam Smith[1] [亚当·斯密] is widely cited as the father of modern economics and capitalism. **The Wealth of Nations**[2] [《国富论》] is considered his **magnum opus** [巨著] and the first modern work of economics. **Invisible hand** [看不见的手], **first coined by Smith** [斯密斯最先创造], use to describe the self-regulating nature of the marketplace.

改写 | Rewrite the Story | in Your Own Words

拯救我的 SAT 写作
Saving My SAT Essay

狄更斯

CHARLES DICKENS[1] (1812–1870)

The pen is mightier than the sword [笔比刀剑更有力]? Perhaps. But it is, at times, mightier than governments. This was certainly the case for Charles Dickens. It was his pen which ***attacked the social evils*** [攻击社会邪恶势力] of Victorian England so effectively that ***successive governments were forced to bring about badly-needed reforms*** [一届届政府被迫实施亟待的改革].

Dickens himself ***born in poverty*** [出身贫苦], was no revolutionary, but he knew only too well from his own experience of the ***misery and squalor of life in the slums*** [贫民窟里穷困的生活].

He was hardly the first to raise the banner of reform [他算不上第一个举起改革大旗的人], but so powerful was his pen that the ***governing classes were compelled to*** [统治阶级被迫] pay attention and ***slowly mitigate the worst conditions of the downtrodden and oppressed*** [逐渐改善被压迫者的困境], including the appalling and widespread use of ***child labor*** [童工].

It was ***not unusual*** [常见的] in industrial society in the 19th century for children even as young as 6 years old to work 10 hours a day ***in mines or factories for starvation wages*** [在矿场或工厂赚钱糊口].

Charles ***received only intermittent schooling*** [断断续续地读了些书] and ***was compelled to go to work at the age of 11 in a shoe factory*** [11 岁被迫到鞋厂工作], ***pasting labels on bottles of polish*** [给鞋油瓶子贴标签]. The experience was so ***traumatic*** [留下创伤的] that he never spoke about it, even to his family.

Righteous anger stemmed from his own situation [自己生活的窘困让他愤由心生] and the conditions under which ***working-class people lived became the major themes of his works*** [劳动阶级成为他作品的主要题材]. It was this unhappy period in his youth to which he alluded in his favorite and most autobiographical, novel, *David Copperfield*[2].

For a time he ***worked as a solicitor's clerk*** [给律师做书记员], ***reading voraciously*** [如饥似渴地读书] and ***learning shorthand with an eye*** [学习速记法] to become a newspaper reporter.

When he was 20 he ***achieved this goal*** [达到目标], ***starting out by covering debates in the House of Commons*** [开始报道下议院的辩论]. He continued to work as a reporter for 16 years while also ***contributing articles to popular periodicals*** [给流行刊物供稿].

A London publisher, planning to publish a book of humorous drawings by a popular artist, invited Dickens to provide a written commentary. This took the form of the *Pickwich Papers*[3] which ***was an instant success*** [一炮走红], and made Dickens famous at 24.

He then ***embarked on*** [着手] his first series of 20 novels which was to make him the 19th century England's most celebrated author. Some of Dickens's novels were also made into

---

1 English novelist, generally considered the greatest of the Victorian Era.

2 译作《大卫·科波菲尔》，本书讲述一个中产阶级饱受心酸、在社会寻求出路的不屈不挠的奋斗故事，本书可以看作是狄更斯对自己的人生道路的总结回顾。

3 译作《匹克威克外传》，本书讲述主人公匹克威克（Samuel Pickwick）与三位朋友外出旅行途中的一连串遭遇。

films, notably *A Tale of Two Cities*[1]. Perhaps Dickens's most famous work is his *Christmas Carol*[2] which has __**been adapted for**__ [被改编成] film, stage, television and radio. This short, __*imaginative story of miserliness and redemption*__ [有关吝啬与赎罪的虚构故事] has become as much a part of the Christmas season as __**Santa Claus**__ [圣诞老人].

Oliver Twist[3] is a story about an orphan named Oliver Twist, who __**endures a miserable existence**__ [过着凄惨生活] in a workhouse and escapes to London where he meets the leader of a __**gang of juvenile pickpockets**__ [少年扒手团伙]. The book exposed the cruel treatment of many a __**waif-child**__ [流浪儿] in London, which increased concern in what is sometimes known as "The Great London Waif Crisis": the large number of orphans in London in the Dickens era. *Great Expectations*[4] is a novel, which __**depicts the growth and personal development of an orphan**__ [描述一个孤儿的成长] named Pip.

Q uotes by Dickens

A wonderful fact to reflect upon, that every human creature is constituted to be that profound secret and mystery to every other.

Have a heart that never hardens, and a temper that never tires, and a touch that never hurts.

No one is useless in this world who lightens the burdens of another.

To conceal anything from those to whom I am attached, is not in my nature. I can never close my lips where I have opened my heart.

改写 | Rewrite the Story | in Your Own Words

---

1 译作《双城记》，本书以法国大革命为背景，讲述为爱而自我牺牲的故事。

2 译作《圣诞颂歌》，是一个圣诞小故事，以吝啬与赎罪为主题。

3 译作《雾都孤儿》，本书揭露许多当时的社会问题，如救济院、童工、以及帮派吸收青少年参与犯罪等，试图唤起大众的注意。

4 译作《远大前程》，本书讲述一个孤儿的跌宕起伏的人生，表达他对生命和人性的看法。

列夫·托尔斯泰
LEO TOLSTOY[1] （1828–1910）

If you were able to assemble a group of ***literary critics*** [文学评论家] in one room and asked them to ***put down a list of*** [写下一个单子] the 10 greatest writers of fiction, it is a reasonably safe bet that the name of Leo Tolstoy would appear on all of them. If you then asked for a list of the 10 greatest novels, you would probably find Tolstoy's ***War and Peace***[2] [《战争与和平》] and ***Anna Karenina***[3] [《安娜·卡列尼娜》] on most, if not all of them.

To a considerable degree [在很大程度上] the reputation of the greatest Russian author ***rests on these two monumental works*** [有赖于这两部不朽的作品]. They have proved so ***remarkably durable*** [它们如此经久不衰] that several films have been made based on the novels.

Born into a wealthy Russian family of aristocrats [出生于富裕的俄罗斯贵族家庭], ***Count*** [伯爵] Leo Tolstoy wrote ***a vast amount of*** [大量的] material in his career. Much of it was not fictional and ***involved his views on philosophy*** [有关他的哲学观点] and especially on art.

After several years of formal education, Tolstoy ***took on the responsibility of running the family estate*** [承担起经营家庭产业的责任] which he did with rather limited success, as he preferred ***social whirl*** [大城市的社会漩涡] of big cities like ***Moscow and St. Petersburg*** [莫斯科和圣彼得堡].

Tiring of this rather pointless existence [厌倦了这种毫无意义的生活], he joined the ***Czarist Army*** [沙俄军队] and ***participated in the siege of Sevastopol*** [参与夺取塞瓦斯托波尔的战斗] during the Crimean War[4] against Britain. ***The experience proved invaluable*** [这些经验弥足珍贵] when he came later to write *War and Peace*.

His ***social conscience led him to a rigorous study of the character and ethics of his society*** [社会良知让他痴迷于钻研社会性格和道德]. He ***could not accept the vast injustices of Czarist society*** [不能接受沙俄社会的大量不公平现象] and ***looked for alternative solutions to these problems*** [寻找解决这些问题的其他办法]. Tolstoy felt he had found answers in Christ's preaching to "resist not evil[5]" and to ***search out the good in every individual*** [寻找每个人身上的善良] flowing from God's love.

Tolstoy ***gave up all his goods and literacy copyrights*** [放弃所有的动产和著作权] to his ***grasping*** [贪婪的] wife and children. ***Penniless*** [身无分文的], he renounced tobacco [戒烟], alcohol and sex. He ***became a vegetarian*** [成为素食主义者] and ***worked in the fields with***

---

1 Russian author, a master of realistic fiction and one of the world's greatest novelists. Tolstoy is best known for his two longest works, *War and Peace* and *Anna Karenina*, which are commonly regarded as among the finest novels ever written.

2 译作《战争与和平》，本书以 1812 年俄国卫国战争为中心，讲述欧洲拿破仑时期的俄罗斯所发生的事。

3 译作《安娜·卡列尼娜》，本书描写不同的婚姻和家庭生活。

4 克里米亚战争，爆发于 1853 年至 1856 年的欧洲，作战的一方是俄罗斯帝国，另一方是奥斯曼帝国（又称土耳其帝国）、法兰西帝国、不列颠帝国。其中最长最重要的战役发生在克里米亚半岛。

5 这句话扩展成 "Resist not evil, but overcome evil with good"，可以理解为，如果我们以牙还牙（An eye for an eye），以其人之道还治其人之身来毁灭邪恶，这样我们本身会变得更加邪恶；所以我们要选择不抵抗，发现每个人身上的善意，让邪恶自生自灭，这种精神类似于甘地（Mohandas Gandhi,1869–1948）、曼德拉（Nelson Mandela, 1918–）、马丁·路德·金（Martin Luther King， 1929–1968）等人 "非暴力不合作（Nonviolence）" 思想。

the peasants [和农民一起耕田], ***rejecting the idea of private property*** [拒绝持有私人财产].

Quotes by Tolstoy

Everyone thinks of changing the world, but no one thinks of changing himself.

Only people who are capable of loving strongly can also suffer great sorrow, but this same necessity of loving serves to counteract their grief and heals them.

All happy families are alike; each unhappy family is unhappy in its own way.

The two most powerful warriors are patience and time.

改写 | Rewrite the Story | in Your Own Words

尼采

FRIEDRICH NIETZSCHE[1] (1844–1900)

"上帝已死"
Famous for the quote "God is dead"

A brilliant young man, he **was appointed professor** [被任命为教授] at the University of Basel aged 24 **having not even finished his degree** [甚至没有完成学位]. His **evanescent philosophical life** [短暂的哲学生命] ended 20 years later when he **went insane** [发疯] and died shortly afterwards.

Nietzsche argued that the Christian system of faith and worship was not only incorrect, but **harmful to society** [对社会有害] because it allowed the weak to rule the strong—it **suppressed the will to power** [抑制对权利的控制] which was the driving force of human character. Nietzsche wanted people to **throw off the shackles** [挣脱枷锁] of our misguided Christian morality and become supermen—**free and titanic** [自由而且强大].

However, without God he felt that the future of man might spiral into **a society of nihilism** [虚无的社会], **devoid of any meaning** [没有任何意义]; his aim was for man to realize the lack of divine purpose and **create his own values** [实现自己的价值].

Nietzsche's father died when Nietzsche was five, and Nietzsche **was raised by his mother** [由母亲抚养成人] in a home that included his grandmother, two aunts, and a sister.

Thus Spake Zarathustra [《查拉图斯特拉如是说》] **articulated Nietzsche's theory of the Übermensch** [阐明了尼采的 "超人理论"], a term translated as "Superman" or "Overman."

One of Nietzsche's fundamental contentions was that traditional values had lost their power in the lives of individuals. He expressed this in his proclamation "**God is dead** [上帝已死]."

He was convinced that traditional values represented a "**slave morality** [奴隶道德]," a morality created by weak and **resentful** [愤恨的] individuals who encouraged such behavior as gentleness and kindness because the behavior served their interests.

Nietzsche claimed that new values could **be created to replace the traditional ones** [创造新的价值代替传统价值], and his discussion of the possibility led to his concept of the overman or superman.

Nietzsche maintained that **all human behavior is motivated by the will to power** [人类所有行为都是被 "权力欲" 所驱使]. The will to power is not simply power over others, but the **power over oneself** [对自己的驾驭] that is necessary for creativity. **Such power is manifested in the overman's independence, creativity, and originality** [这样的能量在 "超人" 的独立性、创造力和创新性等方面得到彰显].

Although Nietzsche **explicitly denied that any overman had yet arisen** [尼采明确地承认 "超人" 至今没有出现], he mentioned several individuals who could serve as models. Among these models he listed **Jesus** [耶稣], Greek philosopher **Socrates** [苏格拉底] (469–399BC), **Florentine thinker** [佛罗伦萨思想家] **Leonardo da Vinci** [达•芬奇] (1452–1519), Italian artist

---

1 German classical scholar, philosopher, and critic of culture, who became one of the most influential modern thinkers. His attempts to unmask the motives that underlie traditional Western religion, morality, and philosophy deeply affected generations of theologians, philosophers, psychologists, poets, novelists, and playwrights.

Michelangelo [米开朗基罗] (1475–1564), English playwright **William Shakespeare** [莎士比亚] (1564–1616), German author Johann **Wolfgang von Goethe** [歌德] (1749–1832), Roman ruler **Julius Caesar** [恺撒大帝] (102–44 BC), and French emperor **Napoléon** [拿破仑] (1769–1821).

Q by Quotes Nietzsche

Without music, life would be a mistake.

That which does not kill us makes us stronger.

The individual has always had to struggle to keep from being overwhelmed by the tribe. If you try it, you will be lonely often, and sometimes frightened. But no price is too high to pay for the privilege of owning yourself.

Sometimes people don't want to hear the truth because they don't want their illusions destroyed.

改写 | Rewrite the Story | in Your Own Words

萧伯纳
GEORGE BERNARD SHAW[1] (1856–1950)

著名剧作家
Famous dramatist

Born in Dublin of middle-class but ***impoverished stock*** [贫困的家世], Shaw ***was forced to leave school*** [被迫离开学校] at 15 to ***take a job as a clerk*** [做一名职员]. His father became an alcoholic and in 1872 his mother left home, going to London with her 2 daughters. Shaw followed them there in 1876.

In London, Shaw regularly went to the British Museum in order to ***educate himself*** [自学], a fact which may partly ***account for*** [说明] the originality and ***independence of his thinking*** [思想的独立性].

In the mid-1880s, he began to ***be active in the Socialist movement*** [在社会主义运动中表现很活跃], ***becoming a noted orator*** [成为知名演说家] and an influential member of the ***recently-founded*** [刚刚成立的] Fabian Society[2], an influential group of middle-class socialists who sought to ***transform society by non-revolutionary means*** [通过非革命方法改造社会]. In 1889, he ***edited and contributed to*** [编辑并供稿] *Fabian Essays in Socialism*[3]. He also became famous for his music, drama and art criticism.

Shaw's comic touch is seen at its best in *Pygmalion*[4] [《卖花女》] (1913), which ***was adapted as the musical comedy and film*** [改编成音乐剧和电影] *My Fair Lady* [《窈窕淑女》]. But the play also ***addresses important issues*** [解决了重要问题] of class, social power and even sexual politics.

In 1923, Shaw produced what many regard as his masterpiece, *Saint Joan*[5] [《圣女贞德》], for which he received the 1925 ***Nobel Prize for Literature*** [诺贝尔文学奖]. ***Witty yet deeply moving*** [机智但又感人的], the play depicts Joan of Arc as a mystic visionary and also as a ***plain-speaking peasant girl*** [直言不讳的农村女孩]. Throughout his long career, Shaw always ***used his plays as a vehicle for his ideas*** [通过剧作来表达自己观点].

Shaw was a ***vegetarian*** [素食主义者] and neither drank nor smoked, but this did not make him any the less attractive to women. Even after his marriage, Shaw ***maintained long correspondences*** [保持长时间通信来往] with several prominent women.

The famous dancer Isadora Duncan[6] even ***proposed having a baby with Shaw*** [提出和萧伯纳造人的想法], hopefully with her looks and his brains. He refused... the baby might turn out to have his looks and her brains.

哲学与文学 PHILOSOPHY AND LITERATURE　Chapter 3

---

1 Irish comic dramatist, literary critic, and socialist propagandist, winner of the Nobel Prize for Literature in 1925.

2 费边社，起源于 19 世纪末，英国的一个社会主义派别，参与协助英国工党的成立，其意识形态称为费边主义 (Fabianism)。费边社的主要思想在于，重在务实的社会建设，倡导互助互爱的社会服务，主张通过温和改良方式走向社会主义，并强调通过教育的途径让权力回到知识精英的手中。

3 《费边社会主义论文集》自 1889 年陆续出版。

4 《卖花女》，原名《皮格马利翁》。本剧曾于 1938 年翻拍成黑白电影，于 1956 年改编为音乐剧《窈窕淑女》(*My Fair Lady*)。

5 《圣女贞德》，是一部萧伯纳创作的历史剧。

6 艾莎多拉·邓肯 (1878–1927)，美国舞蹈家，现代舞的创始人。

Bernard Shaw

Life isn't about finding yourself. Life is about creating yourself.

A life spent making mistakes is not only more honorable, but more useful than a life spent doing nothing.

Animals are my friends...and I don't eat my friends.

If you cannot get rid of the family skeleton, you may as well make it dance.

改写 | Rewrite the Story | in Your Own Words

海明威

ERNEST HEMINGWAY[1] （1899–1961）

"一个人可以被毁灭，但不可以被打倒"
An outstanding creative writer

Hemingway's childhood and adolescence **_gave him an insight into all aspects of life_** [给他机会洞察生活的方方面面]. Being such an **_inquisitive_** [好奇的] person with a determination for details he wanted to try everything and **_be exceptional at_** [出众] everything he did.

He found it very frustrating when his health or **_poor eyesight_** [视力差] **_kept him from fulfilling his goals_** [阻止他实现他的目标]. Right from adolescence when he wanted to **_join the forces_** [参军] he was unable to. His poor eye sight meant he could only join the ambulance corps. Enough for some people, but not Hemingway. He wanted to excel, to be thought of as the best.

After the United States entered the **_First World War_**[2] [第一次世界大战], he joined a volunteer ambulance unit in the Italian army. **_Serving at the front_** [在前线服勤], he **_was wounded_** [受伤] and spent considerable time in hospitals.

Prevented from achieving his first goal of being a war "hero"—**_fulfilling his father's teachings_** [实现父亲的教诲] of being a strong, dominant, fighting man, afraid of nothing, he turned to his mother's loves—culture, and began to write.

His experience of war was **_his initiation into manhood_** [开始成长为男子汉] and, like so many who underwent it, he spent his later life in trying to understand its significance, for the individual and for his generation. He wrote about the war itself most directly and fully in *A Farewell to Arms*[3] [《永别了，武器》], but in all his writings the moral and psychological problems he had been brought face to face with in action were explored, whether in setting of later wars of **_civil violence_** [国内暴动], **_big game hunting_** [大狩猎], or **_bull fighting_** [斗牛].

During his twenties, Hemingway became a member of the group of **_expatriate Americans in Paris_** [移居巴黎的美国人], which he described in his first important work, *The Sun Also Rises*[4] [《太阳照常升起》].

The Old Man and the Sea[5] [《老人与海》] is an **_allegorical account_** [寓言式的故事] of an old fisherman's **_lonely struggle in the Gulf of Mexico_** [在墨西哥湾独自搏斗] to land a huge **_marlin_** [枪鱼]. The tale **_was awarded a Pulitzer Prize_**[6] [获得普利策奖] in 1953. In **_the following year_** [次年], his international standing as a writer was recognized with the award of the Nobel Prize for Literature.

---

1 American novelist and short-story writer, awarded the Nobel Prize for Literature in 1954. He was noted both for the intense masculinity of his writing and for his adventurous and widely publicized life.

2 第一次世界大战，发生在欧洲，波及全世界，导火索是 1914 年 6 月的萨拉热窝事件，战后各国于巴黎凡尔赛宫召开 "巴黎和会 (Paris Peace Conference)"，诸国与德国签订协议和条约《凡尔赛和约》(*Treaty of Versailles*)。

3 译作《永别了，武器》，是海明威于 1929 年写成的半自传体小说。

4 译作《太阳照常升起》，海明威藉此成为 "迷惘一代"(Lost Generation) 的作家中代表人物。

5 译作《老人与海》，写于 1951 年，海明威的作品，作者因本书于 1953 年获得普利策奖 (Pulitzer Prize)，1954 年本书又为海明威夺得诺贝尔文学奖起了重要作用。

6 普利策奖，也称普利策新闻奖，曾是美国新闻界的一项最高荣誉，现已成为全球性的奖项，由哥伦比亚大学的普利策奖评选委员会的十四名会员评定，5 月由哥伦比亚大学 (Columbia University) 校长正式颁发。

 **Hemingway**

A man can be destroyed but not defeated.

A man's got to take a lot of punishment to write a really funny book.

Courage is grace under pressure.

Every man's life ends the same way. It is only the details of how he lived and how he died that distinguish one man from another.

Fear of death increases in exact proportion to increase in wealth.

No weapon has ever settled a moral problem. It can impose a solution but it cannot guarantee it to be a just one.

改写 Rewrite the Story | in Your Own Words

Chapter 4

科学与探索

SCIENCE AND EXPLORATION

本 章 目 录

希波克拉底 HIPPOCRATES (460–377 BC)

阿基米德 ARCHIMEDES (287–212 BC)

哥白尼 NICOLAUS COPERNICUS (1473–1543)

布鲁诺 GIORDANO BRUNO (1548–1600)

伽利略 GALILEO GALILEI (1564–1642)

哈维 WILLIAM HARVEY (1578–1657)

牛顿 SIR ISAAC NEWTON (1642–1727)

瓦特 JAMES WATT (1736–1819)

爱德华•詹纳 EDWARD JENNER (1749–1823)

达尔文 CHARLES DARWIN (1809–1882)

孟德尔 GREGOR MENDEL (1822–1884)

巴斯德 LOUIS PASTEUR (1822–1895)

居里夫人 MARIE CURIE (1867–1934)

爱因斯坦 ALBERT EINSTEIN (1879–1955)

弗莱明 ALEXANDER FLEMING (1881–1955)

波尔 NIELS BOHR (1885–1962)

克里克 FRANCIS CRICK (1916–2004)

霍金 STEPHEN HAWKING (1942–)

希波克拉底

HIPPOCRATES[1] (460-377 BC)

He became known as the ***founder of modern medicine*** [现代医学创始人] and ***was regarded as the greatest physician of his time*** [被看做当时最伟大的医生]. He based his medical practice on observations and on the study of the human body.

He ***held the belief*** [相信] that illness had a physical and a rational explanation. He ***rejected the views of his time*** [拒绝同时代观点] that considered illness to be caused by ***possession of evil spirits*** [中邪] and ***disfavor of the gods*** [失去诸神宠幸].

The body, given half a chance, could often ***heal itself*** [自愈]. "Our natures are the physicians of our diseases", he is quoted as advising. ***His treatments consisted of proper diet, fresh air and changes in living habits*** [他的治疗包括合理饮食、新鲜空气和改变生活习惯].

Hippocrates ***placed great emphasis on prevention*** [特别强调预防], that is adopting healthy living habits rather than looking for ***magical medical cures*** [灵丹妙药].

Hippocrates ***traveled throughout Greece practicing his medicine*** [遍游希腊，四处行医]. He ***founded a medical school*** [成立医校] on the island of Cos, Greece and began teaching his ideas.

The Hippocratic Oath[2] [希波克拉底誓词] has preserved his name for all time. Although not written by him, it ***embodies his principles and ideals*** [体现了他的原则和理想] ***with regard to medical practice*** [有关行医], emphasizing particularly the ethical duty of physicians [医生的道德责任] to act always ***in the best interests of their patients*** [代表患者的最大利益].

 Hippocrates

There are in fact two things, science and opinion; the former begets knowledge, the latter ignorance.

Let food be thy medicine and medicine be thy food.

Declare the past, diagnose the present, foretell the future.

Walking is man's best medicine.

---

1 Ancient Greek physician who lived during Greece's Classical period and is traditionally regarded as the father of medicine.

2 The Hippocratic Oath，希波克拉底誓词，俗称医师誓词，是希波克拉底给医生列出的一些特定伦理规范。本书给出的是原文的英译本，现代医师誓词有很大改动。

阿基米德

ARCHIMEDES[1] (287–212 BC)

"***Eureka! Eureka*** [找到了]! "

This is certainly one of the most famous shouts in history and it was made by a ***naked Greek mathematician*** [赤身裸体的希腊数学家] who had just jumped out of a public bath in Syracuse[2], Sicily[3]. "Eureka!" means simply "I have found it."

What Archimedes had found was the basic ***principle of buoyancy*** [浮力定律]. He had been asked by the King of Syracuse to determine whether a crown, made for the king by a ***goldsmith*** [金匠], was really pure gold.

The simplest schoolboy [最普通不过的学生] ***is now familiar with*** [熟悉] ***truths for which Archimedes would have sacrificed his life*** [阿基米德用生命换来的真理].

As far as we know, Archimedes ***devoted his whole life to experimentation and research*** [将毕生献给实验研究]. Indeed, some historians call him "the father of experimental science" because he always ***put his theories to practical tests*** [用实验测试理论].

He proved that ***the volume of a sphere is two-thirds of that of a cylinder that circumscribes the sphere*** [等圆周的球体与圆柱体体积的大小关系为：二比三].

Archimedes applied geometry to ***hydrostatics*** [流体静力学] and mechanics, ***devised numerous ingenious mechanisms*** [设计大量精巧机构], and ***discovered the principle of buoyancy*** [发现浮力定律]. In ***mechanics*** [机械学], Archimedes ***defined the principle of the lever*** [定义了杠杆原理].

During the ***Roman conquest of Sicily*** [罗马入侵西西里岛], some of his mechanical devices were employed in the defense of Syracuse, for instance, ***catapult*** [弹射器] and a mirror system for ***focusing the sun's rays on the invaders' boats and igniting them*** [聚焦太阳光线点燃敌军船只].

Archimedes was killed by a Roman soldier who found him drawing a mathematical diagram in the sand. It is said that Archimedes ***was so absorbed in calculation*** [全神贯注于计算] that he offended the ***intruder*** [入侵者] ***merely by remarking*** [仅仅说了句], "***Do not disturb my diagrams*** [别弄乱我画的图]."

When scientists ***make an important discovery*** [做出重大发现] they still shout "Eureka".

科学与探索 SCIENCE AND EXPLORATION

Chapter 4

---

1 The most famous mathematician and inventor of ancient Greece.

2 锡拉库扎，又译叙拉古（Siracusa），意大利西西里岛东部一港市。

3 西西里岛，意大利南部的一个自治区，地中海最大的岛，曾属于古希腊殖民区。

Q by Quotes **Archimedes**

Eureka!—I have found it!

Give me a lever long enough and a fulcrum on which to place it, and I shall move the world.

改写 **Rewrite the Story** | **in Your Own Words**

哥白尼

NICOLAUS COPERNICUS[1] (1473–1543)

提出日心说观点
Proposed a sun-centered model

Before Copernican theory was accepted, **_astronomers_** [天文学家] believed that the **_Earth was stationary at the center of the solar system_** [地球在太阳系中心静止不动], and the **_Sun and planets revolved around it_** [太阳及其他行星绕其旋转].

Geocentrism[2] [地心说], or the **_Ptolemaic system_**[3] [托勒密体系] long **_served as the predominant cosmological system_** [占主导地位的宇宙论体系] in many ancient civilizations such as ancient Greece.

Copernicus is best known for his astronomical theory that the sun is **_at rest_** [静止] near the center of the universe, and that the earth, **_spinning on its axis_** [绕轴自转] once daily, revolves **_annually_** [一年一次] around the sun. This is called the **_Heliocentric_** [日心说], or **_sun-centered_** [日心说] system.

Fearing his theory would be judged **_heretical_** [异端的] by the **_Roman Catholic Church_** [罗马天主教], Copernicus **_delayed the publication_** [推迟出版] of **_On the Revolution of Heavenly Bodies_**[4] [《天体运行论》] until shortly before his death in 1543. This **_challenged the long held view_** [挑战了长期持有的观点] that the Earth was stationary at the centre of the universe with all the planets, the Moon and the Sun rotating around it.

Copernican theory **_was not widely accepted until the late 17th century_** [直到十七世纪末才被广泛接受]—over 100 years after Copernicus's death.

Copernicus

To know that we know what we know, and to know that we do not know what we do not know, that is true knowledge.

In the midst of all dwells the Sun. For who could set this luminary in another or better place in this most glorious temple, than whence he can at one and the same time brighten the whole.

Chapter 4　科学与探索　SCIENCE AND EXPLORATION

---

1 Polish astronomer who proposed that the planets have the Sun as the fixed point to which their motions are to be referred; that the Earth is a planet which, besides orbiting the Sun annually, also turns once daily on its own axis; and that very slow, long-term changes in the direction of this axis account for the precession of the equinoxes.

2 地心说(或称天动说)，是古人认为地球是宇宙的中心，而其他的星球都环绕着她而运行的一种学说。

3 古希腊的托勒密(Claudius Ptolemy,，约 90–168)发展完善了地心说的模型。

4 《天体运行论》，作者是波兰天文学家哥白尼，书中创立"日心说"，本书是天文学上的一次革命，改革了人类的宇宙观，天主教于 1616 年将其列为禁书。

布鲁诺

Giordano Bruno[1] (1548–1600)

为科学信仰现身
A precursor of modern civilization

Filippo Bruno was born at Nola[2] in southern Italy, in 1548. He took the name Giordano when **_entering a monastery_** [进入修道院] in Naples[3] in 1565. While there, he studied philosophy, theology and science. He developed **_unorthodox views_** [非正统的观点] on some Catholic teachings, **_was suspected of heresy_** [被怀疑涉嫌异教] and had to **_flee monastic life_** [逃离修道院生活] in 1576.

With a love of knowledge and a hatred of ignorance [热爱知识，憎恨无知], he **_became a rebel_** [成为造反派] **_unwilling to accept traditional authority_** [拒绝接受正统权威]. **_The price he paid for his beliefs was persecution and condemnation_** [他为信仰付出的代价是深受迫害和谴责] in many countries, and ultimately, **_his beliefs cost him his life_** [他为信仰付出了生命].

Giordano **_attempted to deal with the implications of the Copernican universe_** [试图讨论哥白尼宇宙观的含义]. He believed that all the stars in the sky were actually suns like our own; **_each of them having their own planets_** [都有自己的行星] and **_possibly supporting life_** [可能孕育生命].

After **_a trial for heresy_** [异教审判] and **_a lengthy confinement_** [长期监禁], on 17 February, 1600, Giordano Bruno **_was burned at the stake_** [在火刑柱上被执行火刑] in Rome, Italy, after **_consistently refusing to recant his beliefs_** [坚持不放弃自己的信仰].

This happened in a place that is known today as the Campo dei Fiori[4] ("Flower Square or Field of Flowers"). **_A statue of Giordano Bruno is still visible there_** [布鲁诺的雕像至今屹立于此].

Bruno was a pioneer who **_roused Europe from its long intellectual sleep_** [唤醒了沉睡的欧洲知识界]. He **_was martyred for his beliefs_** [为信仰殉难]. He was a sensitive, imaginative poet, **_fired with the enthusiasm_** [有火一般的热情] of a larger vision of a larger universe.

 Bruno

Truth does not change because it is, or is not, believed by a majority of the people.

They dispute not in order to find or even to seek Truth, but for victory, and to appear the more learned and strenuous upholders of a contrary opinion. Such persons should be avoided by all who have not a good breastplate of patience.

1 Italian philosopher, astronomer, mathematician, and occultist whose theories anticipated modern science.
2 诺拉，意大利坎帕尼亚大区那不勒斯省的一个镇。
3 那不勒斯，意大利西南部港市。
4 罗马百花广场，19世纪末，布鲁诺的雕像矗立于此。

科学与探索 SCIENCE AND EXPLORATION

Chapter 4

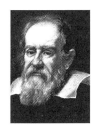

伽利略

GALILEO GALILEI[1] (1564–1642)

He is known as one of the towering figures of science [他是科学史上一座丰碑], considered by many as the father of modern science. Science ***depends heavily on testing and experimentation*** [科学依赖实验]. Modern scientists try to ***devise methods of testing their hypotheses in practical ways*** [设计实验方法测试自己的假说]. ***This seems only common sense*** [这看似不足为奇], but up until Galileo's time, "scientific" knowledge was more a matter of traditional theories that ***could be traced back to Aristotle*** [追溯到亚里士多德], ***whose views were considered almost as sacred as the Bible*** [他的观点如圣经般神圣].

In the history of culture, Galileo ***stands as a symbol of*** [作为象征] the ***battle against authority*** [挑战权威] for ***freedom of inquiry*** [自由质疑]. He put his questions to nature instead of to the ancients and ***drew conclusions fearlessly*** [无畏地下结论]. He has been the first to turn a telescope to the sky and had seen there evidence and collected enough data to ***cause a downfall of*** [垮台] Aristotle's theory.

In ***astronomy*** [天文学], he ***used the telescope in observation*** [使用望远镜观测] and the ***discovery of sunspots*** [发现太阳黑子], ***lunar mountains and valleys*** [月球山系], the four largest ***satellites of Jupiter*** [木星卫星], and etc.

Galileo's most valuable scientific contribution was his founding of physics on ***precise measurements*** [精确地测量] rather than on ***metaphysical*** [纯粹哲学的] principles and formal logic.

Aristotle taught that heavier objects fall faster than lighter ones. For some 1800 years, this view went unchallenged, until Galileo climbed the ***Leaning Tower of Pisa*** [比萨斜塔] and ***dropped various weights from the top*** [从塔顶抛下不同重量的重物], and ***rolled balls down the inclined planes*** [球体从斜面上滚下], and then ***generalized the results of his many experiments*** [总结实验结果] into the famous ***law of free fall*** [自由落体运动定律].

Galileo discovered that all objects ***fall toward the earth*** [落体运动] ***with the same acceleration*** [以相同加速度], ***regardless of*** [无论] their weight, size, or shape, ***when gravity is the only force acting on*** [当重力是唯一的作用力] them.

In 1614, Galileo ***was accused of heresy*** [被指控异教] for ***his support of the Copernican theory*** [支持哥白尼理论] that the sun was at the centre of the solar system. This was revolutionary at a time when most people believed the Earth was in this central position. In 1616, he ***was forbidden by the church from teaching or advocating these theories*** [被教堂禁止教授和支持这些理论].

In 1632, ***he was again condemned for heresy*** [再次被定罪为异教] after his book *Dialogue Concerning the Two Chief World Systems*[2] was published. This set out the arguments for and against the Copernican theory ***in the form of a discussion between two men*** [以两个

---

1 Italian natural philosopher, astronomer, and mathematician who made fundamental contributions to the sciences of motion, astronomy, and strength of materials and to the development of the scientific method.

2 《关于托勒密和哥白尼两大世界体系的对话》，本书采用对话的形式，是伽利略撰写的一部天文学著作，于 1632 年在意大利出版。

人对话的形式].

Galileo ***was summoned to appear before the Inquisition in Rome*** [被罗马宗教法庭传唤]. He ***was convicted and sentenced to life imprisonment*** [被判有罪，被处以终身监禁], ***later reduced to permanent house arrest*** [后减刑为永久软禁] at his villa in Arcetri, south of Florence. He ***was also forced to publicly withdraw his support for Copernican theory*** [被迫公开撤销对哥白尼理论的支持].

In 1992, the Church ***acknowledged*** [公开承认] that its ***condemnation*** [责难] of Galileo was a mistake.

 **Galileo**

In questions of science, the authority of a thousand is not worth the humble reasoning of a single individual.

All truths are easy to understand once they are discovered; the point is to discover them.

Mathematics is the language with which God has written the universe.

Passion is the genesis of genius.

I have never met a man so ignorant that I couldn't learn something from him.

改写 | Rewrite the Story | in Your Own Words

哈维

WILLIAM HARVEY[1] (1578–1657)

发现血液循环
Discoverer of blood circulation

The Hippocratic school dominated Western medicine [希波克拉底学派统治西方医学] for the next 500 years, ***until another Greek came onto the scene*** [直到另外一位希腊人登场], namely ***Galen***[2] [盖伦].

According to Galen, ***blood was formed in the liver*** [血液形成于肝脏] from food which was carried to that organ ***from the stomach and intestines*** [从胃和肠道]. This blood then was carried to all parts of the body where it ***was consumed as nutrient*** [作为营养被消耗] or ***was transformed into flesh*** [转化成肉]. Thus blood ***was not conserved*** [血液没被保存].

At this time, ***the church strongly controlled much of medicine and its treatments*** [教堂强有力地掌控着医疗]. The church believed that Galen was right, and ***the consequence of disagreement was to be classed as a heretic*** [有异议者的下场就是被判处异教] and ***be burned at the stake*** [执行火刑].

Harvey was a very curious man and ***carried out a number of dissections*** [完成大量解剖]. Refusing to ***accept traditional beliefs*** [拒绝接受传统观点], he ***took a scientific approach*** [采用科学的方法], and carried out his own experiments..

Harvey ***was fascinated by*** [着迷于] the way blood flowed through the human body. Most people of the day believed that ***food was converted into blood by the liver*** [食物在肝脏被转化成血液], then ***was consumed as fuel by the body*** [像燃料一样被人体消耗].

Harvey knew this was untrue ***through his firsthand observations of human and animal dissections*** [通过他对人体和动物解剖的第一手观察]. In 1628 Harvey published ***An Anatomical Study of the Motion of the Heart and of the Blood in Animals***[3] which explained ***how blood was pumped from the heart throughout the body*** [心脏搏动促使血液在全身循环流动], then returned to the heart and recirculated.

The views this book expressed were very ***controversial*** [有争议的] and ***lost Harvey many patients*** [让哈维失去很多患者], but it became the basis for all modern research on the heart and blood vessels.

A second ***ground-breaking*** [独创性的] book published by Harvey in 1651, Essays on the ***Generation of Animals***[4], is considered the ***basis for modern embryology*** [现代胚胎学基础].

Despite the uproar over each of Harvey's unconventional anatomical theories [尽管哈维与众不同的解剖理论引起了巨大的争议], he was recognized as a medical leader in his day. At the time of his death in 1657, Harvey's medical and scientific genius were celebrated throughout the European medical community.

科学与探索 SCIENCE AND EXPLORATION

Chapter 4

---

1 English physician who was the first to recognize the full circulation of the blood in the human body and to provide experiments and arguments to support this idea.

2 盖伦 (Galen, 129–200)，古希腊医学家。他的见解和理论在他生后的一千多年里在欧洲是起支配性的医学理论。

3 《关于动物心脏与血液运动的解剖研究》，发表于 1826 年。本书观点从根本上推翻了统治千年的关于心脏运动和血液运动的经典观点，提出血液是循环运行的，心脏有节律的持续搏动是促使血液在全身循环流动的动力源泉。

4 《动物的生殖》，发表于 1651 年。本书的内容对生理学和胚胎学的发展起了很大作用。

牛顿

Sir Isaac Newton[1] (1642–1727)

One of the "mountain peaks" in the history of science [科学史上一座高峰], Newton was born in ***Woolsthorpe, England*** [英格兰，埃尔斯索普], and educated at Cambridge University. In fact, he became a professor of mathematics there at only 27.

Between the ages of 22~24, Newton made his three great discoveries—***calculus*** [微积分], the ***nature of white light*** [自然光的本质], and the ***law of gravity*** [万有引力定律]. The greatness and originality of Newton's genius lay in his power of ***seeing beyond the happening of things*** [看透事物本质], which ***were not curbed by*** [没有被制约] some old principles.

Everyone knows the story of Newton observing an apple fall from a tree, which ***suggested the principle of gravitation to him*** [为他发现万有引力定律提供了灵感]. The story may or may not be true, but it has become part of the folklore of science.

By 1666, he had formulated his law of gravitation ***upon which much of the physics of subsequent centuries was based*** [以后几个世纪的物理学都以此为基础]. This law ***was of immense importance to*** [极为重要] astronomers as well, and ***enabled scientists to accurately predict the motions of the planets in the solar system*** [使得科学家准确地预测太阳系行星的运动].

Although partially modified by Einstein's Theory of Relativity [尽管被爱因斯坦相对论部分地改进], Newtonian physics is still very useful in solving many practical problems of physicists and engineers.

Newton devised an ***analytic method*** [分析方法] more ***rigorous*** [严格的] than that of any scientist before him, and his ***experimental method*** [试验方法] ***is still practiced today*** [至今仍然被使用]. His contributions to mathematics, physics, and ***the study of natural phenomena*** [对自然现象的研究] have proven extremely ***far-reaching*** [影响深远] and valuable.

Newton was a difficult man, ***prone to depression*** [容易抑郁] and often ***involved in bitter arguments with other scientists*** [和其他科学家争论不休], but by the early 1700s he was the ***dominant figure*** [权威人物] in British and European science. He died on 31 March, 1727 and ***was buried in Westminster Abbey***[2] [被安葬在威斯敏斯特大教堂].

---

1 English physicist and mathematician, who was the culminating figure of the scientific revolution of the 17th century.

2 威斯敏斯特大教堂。这里一直是英国君主安葬或加冕登基的地点。乔叟（Geoffrey Chaucer，1343–1400），查尔斯•达尔文（Charles Darwin，1809–1882），查尔斯•狄更斯（Charles Dickens，1812–1870），丘吉尔（Winston Churchill，1874–1965）等人都安葬于此地。

If I have seen further... it is by standing upon the shoulders of giants.

I seem to have been only like a boy playing on the seashore, and diverting myself in now and then finding a smoother pebble or a prettier shell than ordinary, whilst the great ocean of truth lay all undiscovered before me.

If I have made any valuable discoveries, it has been owing more to patient attention than to any other talent.

I keep the subject of my inquiry constantly before me, and wait till the first dawning opens gradually, by little and little, into a full and clear light.

改写 | Rewrite the Story | in Your Own Words

瓦特
JAMES WATT[1] (1736–1819)

If iron was the key metal of the ***Industrial Revolution***[2] [工业革命], the ***steam engine*** [蒸汽机] was perhaps the most important machine technology.

The first working steam engine ***had been patented*** [被注册] in 1698 and ***by the time of Watt's birth*** [在瓦特出生的时候], Newcomen[3] engines were ***pumping water from mines*** [从矿山抽水] all over the country.

In around 1764, Watt was given a model Newcomen engine to repair. He realized that it was ***hopelessly inefficient*** [无望地低效率] and began to work to ***improve the design*** [改进设计].

He designed ***a separate condensing chamber*** [分离压缩缸] for the steam engine that ***prevented enormous losses of steam*** [避免蒸汽泄漏]. His first patent in 1769 covered this device and other improvements on Newcomen's engine.

James Watt ***improved the steam engine*** [改良蒸汽机], allowing it to be used in many industrial settings, not just in ***mining*** [采矿]. Early mills had run successfully with ***water power*** [水力], but the advancement of using the steam engine meant that ***a factory could be located anywhere*** [工厂可以建在任何地方], not just close to water. It helped ***advance the Industrial Revolution*** [推进工业革命].

He invented the ***flyball governor*** [飞球调速器] in 1788, and which ***automatically regulated the speed of an engine*** [自动调节发动机转速]. It is ***the basic concept of automation*** [自动控制基本概念].

A unit of measurement of electrical and mechanical power [电力和机械功率单位] —the watt—***is named in his honor*** [以他的名字命名].

Industrial Revolution

By the mid-eighteenth century, a new ***technological revolution*** [科技革命] ***was under way*** [进行中], first in England and then in America. The development of industry was even more powerful than the rise of agriculture in bringing change to the economy.

Throughout history, "energy" had meant the ***muscle power of people or animals*** [人力畜力]. But in 1765, the English inventor James Watt introduced the ***steam engine*** [蒸汽机]. One hundred times stronger than muscle power, early steam engines soon ***drove***

科学与探索
SCIENCE AND EXPLORATION

Chapter 4

1　Scottish instrument maker and inventor whose steam engine contributed substantially to the Industrial Revolution.

2　工业革命，18 世纪中叶，瓦特改进蒸汽机，19 世纪传播到北美。工业革命的主要特点是用机器取代人力，以大规模工厂化生产取代个体手工生产。

3　纽科门 (Thomas Newcomen，1663–1729)，英国工程师，蒸汽机发明人之一。他发明的蒸汽机是瓦特蒸汽机的前身。

heavy machinery [驱动笨重机械].

Steam engine [蒸汽机], ***factory production*** [工厂化生产], ***advances in metallurgy and textile manufacturing*** [冶金和纺织业的进步]—***all were hallmarks of the Industrial Revolution*** [工业革命的特点].

During the 18th century, ***water was an important source of power for industry*** [水是工业的重要动力来源], and ***many machines were driven by waterwheels*** [很多机器由水车驱动]. Steam power was also developed at that time. Engines and furnaces ***were all fueled by coal*** [以煤炭作为燃料]. By the 19th century, coal was being transported to the factories by ship or rail.

Before the Industrial Revolution, ***most goods were produced in small workshops or at home*** [产品在小作坊或家庭作坊里生产]. ***Mass production in factories*** [工厂化大规模生产] made it possible to ***manufacture goods*** [制造产品] more cheaply and quickly. ***Huge markets for these goods were opening up in the new cities*** [在新兴城市为产品开辟广阔市场], and in the lands that the ***European nations were conquering and settling overseas*** [欧洲国家在海外占领并定居的殖民地].

The Industrial Revolution ***created a completely new way for people to live*** [为人们创造全新的生活方式]. For many it provided more leisure, new goods and services, and ***far greater mobility*** [出行极为方便] than was enjoyed by common people of earlier ages.

改写 | **Rewrite the Story** | **in Your Own Words**

爱德华·詹纳
EDWARD JENNER[1] (1749–1823)

For many centuries, smallpox **_devastated mankind_** [摧残着人类]. In modern times we do not have to worry about it **_thanks to_** [由于] the remarkable work of Edward Jenner and later developments from his endeavors. **_With the rapid pace of vaccine development_** [疫苗的快速发展] in recent decades, the historic origins of immunization are often forgotten.

At the time, one of the most feared diseases was smallpox. The disease was common and killed up to 33% of those who **_contacted_** [感染] it. At the time, **_there was little known treatments or vaccinations_** [很少有治疗或预防方法] that could prevent it.

In 1796, an English doctor named Edward Jenner **_performed an experiment_** [做实验] to expose a healthy eight-year-old boy named James Phipps to **_the deadly smallpox virus_** [致命性天花病毒]. The boy came down with **_cowpox_** [牛痘], but he recovered. Then, Jenner scratched smallpox matter into the boy's arm. Amazingly, the boy stayed healthy.

Actually, Jenner had noticed that **_milkmaids_** [挤奶女工] did not often get smallpox. The milkmaids did catch cowpox but they recovered quickly. He discovered the vaccine that is used against smallpox and **_laid the groundwork for the science of immunology_** [为免疫学奠定基础].

改写 | Rewrite the Story | in Your Own Words

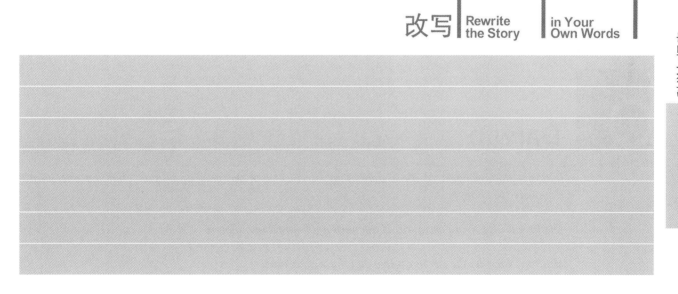

科学与探索 SCIENCE AND EXPLORATION

Chapter 4

---

1 English surgeon and discoverer of vaccination for smallpox.

达尔文

CHARLES DARWIN[1] （1809–1882）

Prior to the publication of Darwin's evolutionary theory [在达尔文的进化论提出之前], most people believed that ***species were eternally unchanging*** [物种是永恒不变的].

Charles Darwin, British scientist, ***laid the foundations of*** [奠定基础] ***modern evolutionary theory*** [现代进化论] with his concept of all forms of life evolving through the ***slow-working process of natural selection*** [漫长的自然选择过程].

In 1831 at the age of 22, Darwin sailed aboard the ***H.M.S. Beagle*** [英国海军勘探船 "贝格尔号"]（H.M.S.: His /Her Majesty's Ship）—***a scientific expedition*** [科学探险] that studies plant and animal species around the world. ***Upon his return to England*** [一回到英国后] in 1836, Darwin wrote extensively about his voyages.

Natural selection thus tends to ***promote adaptation*** [促进适应] by ***maintaining favorable adaptations*** [维持有益的进化] in a constant environment [不变的环境] or ***improving adaptation*** [改善适应性] in a direction appropriate to ***environmental changes*** [环境变化].

There was a tremendous uproar in both scientific and religious circles [在科学和宗教界引起了巨大震动], theologians arguing that Darwin's theories contradicted *the Bible*. By ***implying*** [暗示] that ***humans had evolved just like other species*** [人类也像其他物种一样进化], ***On the Origin of Species***[2] [《物种起源》] ***directly contradicted orthodox theological opinion*** [与正统的神学观点相矛盾]. The thought that ***living things had evolved by natural processes*** [生物体通过自然选择方式进化] denied the special ***creation of humankind*** [创造人类].

 Darwin

It is not the strongest of the species that survives, nor the most intelligent, but the one most responsive to change.

The love for all living creatures is the most noble attribute of man.

Multiply, vary, let the strongest live and the weakest die.

---

1 English naturalist whose theory of evolution by natural selection became the foundation of modern evolutionary studies.

2 译作《物种起源》，全称《论借助自然选择（即在生存斗争中保存优良种群）的方法的物种起源》（*On the Origin of Species by Means of Natural Selection, or the Preservation of Favored Races in the Struggle for Life*），于 1859 年出版，在该书中，达尔文首次提出进化论观点。

Chapter 4

科学与探索
SCIENCE AND EXPLORATION

孟德尔

GREGOR MENDEL[1] （1822–1884）

Although some leading scientists in the late nineteenth century considered ***religion to be an impediment to progress in science*** [宗教是阻碍科学进步的因素], the life of the monk Gregor Mendel ***serves as an important counter-example*** [却是一个重要的反例].

The fact that a monk initiated one of the greatest advances in biology demonstrates ***the poverty of the notion*** [见解不充分] of ***there being a perpetual war between science and religion*** [宗教和科学之间的战争无休无止]. In Mendel's case, ***rather than hindering science*** [没有阻碍科学], religious institutions promoted scientific knowledge, experimentation, and progress.

Mendel ***was born into a poor farming family*** [生在一个穷苦的农民家庭]. At that time it was difficult for poor families to ***obtain a good educatio***n [获得好的教育] and the young Mendel saw ***the only way to escape a life of poverty*** [逃脱贫困生活的唯一出路] was to enter the monastery. Here he was given the name Gregor.

To enable him to ***further his education*** [深造], the abbot arranged for Mendel to ***attend the University of Vienna*** [就读维也纳大学] to ***get a teaching diploma*** [获得教师资格].

However, Mendel did not perform well. He was nervous and the university did not consider him a clever student. Mendel's examiner failed him with the comments, "he ***lacks insight and the requisite clarity of knowledge*** [缺乏洞察力和基础知识不清晰] ". This must have been devastating to the young Mendel who in 1853 had to return to the monastery as a failure.

He ***could not pass the test to be certified as a biology teacher*** [没能通过考试成为一名有资格的生物教师], but Gregor Mendel, a 19th century monk, discovered a basic principle of biology. ***Cross-breeding peas*** [杂交豌豆] in the garden of his monastery in Austria, he learned how to ***predict the features of the hybrids*** [预测杂交豌豆的特点].

Knowing he had ***achieved a scientific breakthrough*** [完成一项科学突破], he presented his work to the Natural Science Society in Brunn[2] and published his results, but his ***research was ignored*** [研究被忽视]. Not until 16 years after his death was he recognized for having discovered the ***fundamentals of genetics*** [遗传学基础].

The rediscovery of Mendel's work in 1900 by three different scientists ***occurred in the context of debates over evolution*** [发生在对进化论争论不休的大背景下]. Biological evolution was widely accepted by European scientists by 1900.

Once his work was independently replicated in the 20th century, the modern field of genetics ***began to fully sprout*** [开始萌芽].

拯救我的 SAT
写作
Saving My SAT
Essay

---

1 Austrian botanist, teacher, and Augustinian prelate, the first to lay the mathematical foundation of the science of genetics, in what came to be called Mendelism.

2 布吕恩自然科学研究协会。

科学与探索 SCIENCE AND EXPLORATION

Chapter 4

巴斯德

LOUIS PASTEUR[1] （1822–1895）

Louis Pasteur ***founded the science of microbiology*** [创立微生物科学], proved the ***germ theory of disease*** [微生物病原理论], ***invented the process of pasteurization*** [发明巴斯德杀菌法], and ***developed vaccines for several diseases*** [研究疾病疫苗], including ***rabies*** [狂犬病].

Rabies is a ***fatal disease*** [致命的疾病] that ***spreads to people*** [传染人类] through ***the bite of an infected animal*** [被染病动物咬伤]. In 1885, Pasteur ***isolated a weak form of a rabies virus*** [分离出毒性较弱的狂犬病病毒] in rabbits.

Pasteur used this to save a nine-year-old boy bitten by a rabid dog. The vaccine transferred ***antibodies*** [抗体] from the rabbit to the boy's ***immune system*** [免疫系统]. The boy, who would likely have died otherwise, survived.

The ***souring of wine*** [葡萄酒发酸] and beer had been a major economic problem in France; Pasteur ***contributed to solving the problem*** [提供解决办法] by showing that bacteria can be eliminated by ***heating wine to a high temperature*** [通过高温加热方法消除细菌].

Pasteur ***extended these studies to*** [扩展研究] the ***souring of milk*** [牛奶变酸], and he ***proposed a similar solution*** [提出相似解决办法]. This process is now called ***pasteurization*** [巴斯德杀菌法]. We now, benefiting from his invention, take advantage of drinking ***pasteurized milk*** [巴氏灭菌牛奶].

Pasteur ***saved France's silk industry from disaster*** [将法国丝绸工业从灾难中拯救了出来] when he discovered that some ***silkworms*** [桑蚕] ***were infected with a disease-causing microorganism*** [被致病微生物感染], and recommended that those infected be destroyed.

 Pasteur

_____ *Chance favors the prepared mind.*

_____ *Let me tell you the secret that has led me to my goal: my strength lies solely in my tenacity.*

_____ *Do not let yourself be tainted with a barren skepticism.*

_____ *Science knows no country, because knowledge belongs to humanity, and is the torch which illuminates the world. Science is the highest personification of the nation because that nation will remain the first which carries the furthest the works of thought and intelligence.*

---

1 French chemist and microbiologist who was one of the most important founders of medical microbiology.

居里夫人

MARIE CURIE[1] （1867–1934）

The door to the world of science was long marked "Men Only" [科学界一直都是男人统治的世界] and ***was firmly closed to women*** [大门从来没有向女人敞开过]—until the 19th century when a young Polish immigrant began to ***pry it open in France*** [在法国撬开这扇大门].

Marie Curie ***had a world-wide reputation*** [获得世界声誉] as the most distinguished woman investigator of our times. Her claim to fame rests primarily on ***her researches in connection with the radioactive elements*** [她的研究和放射性元素有关] and particularly for her ***discovery and separation of the new element radium*** [发现并分离新元素镭], which ***showed radioactive properties to a marked degree*** [表现出显著放射性].

Born in Warsaw[2] [生在华沙], Marie ***was fascinated by science even as a child*** [儿时就痴迷科学]. ***Poland was in the possession of Imperial Russia at the time*** [波兰当时被沙俄占领] and ***women were not permitted to enter university*** [女人不允许读大学], so Marie became a teacher.

Determined to acquire a university education [决心要获得大学学位], Marie saved her money and ***emigrated to France*** [移民法国] in 1891 where she ***was accepted at the Sorbonne***[3] [被索邦大学录取]. Despite her poverty she was happy in her scientific studies.

The Curies worked together investigating radioactivity, building on the work of the German physicist ***Roentgen***[4] [伦琴] and the French physicist ***Becquerel***[5] [贝克勒尔]. In July 1898, the Curies announced the discovery of a new chemical element, ***polonium*** [钋元素]. At the end of the year, they announced the discovery of another, radium. The Curies, along with Becquerel, were awarded the Nobel Prize for Physics in 1903.

Curies' husband—Pierre's ***life was cut short*** [被缩短] in 1906 when he was knocked down and killed by a carriage. Marie ***took over his teaching post*** [接过他的教鞭], becoming the first woman to teach at the Sorbonne, and devoted herself to continuing the work that they had begun together. She received a second Nobel Prize, for Chemistry, in 1911.

The Curie's research was crucial in the development of ***x-rays in surgery*** [外科手术使用 X 射线]. During World War I, Curie begged money, supplied and helped to ***equip ambulances with x-ray equipment*** [用 X 射线仪器装备救护车], which ***she herself drove to the front lines*** [亲自驾车到前线]. Over the four years, more than a million soldiers were examined by units she set up in France.

At the end of the war, she was persuaded to ***make a tour of the United States to raise funds for her research*** [到美国巡回演讲为研究募集资金]. She ***was enormously successful*** [获得巨大成功] and returned to France as a hero. The ***International Red Cross*** [国际红十字会] made her head of its radiological service and she ***held training courses*** [主持培训课程] for medical orderlies and doctors in the new techniques.

---

1 Polish-born French physicist, famous for her work on radioactivity and twice a winner of the Nobel Prize.

2 华沙，波兰首府。

3 索邦大学（La Sorbonne）是巴黎一所历史悠久的大学，也是现在巴黎大学系统的一部分。

4 伦琴（1845–1923），全名威廉·康拉德·伦琴，德国物理学家，发现"X 射线"，1901 年获得首届诺贝尔物理学奖。

5 亨利·贝可勒尔（1852–1908），法国物理学家，因发现天然放射性现象，1903 年获得诺贝尔物理学奖。

Despite her success, Marie continued to **_face great opposition from male scientists in France_** [继续面对法国男性科学家的抵制], and she never received significant financial benefits from her work.

Unfortunately **_her exposure to radioactive substances over the years_** [常年接触放射性物质] **_was taking a severe toll on her health_** [对她健康造成严重伤害]. By the late 1920s **_her health was beginning to deteriorate_** [健康情况恶化]. She died on 4 July 1934 from **_leukemia_** [白血病].

Both her daughters became scientists. Irene[1] married another famous scientist, Frederic Joliot, and the couple won the Nobel Prize for Chemistry in 1935. Marie's second daughter Eve also **_became a world-famous symbol_** [成为世界著名标志] of the scientific ability of women.

Quotes by Marie

All my life through, the new sights of Nature made me rejoice like a child.

I am among those who think that science has great beauty. A scientist in his laboratory is not only a technician: he is also a child placed before natural phenomena which impress him like a fairy tale.

Nothing in life is to be feared, it is only to be understood. Now is the time to understand more, so that we may fear less.

You cannot hope to build a better world without improving the individuals. To that end each of us must work for his own improvement, and at the same time share a general responsibility for all humanity, our particular duty being to aid those to whom we think we can be most useful.

After all, science is essentially international, and it is only through lack of the historical sense that national qualities have been attributed to it.

改写 | Rewrite the Story | in Your Own Words

科学与探索 SCIENCE AND EXPLORATION

Chapter 4

---

1 伊雷娜·约里奥-居里(1897–1956),法国物理学家,居里夫妇的长女,1935 年与丈夫弗雷德里克·约里奥-居里(Jean Frédéric Joliot-Curie, 1900–1958)一同获得诺贝尔化学奖。

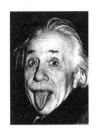

爱因斯坦

ALBERT EINSTEIN[1] (1879–1955)

提出相对论
The most famous scientist of the 20th century

The most famous scientist of the 20th century was actually born in the 19th, in Ulm[2], Germany, but ***he was educated mainly in Switzerland*** [主要在瑞士接受教育]. Albert Einstein ***was not considered an exceptional student*** [没有被当做一位优秀的学生], and ***was rather weak in mathematics*** [数学尤其差]. He became a naturalized Swiss citizen in 1902, and ***worked as a patent examine***r [做了一份专利鉴定员的工作] while ***qualifying for a doctorate from the University of Zurich*** [从苏黎世大学获得博士学位].

Three years later, Einstein ***published his first three papers*** [发表了他的前三篇论文] on physics, which ***exploded on the scientific world like an atom bomb*** [像一颗原子弹在科学界炸开], so advanced and radical were his ideas. One introduced his ***special theory of relativity*** [狭义相对论] and another his equation "E = mc[2]" which related mass and energy.

In 1914, he was appointed director of the ***Kaiser Wilhelm Institute for Physics*** [威廉皇家物理研究所] in Berlin. He became a German citizen in the same year. In 1916 he published his ***theory of general relativity*** [广义相对论].

Einstein received the 1921 ***Nobel Prize in Physics*** [物理学诺贝尔奖] for his ***discovery of the law of the photoelectric effect*** [发现光电效应] and his work in the field of theoretical physics.

In 1933, the year the ***Nazis took power in Germany*** [纳粹掌握德国政权], Einstein ***emigrated to America*** [移民美国]. He accepted a position at the ***Institute of Advanced Study in Princeton*** [普林斯顿高级研究院] and ***took US citizenship*** [获得美国国籍].

Einstein retired from the institute in 1945 but worked for the rest of his life towards a unified field theory to ***establish a merger between quantum theory and his general theory of relativity*** [建立量子理论和广义相对论的结合].

On the outbreak of war [战争爆发时] in 1939, Einstein wrote to ***President Roosevelt*** [罗斯福总统] about the ***prospect of atomic bomb*** [对原子弹的预期]. He warned Roosevelt the Germans were working on it. Roosevelt headed his advice and started the ***Manhattan project***[3] [曼哈顿计划]. But, after the war ended, Einstein ***reverted to his pacifist views*** [重拾他的和平主张].

Einstein died in 1955, ***at his request his brain and vital organs were removed for scientific study*** [要求捐献自己的大脑和重要器官用作科学研究].

A pacifist, a humanitarian and a music lover (he played the violin), he ***was offered the presidency of Israel*** [被邀请担任以色列的总统] when that state came into existence [成立] in 1948, but he ***declined on the grounds that*** [拒绝的理由是] he was not qualified for the

---

1 German-born physicist who developed the special and general theories of relativity and won the Nobel Prize for Physics in 1921 for his explanation of the photoelectric effect. Einstein is generally considered the most influential physicist of the 20th century.

2 乌尔姆，德国巴登-符腾堡州的一座城市，位于多瑙河畔。

3 曼哈顿计划，自 1942 年，第二次世界大战期间美国陆军研究核武器计划的代号。曼哈顿计划的负责人为美国物理学家罗伯特•奥本海默（J. Robert Oppenheimer，1904–1967），此计划获得美国总统富兰克林•罗斯福（Franklin Delano Roosevelt，1882–1945）的批准。

position and went on working for the world government, which he saw as the answer to the world's problems. To date it has not arrived.

Q by Quotes | Einstein

Imagination is more important than knowledge. For knowledge is limited, whereas imagination embraces the entire world, stimulating progress, giving birth to evolution.

I, at any rate, am convinced that He (God) does not throw dice.

Falling in love is not at all the most stupid thing that people do, but gravitation cannot be held responsible for it.

Try not to become a man of success, but rather try to become a man of value.

The secret to creativity is knowing how to hide your sources.

改写 Rewrite the Story | in Your Own Words

科学与探索 SCIENCE AND EXPLORATION

Chapter 4

弗莱明

ALEXANDER FLEMING[1] (1881–1955)

Today, ***the use of penicillin and other antibiotics is a commonplace*** [使用盘尼西林等抗生素已不再稀奇]. The various antibiotics are used to treat a number of what are now common diseases and to ***prevent the onset of infections*** [避免感染发作] when our skin, our ***first barrier to fight off disease*** [抵抗病毒的第一道防线], is somehow broken through a simple cut or a more serious wound.

It is something that ***we all take for granted*** [习以为常], today. However, many diseases and simple wounds that are so easily treated today because of the availability of antibiotics has not always been available. ***Antibiotics are a relatively recent discovery*** [相对来说，抗生素是最近的发现] and the first practical one, penicillin, was not available until the early 1940s.

In 1928, while ***studying influenza*** [研究流感], Fleming noticed that ***mould had developed accidentally on a set of culture dishes*** [霉菌意外地在一组培养基上生长] being used to ***grow the staphylococci germ*** [培育葡萄状球菌]. The mould had created a ***bacteria-free circle*** [无菌环] around itself. Fleming experimented further and named the active substance penicillin.

It was two other scientists however, Australian Howard Florey[2] and Ernst Chain[3], a ***refugee from Nazi Germany*** [来自纳粹德国的避难者], who developed penicillin further so that it could be produced as a drug. At first, supplies of penicillin were very limited, but by the 1940s it was being ***mass-produced*** [大规模生产] by the American drugs industry.

The discovery, ***development and subsequent use of penicillin*** [青霉素的开发和后继应用] can be considered to be ***one of the most important breakthroughs in medical history*** [是医学史上的重大突破之一]. Penicillin prevents a large number of germs from growing.

The immediate impact of the discovery is obvious [这项发现的直接影响立竿见影]. The drug was developed quickly in the War years by the American government. By developing the drug so readily and so quickly, the US Government helped many soldiers prevent their war wounds from becoming infected: the drug therefore saved a lot of lives and, it could be argued, played a role in ***helping to win the war for the Allies*** [帮助同盟国赢得一战胜利].

 Fleming

It is the lone worker who makes the first advance in a subject; the details may be worked out by a team, but the prime idea is due to enterprise, thought, and perception of an individual.

1 Scottish bacteriologist best known for his discovery of penicillin. Fleming had a genius for technical ingenuity and original observation.

2 弗洛里(1898–1968)，英国牛津大学病理学系主任

3 钱恩(1906–1979)，德国生物化学家，他因为有关盘尼西林的研究，而与亚历山大•弗莱明及霍华德•弗洛里共同获得 1945 年的诺贝尔生理学或医学奖。

I have been trying to point out that in our lives chance may have an astonishing influence and, if I may offer advice to the young laboratory worker, it would be this—never to neglect an extraordinary appearance or happening.

改写 | Rewrite the Story | in Your Own Words

波尔
NIELS BOHR[1] （1885–1962）

Niels Bohr's work ***laid the foundation*** [奠定基础] that led to a ***better understanding of the atomic structure and quantum mechanics*** [更好地理解原子结构和量子力学], a feat that fetched him the Nobel Prize for Physics in 1922. His work made it possible to solve many of the problems regarding the nuclear model of an atom that classical physics was unable to.

After Hitler took power in Germany [希特勒在德国登台], Bohr ***was deeply concerned for*** [担忧] his colleagues there, and offered a place for many ***escaping Jewish scientists*** [逃亡的犹太裔科学家] to live and work. He later ***donated his gold Nobel medal*** [捐出自己的诺贝尔奖金质奖章] to the Finnish war.

Three years later ***Bohr's family fled to Sweden in a fishing boat*** [举家坐渔船逃亡到瑞典]. Then Bohr and his son Aage left Sweden traveling ***in a British military plane*** [乘坐英国军事飞机]. They ultimately went to the United States, where both joined the government's team of physicists ***working on atomic bomb*** [研制原子弹].

Bohr ***had qualms about the disastrous consequences of the bomb*** [因原子弹带来的灾难性后果感到良心不安]. He angered Winston Churchill by wanting to ***share information with the Soviet Union*** [和苏联分享信息] and ***supporting postwar arms control*** [支持战后军备控制].

Bohr

An expert is a person who has made all the mistakes that can be made in a very narrow field.

Never express yourself more clearly than you are able to think.

---

1 Danish physicist who is generally regarded as one of the foremost physicists of the 20th century. He was the first to apply the quantum concept, which restricts the energy of a system to certain discrete values, to the problem of atomic and molecular structure. For this work he received the Nobel Prize for Physics in 1922.

克里克
FRANCIS CRICK[1] (1916–2004)

解密遗传物质结构
Biologist unlocked the 'secret of life'

To the public [对公众而言], Francis Crick was one of the men who, with the American J. D. Watson[2], ***discovered the structure of DNA***[3] [发现 DNA 结构] and ***received a Nobel Prize*** [获得诺贝尔奖] for it.

To his colleagues and students, he was one of the most distinguished and influential biologists in the 20th century, as well as one of the most ***flamboyant*** [光芒耀眼的]. Scientists would tell stories about Crick the way politicians once told stories about Churchill.

In 1947, Crick knew no biology and practically no ***organic chemistry*** [有机化学] or ***crystallography*** [结晶学], so that much of his next few years was spent in learning the elements of these subjects.

A critical influence on Crick's career [对克里克事业的一个重要影响] was his friendship, beginning in 1951, with J. D. Watson, then a young man of 23, leading in 1953 to the proposal of the ***double-helical structure*** [双螺旋结构] for DNA and the ***replication scheme*** [复制方法].

The story goes that on 28 February 1953, Francis Crick walked into the Eagle pub in Cambridge and announced that he and his American colleague James Watson "had ***found the secret of life*** [发现了生命的秘密]". In fact, they had.

That morning, Crick and Watson had worked out the structure of DNA (deoxyribonucleic acid). They had discovered its "double helix" form, one which could ***replicate itself*** [自我复制], confirming theories that it ***carried life's hereditary information*** [承载着遗传信息].

It was a ***revolutionary discovery*** [革命性的发现], the ***most significant contribution to science*** [对科学做出了最重大的贡献], in the view of many, since ***Darwin's theory of evolution*** [达尔文的进化理论]. ***It earned Crick and Watson a Nobel Prize*** [为二人赢得了诺贝尔奖].

Francis Crick was 38 and didn't even have a ***PhD*** [博士学位] (Doctor of Philosophy). His studies had been interrupted by World War II during which he helped ***develop torpedoes for the Royal Navy*** [在皇家海军研发鱼雷].

The discovery spawned an entire (biotechnology) industry [这项发现孕育了整个(生物技术)产业] and hardly a day seems to go by when some aspect of genetic research, be it in medicine, agriculture, forensic science or ethical debate, is not in the news.

拯救我的 SAT 写作
Saving My SAT Essay

---

1 Danish physicist who is generally regarded as one of the foremost physicists of the 20th century. He was the first to apply the quantum concept, which restricts the energy of a system to certain discrete values, to the problem of atomic and molecular structure. For this work he received the Nobel Prize for Physics in 1922.

2 詹姆斯•杜威•沃森(James Dewey Watson，1928–)，美国分子生物学家，与弗朗西斯•克里克共同发现 DNA 的双螺旋结构。

3 脱氧核糖核酸(Deoxyribonucleic Acid)，缩写为 DNA，保存生物体遗传信息。

Quotes by Crick

A busy life is a wasted life.

Chance is the only source of true novelty.

Exact knowledge is the enemy of vitalism.

改写 | Rewrite the Story | in Your Own Words

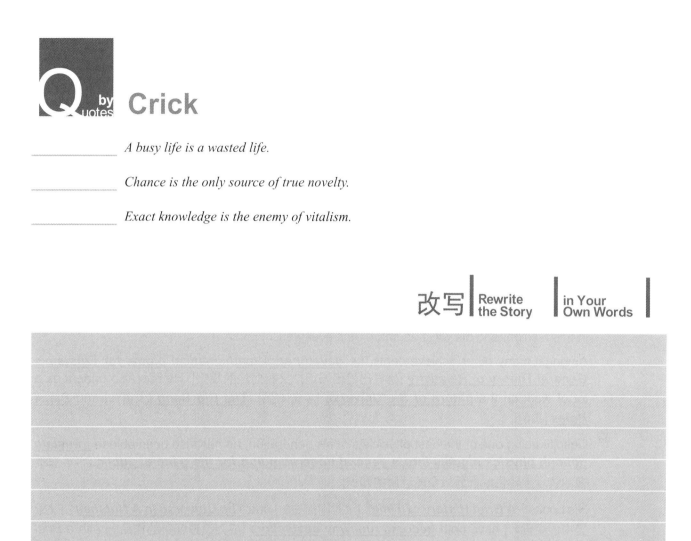

霍金
STEPHEN HAWKING[1] （1942–）

Professor Hawking ***has combated Motor Neurone Disease*** [一直在和神经元疾病抗争] ***despite the odds associated with the disease*** [与此疾病抗争非常困难]. It is thought that he is the longest survivor in the world.

He ***was officially diagnosed*** [被确诊] at the age of 21 whilst studying at Cambridge. Over the years his ***ability to communicate has deteriorated*** [交流能力退化], but he is now able to speak through a computer at the speed of 15 words a minute. ***Despite the laborious task of replying in this fashion*** [尽管这是一种费劲的应答方式], he has managed to relay books in this fashion, and his wit is as sharp as it ever was.

Amongst many other achievements, he ***developed a mathematical model for Einstein's General Theory of Relativity*** [推导出爱因斯坦广义相对论的模型]. He has also undertook a lot of work on the ***nature of the Universe*** [宇宙本质], ***The Big Bang*** [大爆炸] and ***Black Holes*** [黑洞].

Despite being one of the best physicists of his generation, he has also been able to ***translate difficult physics models into a general understanding for the general public*** [将艰涩难懂的物理学转化成普通大众能理解的知识].

His books—***A Brief History of Time***[2] [《时间简史》] and ***The Universe in A Nutshell***[3] [《果壳中的宇宙》] have both ***become runaway bestsellers*** [成为迅速畅销的作品]—with *a Brief History of Time* being in the bestseller lists for over 230 weeks. Despite suffering from the debilitating illness, Motor Neurone Disease, he has appeared on the TV programs ***Star Trek*** [《星际迷航》] and ***The Simpsons*** [《辛普森一家》].

Hawking

The greatest enemy of knowledge is not ignorance, it is the illusion of knowledge.

One, remember to look up at the stars and not down at your feet. Two, never give up work. Work gives you meaning and purpose and life is empty without it.

My goal is simple. It is a complete understanding of the universe, why it is as it is and why it exists at all.

---

1 English theoretical physicist whose theory of exploding black holes drew upon both relativity theory and quantum mechanics. He also worked with space-time singularities.

2 全名是《时间简史：从大爆炸到黑洞》（*A Brief History of Time: From the Big Bang to Black Holes*），英国物理学家霍金于 1988 年编写的一本科普图书，本书讲述了关于宇宙的起源和命运，介绍了什么是宇宙、宇宙发展的最新状况和关于宇宙本性的最前沿知识，解释了黑洞和大爆炸等天文物理学理论。

3 《果壳中的宇宙》，霍金为其成名著作《时间简史》在 2001 年写的续篇。

The victim should have the right to end his life, if he wants. But I think it would be a great mistake. However bad life may seem, there is always something you can do, and succeed at. While there's life, there is hope.

改写 Rewrite the Story | in Your Own Words

Notes

Chapter 5

政治与权力

POLITICS AND POWER

本 章 目 录

恺撒大帝
Julius Caesar[1] (100–44BC)

If there is **_a single name associated with the Roman Empir_**e [一个和罗马帝国联系起来的名字], it has to be that of Julius Caesar. He himself was known as **_imperator_** [古罗马大将] which usually was reserved for Roman generals in the field. Rome was actually a **_republic_** [共和国] during Caesar's lifetime.

Gaius Julius Caesar was born 100 years **_before the birth of Christ_** [早于耶稣诞生], on the twelfth day of the month which **_was later renamed July in his honor_** [为纪念他而被命名为 "July"].

His family **_were closely connected with_** [联系紧密] Roman politics. Caesar himself **_progressed within the Roman political system_** [在罗马政治体制内仕途步步高升], becoming **_in succession_** [连续地] **_quaestor_** [财务官] (69 BC), and **_aedile_** [营造官] (65 BC). He served as governor of the Roman province of Spain from 61BC to 60 BC.

Back in Rome in 60 BC, Caesar **_made a pact_** [立下契约] with Pompey[2] and Crassus[3], who helped him to **_get elected as consul_** [当选为执政官] for 59 BC. The following year he was appointed **_governor of Roman Gaul_** [罗马高卢地区总督] where he stayed for eight years, **_adding the whole of modern France and Belgium to the Roman empire_** [将面积相当于整个现代法国和比利时的领土纳入了罗马帝国], and making Rome safe from the possibility of **_Gallic invasions_** [高卢入侵].

Caesar then returned to Italy, **_disregarding the authority of the senate_** [不顾元老院权威] and famously **_crossing the Rubicon River_**[4] [强渡卢比孔河] without **_disbanding his army_** [没有解散军队].

In the ensuing civil war [在接下来的内战中], Caesar defeated the republican forces. Pompey, their leader, **_fled to Egypt_** [逃亡埃及] where he **_was assassinated_** [被刺杀].

Caesar was now master of Rome and made himself consul and **_dictator_** [独裁官]. He **_used his power to carry out much-needed reform_** [利用他的权力推动势在必行的社会改革], **_relieving debt_** [减轻债务], and **_revising the calendar_** [修制儒略历]. Dictatorship was always regarded a temporary position but in 44 BC, Caesar **_took it for life_** [改为终身制]. His success and ambition strongly alienated republican senators.

Alarmed by Caesar's increasing dictatorial power, republicans, led by Caesar's old colleague Marcus Brutus[5], plotted his assassination. Caesar **_was stabbed to death_** [被刺死].

---

1 Celebrated Roman general and statesman, the conqueror of Gaul (58–50 BC), victor in the Civil War of 49–45 BC, and dictator (46–44 BC), who was launching a series of political and social reforms when he was assassinated by a group of nobles in the Senate House on the Ides of March.

2 庞培(Pompey the Great, 106–48BC)，古罗马政治家、军事家。

3 克拉苏(Marcus Licinius Crassus, 115–53BC)，古罗马军事家、政治家，曾镇压过斯巴达克起义(War of Spartacus)，后和庞培、凯撒合作，组成三头政治同盟。

4 卢比孔河，意大利北部的一条河流。罗马法律规定，任何指挥官皆不可带着军队渡过卢比孔河，否则就是背叛罗马。凯撒在此讲出一句广为流传的名言："Alea iacta est(拉丁文)"（英语：The die has been cast.）。因此"渡过卢比孔河"(Crossing the Rubicon)常用来表示"破釜沉舟"之意。

5 马尔库斯·尤尼乌斯·布鲁图(Marcus Junius Brutus Caepio, 85–42 BC)，罗马共和国晚期的一名元老院议员，组织并参与对恺撒的谋杀。

Caesar, in addition to his ***military and political talents*** [军事政治才干], was a brilliant writer of Latin, a ***perceptive historian*** [有洞察力的历史学家], a clever ***lawmaker*** [法律制定者] and a fine ***orator*** [演讲家].

A man of ***limitless ambition*** [无限的野心], ***highly promiscuous in his personal life*** [私生活混乱], he ***used his marriages as political tools*** [把婚姻当做政治工具]. And like other great conquerors, he was responsible for the spilling of oceans of blood.

Q by Quotes Caesar

I came, I saw, I conquered.

No one is so brave that he is not disturbed by something unexpected.

It is better to create than to learn! Creating is the essence of life.

I love treason but hate a traitor.

It is easier to find men who will volunteer to die, than to find those who are willing to endure pain with patience.

改写 Rewrite the Story | in Your Own Words

亚历山大大帝
ALEXANDER THE GREAT[1] (356–323 BC)

"My father will get ahead of me in everything and will leave nothing great for me to do." The father: Philip II of ***Macedonia***[2] [马其顿王国]. The son: Alexander, his ***heir and successor*** [子嗣和继任者].

Philip, a brilliant general and organizer, had already made Macedonia ***the dominant power in the region*** [区域里占支配地位的政权] by the time his ambitious young son ***appeared on the stage of history*** [登上历史舞台].

Alexander was ***astonishingly gifted*** [极有天赋]. Of ***average height*** [身材中等], ***strikingly handsome*** [非常英俊], with huge eyes, fine features and ***blond curling hair*** [金色卷发], he ***played the lyre*** [演奏七弦琴] so well that his father teased him about it; his ***scholarly passion for history, literature and science*** [对历史、文学和科学研究热情] was ***insatiable*** [不知足的] and from it he ***developed an intense and permanent love for*** [培养了强烈和持久的热爱] the culture of central Greece.

Alexander had ***inherited his father's pride*** [继承了他父亲的荣耀] and ***his mothers' fiery temper*** [妈妈暴躁的脾气], but he was also ***warm-hearted*** [热心的]. He admired his father as a soldier and he ***was always deeply devoted to his mother*** [深爱着他的母亲].

As a ***lad*** [少年], Alexander ***proved his mettle*** [证明他的勇气] by ***taming a magnificent horse*** [驯服一头骏马] named ***Bucephalus***[3], previously quite ***untameable*** [不被驯服的]. It was this animal which was later to carry him all the way to India.

Under Aristotle's guidance [在亚里士多德指导下], Alexander ***developed all the intellectual and moral virtues*** [培养智力和道德的美德] which the ***Athenians*** [雅典人] believed to be the ***hallmarks of the ideal man*** [完美人类的标志], and combined them with the ***dignity*** [高尚] and responsibility of his ***noble birth*** [贵族血统].

Philip ***was assassinated*** [被暗杀] in 336 BC and Alexander ***inherited a powerful yet volatile kingdom*** [继承一个强大但又不稳定的王国]. He quickly dealt with his enemies at home and ***reasserted Macedonian power within Greece*** [要求马其顿政权统治全希腊]. He then ***set out to conquer the massive Persian Empire*** [征伐强大的波斯帝国].

Against overwhelming odds [面对压倒性的优势], he ***led his army to victories*** [率领军队接连胜利] across the Persian territories of ***Asia Minor*** [小亚细亚], ***Syria*** [叙利亚] and Egypt ***without suffering a single defeat*** [从没吃过一次败仗]. His greatest victory was at the ***Battle of Gaugamela***[4] [高加米拉战役], in what is now northern Iraq, in 331 BC.

---

1 King of Macedonia (356–323 BC). He overthrew the Persian empire, carried Macedonian arms to India, and laid the foundations for the Hellenistic world of territorial kingdoms.

2 马其顿位于希腊北部，境内山区称上马其顿，滨爱琴海地带称下马其顿。腓力二世(亚历山大大帝父亲)最终统一了上、下马其顿。亚历山大大帝于公元前 330 年灭亡波斯帝国，而后建立起横跨欧、亚、非的马其顿亚历山大大帝国。

3 布西发拉斯，它是亚历山大大帝的爱马。

4 高加米拉战役，在公元前 331 年 10 月 1 日发生，是马其顿与波斯之间的一场战役。据记载，波斯军损失超过 10 万人，远征军则仅以数百人的代价赢得这场重要战役。大流士三世(Darius III)不久后被部将杀害。

The young king of Macedonia, leader of the Greeks, _**overlord**_ [最高君主] of Asia Minor and _**pharaoh of Egypt**_ [埃及法老] became "great king" of Persia at the age of 25.

Over the next eight years, in his capacity as king, commander, politician, scholar and explorer, Alexander led his army a further 11,000 miles, founding over 70 cities and _**creating an empire that stretched across three continents**_ [建立了一个横跨三个大陆的帝国] and covered around two million square miles.

The entire area from Greece in the west, north to the _**Danube**_ [多瑙河], south into Egypt and as far to the east as the Indian _**Punjab**_[1] [旁遮普], was linked together in a _**vast international network of trade and commerce**_ [巨大的国际性商业贸易网络]. This was united by a common Greek language and culture, while the king himself _**adopted foreign customs**_ [采纳外国习俗] in order to _**rule his millions of ethnically diverse subjects**_ [统治成千上万种族多元化的子民].

Alexander had a love of music and books, when asked what was his greatest possession, Alexander replied _**Homer's Iliad**_ [荷马的《伊利亚特》]. However, he _**enjoyed a passionate life of drinking and reveling**_ [享受着喝酒与狂欢的激情生活]. For _**a man seemingly invincible on the battlefield**_ [一个沙场上战无不克的人], he _**ironically**_ [讽刺地] died at the early age of 32.

Within a dozen years, _**his empire broke down into its former squabbling states**_ [他的帝国瓦解成之前征战不休的小国].

Q by Quotes Alexander

Were I not Alexander, I would be Diogenes.

How great are the dangers I face to win a good name in Athens.

I am not afraid of an army of lions led by a sheep; I am afraid of an army of sheep led by a lion.

There is nothing impossible to him who will try.

改写 | Rewrite the Story | in Your Own Words

---

1 旁遮普，印度西北部一地方。

武则天
EMPRESS WU[1] (624–705)

中国古代唯一女皇
The Only Empress in the history of ancient China

Empress Wu was the only throned woman in the long history of ancient China [中国漫漫历史长河中唯一的女皇]. She ***was not born noble*** [并非含着金钥匙出生].

Empress Wu ***entered the palace*** [进宫] of the second Tang emperor, *Taizong* [唐太宗李世民] (599–649, ruled 626–649), as a ***junior concubine*** [才人] in 638, at age 13.

Relegated to a Buddhist convent [被送至尼姑庵雪藏] on the death of Taizong, ***as custom required*** [依照惯例], the Empress Wu was visited there by the new emperor—***Gaozong*** [唐高宗李治] (628–683, ruled 649–683), who had her brought back to the palace to be his own favorite concubine.

Empress Wu ***eliminated her female rivals within the palace one after another*** [接连铲除后宫竞争对手], and in 655 ***gained the position of empress for herself*** [加封皇后].

Empress Wu used her authority to ***bring about the fall of the elder statesmen*** [扳倒朝中老臣], all of whom had ***served Taizong*** [辅佐太宗] and still ***exercised great influence over the government*** [依然权倾朝野].

The power was exercised by the empress [武则天掌权] in the name of the sickly Gaozong, who ***was often too ill to attend to state affairs for long periods*** [终日抱病，不问朝政]. After Gaozong's death, in 690, at age 65, the empress ***usurped the throne itself*** [篡权登基].

Empress Wu was ***a highly competent ruler*** [励精图治的统治者], using men of her own choice, ***regardless of their social standing*** [不论出身贵贱]. Although her motives were to ***secure her own authority*** [巩固统治], the consequences of her policies were to ***be of great historical importance*** [具有重要的历史意义].

The early part of her reign was characterized [统治初期的特点是] by secret police terror, which ***moderated as the years went by*** [随着时间流逝有所缓和].

She ***established the new unified empire on a lasting basis*** [建立了一个长治久安的统一帝国] and ***brought about needed social changes*** [推行符合时代要求的社会变革] that ***stabilized the dynasty*** [稳定王朝] and ***ushered in one of the most fruitful ages of Chinese civilization*** [为大唐盛世、文化昌明揭开了序幕].

政治与权力 POLITICS AND POWER

Chapter 5

---

1 The woman who rose from concubinage to become empress of China during the Tang dynasty (618–907). She ruled effectively for many years, the last 15 years (690–705) in her own name. During her reign, Tang rule was consolidated, and the empire was unified.

成吉思汗
GENGHIS KHAN[1] (1162?–1227)

Who built the largest empire ever developed in the lifetime of one man? ***Alexander the Great*** [亚历山大大帝]? ***Julius Caesar*** [恺撒大帝]? ***Napoleon*** [拿破仑]? None of the above. Rather, it was a man whose name was ***Temujin*** [铁木真], also known to us as Genghis Khan (He was proclaimed Genghis Khan in 1206.).

Khan was born in 1167, the son of ***a powerful tribal chief*** [强大的部落首领]. At the age of 3, he ***was strapped into a saddle*** [用皮绳捆在马鞍上] and placed on a powerful horse. The lads who ***survived this education*** [在训练中存活下来] became the most skilled ***horsemen*** [骑兵] of their time, well-prepared for ***military service*** [军事训练] which was mandatory.

To further enhance their warlike upbringing, his tribe organized an ***annual hunt of wild animals*** [一年一度的狩猎]. Bears, tigers, wolves, leopards [豹], as well as less dangerous creatures, were driven into a small circle and after Genghis had made the first kill, the hunting began ***in earnest*** [认真地] and continued for days.

At the tender age of 13, Genghis ***succeeded to his father's position of chief*** [继承父亲首领的头衔]. He immediately ***became the target of subject tribes*** [成为部落的目标] who ***instigated military action*** [挑唆军事行动] against the ***stripling chieftain*** [年轻的首领].

But Khan soon ***proved his prowess*** [证明自己的能力] by ***subduing these tribes*** [驯服这些部落] and ***conquering hostile neighbors*** [征服敌对的强邻] as well.

His huge neighbor's emperor still ***demanded the traditional payment of tribute*** [要求传统上的进贡] from the peoples of the region. Genghis ***contemptuously refused*** [轻蔑地拒绝].

His succession adapted his method of warfare, moving from ***depending solely on cavalry*** [仅仅依靠骑兵] to using ***sieges*** [围攻], ***catapults*** [石弩], ladders, and other equipment and techniques suitable for the capture and destruction of cities.

Genghis Khan was a brilliant organizer, a ***master military tactician*** [精明的战术家], a ***disciplinarian*** [严格执行纪律者]. His standing order to his troops remained—soldiers "having ***retreated*** [退却] who ***do not resume their advance*** [没有继续前进] will ***be beheaded*** [被砍头]."

---

1 Mongolian warrior-ruler, one of the most famous conquerors of history, who consolidated tribes into a unified Mongolia and then extended his empire across Asia to the Adriatic Sea.

本杰明·富兰克林
BENJAMIN FRANKLIN[1] (1706–1790)

第一个真正的美国人
A leader in the American struggle for independence

An ***exceptionally well-rounded*** [多姿多彩的] man, Franklin ***worked in numerous fields and succeeded in all of them*** [在自己所有工作过的领域都获得了成功]. Franklin ***was noted for his curiosity*** [因他的好奇心而出名], ***ingenuity*** [独创性] and ***diversity of interests*** [兴趣广泛].

He ***wrote a classic autobiography*** [撰写一流的自传] and ***devised many practical inventions*** [设计了许多实用的发明]. He ***invented the lightning rod*** [发明避雷针] and ***bifocals*** [双焦点透镜]; he invented the idea of America.

He devised means to correct the excessive smoking of chimneys, and invented the Franklin stove, which ***supplied greater heat*** [提供更多热量] with ***a reduced consumption of fuel*** [减少燃料消耗].

He is also a brave scientist; he ***demonstrated to the public*** [向公众展示] that lightning was a form of electricity. He constructed a kite and ***flew it during the storm*** [在暴风雨中放风筝].

Served as ambassador to France [作为驻法大使], ***his success in securing French military and financial support for the newly formed United States*** [成功地保障法国对新生美国的军事和财政支持] ***was decisive for American victory over Britain*** [在美国对英国斗争的胜利上起了决定性作用].

He became one of the committee of five chosen to ***draft the Declaration of Independence***[2] [起草《独立宣言》] and became one of the signers of the historic document.

During the War of Independence[3] [美国独立战争期间]（1775–1783），Benjamin Franklin once said "gentlemen, we must all hang together or we will surely all hang separately".

Benjamin Franklin

Many people die at twenty five and aren't buried until they are seventy five.

Fear not death for the sooner we die, the longer we shall be immortal.

By failing to prepare, you are preparing to fail.

1 American printer and publisher, author, inventor and scientist, and diplomat. As one of the foremost of the Founding Fathers, Franklin helped draft *the Declaration of Independence* and was one of its signers, represented the United States in France during the American Revolution, and was a delegate to the Constitutional Convention.

2 《美国独立宣言》，1776 年 7 月 4 日，通过此宣言北美洲十三个英属殖民地宣告独立。

3 美国独立战争（1775–1783），战争始于北美十三个殖民地对抗英国的经济政策，之后有几个欧洲强国加入战争。

Chapter 5　政治与权力 POLITICS AND POWER

_____ *Instead of cursing the darkness, light a candle.*

_____ *An investment in knowledge pays the best interest.*

_____ *It is the first responsibility of every citizen to question authority.*

_____ *Early to bed and early to rise makes a man healthy, wealthy, and wise.*

改写 | **Rewrite the Story** | **in Your Own Words**

华盛顿
GEORGE WASHINGTON[1] (1732–1799)

美国国父
The first President of US

George Washington was ***America's first national hero*** [美国第一位国家英雄]. The man who ***was called on*** [被请求] to become the ***commander-in-chief of the colonies*** [殖民地的统帅] in their fight against their mother country was no military genius like ***Napoleon*** [拿破仑] or ***Caesar*** [恺撒]; but unlike many more brilliant commanders he always ***kept the issue he was fighting for clear in his own mind*** [明确战斗目标] and ***did not seek to feed his personal ambitions*** [没有试图满足个人野心].

During eight and a half years of war, George Washington always had one aim: to ***liberate the colonies from British rule*** [从英国的统治下解放殖民地]; once this object had been achieved, he ***was positively eager to relinquish his command*** [急迫地打算放弃他的统帅权].

When one of his officers suggested that George Washington become king, he ***firmly put a stop to any further ideas of that sort*** [坚决地停止类似念头]. Through it all, Washington ***advocated for*** [主张] ***civilian control of the military*** [民众控制军队], and at the end of the conflict, he gave up power [放弃权力], by personally ***resigning his military commission*** [辞去军事职务] before the Congress.

After his military career, Washington ***was chosen to lead the Constitutional Convention*** [被选中领导制宪议会], which developed the guidelines for a new form of government—a republic. ***Elected the country's first president*** [选举成为国家第一任总统], Washington had to work out this new kind of job ***step by step*** [一步步地], knowing that he was ***setting precedents*** [设定先例] for those who would follow him in office.

The Bill of Rights[2] [《权力法案》] became law during his first term, ***guaranteeing American citizens protection*** [保证美国公民享有保护] from ***an over-reaching federal government*** [无孔不入的联邦政府].

In his second term, Washington personally took to the field to put down ***Whiskey Rebellion***[3] [威士忌暴动] and show that the federal government had the right to make and collect taxes. He ***set the precedent of relinquishing office after two terms*** [设定先例最多连任两届], ***underscoring the fact that*** [强调一个事实] the ***presidency was not a life-time appointment*** [总统绝非终身制].

In private life, he led by example, striving to make ***Mount Vernon*** [弗农山] ***a model of new, science-based agriculture*** [新农业科技的典范], in order to benefit other farmers. He ***experimented with crops and fertilizers*** [试验新作物和化肥] and ***continually sought the best innovations*** [不断找到新方法].

As a businessman, he ***took advantage of the opportunities*** [抓住机会] provided by his

---

1 American agricultural chemist, agronomist, and experimenter whose development of new products derived from peanuts (groundnuts), sweet potatoes, and soybeans helped revolutionize the agricultural economy of the South.

2 《权利法案》，又译《人权法案》，指的是美国宪法中第一至第十条宪法修正案。

3 威士忌暴动，美国第一任财长、美国国父之一的亚历山大•汉密尔顿（Alexander Hamilton，1755–1804）为弥补财政赤字，打算征收威士忌消费税，并游说国会成功，美国百姓于 1794 年发起暴动，后来暴动被政府军镇压。

environment, eventually **_running flourishing fisheries_** [经营生意红火的渔场], a **_gristmill_** [磨坊], and the largest **_distillery_** [酿酒厂] in the country.

Washington had **_called for the abolition of slavery_** [要求废除奴隶制度] in 1786, but Congress did not respond. **_In his will_** [他的遗嘱中], he **_decreed_** [命令] that his 124 **_slaves be emancipated on his wife's death_** [妻子死后将奴隶释放].

Washington, one of the most important figures in American history, has earned the title of "Father of His Country" and **_a hallowed place in America's national psyche_** [美国民族精神神圣的地方].

Washington

It is better to offer no excuse than a bad one.

It is impossible to rightly govern a nation without God and the Bible.

Government is not reason, it is not eloquence—it is force. Like fire, it is a dangerous servant and fearful master.

99% of failures come from people who make excuses.

War of Independence

For more than **_a decade before the outbreak of the American Revolution_** [美国独立战争爆发前十年] in 1775, **_tensions had been building between colonists and the British authorities_** [殖民地和英国当局之间的矛盾日趋紧张].

Attempts by the British government to **_raise revenue_** [增加收入] by **_taxing the colonies_** [对殖民地征税] (notably the **_Stamp Act_**[1] [印花税法案] of 1765, the **_Townshend Tariffs_**[2] [汤申德关税] of 1767 and **_the Tea Act_**[3] [茶叶专卖法案] of 1773) met with **_heated protest_** [激烈的抵抗] among many colonists, who resented their **_lack of representation in Parliament_** [在议会缺少代表] and demanded the same rights as other **_British subjects_** [大英属国].

Colonial resistance led to violence [殖民地抵抗导致暴力发生] in 1770, when British soldiers **_opened fire on a mob of colonists_** [向殖民地居民开火], killing five men in what was known as the **_Boston Massacre_** [波士顿大屠杀].

---

1 印花税法案，是英国议会对美国殖民地印刷品直接实施的征税办法，英国想通过该方法来增加国家收入。这一政策遭到殖民地人民的一致强烈抗议。

2 汤申德关税，汤申德·查尔斯（Charles Townshend, 1725–1767）为英国政治家，1766 年任财政大臣及代理首相期间，倡议对从美洲殖民地进口的许多物品（玻璃制品、纸张、铅、颜料、茶、糖、朗姆酒、铁、棉花）征收关税。

3 茶叶专卖法案，英国国会于 1773 年通过的法案，为美国革命的导火线。

After December 1773, when a band of Bostonians ***dressed as Indians*** [化装成印第安人] ***boarded British ships*** [登上英国船只] and ***dumped 342 chests of tea into Boston Harbor*** [将 342 箱茶叶抛入波士顿港], an outraged Parliament passed a series of measures（known as ***Coercive Acts*** [强制法案]）***designed to*** [目的是] ***reassert imperial authority in Massachusetts*** [加强大英对马萨诸塞州的控制].

A group of ***colonial delegates*** [殖民地代表]—***First Continental Congress*** [第一届大陆会议] met in ***Philadelphia*** [费城] in September 1774 to ***give voice to their grievances against the British crown*** [表达他们对英国的愤恨].

On April 19, local ***militiamen*** [民兵] ***clashed with British soldiers*** [和英军士兵发生冲突] in ***Lexington*** [莱克星顿], Massachusetts, ***marking the first shots fired in the Revolutionary War*** [打响独立战争第一枪].

When the ***Second Continental Congress*** [第二届大陆会议] ***convened in Philadelphia*** [在费城召开], delegates—including new additions ***Benjamin Franklin*** [本杰明•富兰克林] and ***Thomas Jefferson***[1] [托马斯•杰斐逊]—voted to ***form a Continental Army*** [组建正规大陆军], with ***Washington as its commander in chief*** [华盛顿为大统帅].

By June 1776, with the Revolutionary War ***in full swing*** [如火如荼], ***a growing majority of the colonists*** [越来越多的殖民地居民] had come to favor independence from Britain.

On July 4, the ***Continental Congress*** [大陆会议] voted to adopt the ***Declaration of Independence*** [《独立宣言》], drafted by a five-man committee including Franklin and John Adams but written mainly by Jefferson.

In 1778, France ***recognized the United States as an independent country*** [法国承认美国作为一个独立国家] and ***signed a treaty of alliance*** [签署同盟合约]. France helped the United States as a way to weaken Britain, its long-time enemy.

The war ended when a peace treaty was signed in Paris on April 15, 1783. In this treaty, Britain and other nations recognized the United States as an independent nation. ***The Treaty of Paris*** [《巴黎和约》] turned the 13 colonies into states, but the job of becoming one nation remained.

改写 | Rewrite the Story | in Your Own Words

政治与权力 POLITICS AND POWER

Chapter 5

---

1 托马斯•杰斐逊（Thomas Jefferson，1743–1826），美国第三任总统，《独立宣言》的起草人。

拿破仑

NAPOLEON BONAPARTE[1] （1769–1821）

科西嘉人
A brilliant military commander

In 1779, young **Napoleon Bonaparte** [拿破仑•波拿马] was sent from the small island of **Corsica** [科西嘉岛] to a military school in France. He graduated in 1785, at the age of 16, **joined the French artillery** [入伍法国炮兵], and **began a military career that would change history** [开始了改写历史的戎马生涯].

During the **French Revolution** [法国大革命] （1789–1799）, France **was at war with its neighbors in Europe** [和欧洲邻国交战]. These wars resumed in 1800 **under the leadership of Napoleon** [在拿破仑的领导下], who **was crowned French emperor** [加冕称帝] in 1804. *A series of great victories* [接二连三的胜利] soon **brought much of Europe under his control** [将欧洲大部分版图收入囊中].

Starting as a second lieutenant [少尉] in the French **artillery** [炮兵], he **rose quickly through the ranks** [快速升职] until he **staged a 1799 coup** [策划了 1799 年的政变] that made him **First Consul of France** [法兰西共和国第一执政官].

In 1804 he **went further** [更进一步], **proclaiming himself emperor** [称帝]. Though **tradition called for the pope to crown the emperor** [传统习俗要求由教皇为皇帝加冕], Napoleon **took the crown from Pope Pius VII's hands** [从教皇庇护七世手中抓过皇冠] and placed it on his own head.

Napoleon created French **satellite kingdoms** [卫星属国] in **Holland** [荷兰], Italy, **Germany** [德国], and **Spain** [西班牙], and made his brothers and other relatives rulers in these places.

He **led his armies to victory after victory** [带领军队接连取得胜利]. But Napoleon's attempts to conquer the rest of Europe failed; His armies reached Moscow in 1812, only to be beaten back by the harsh winter weather. In 1814 he **was deposed** [被废黜] and **exiled** [流放] to the **island of Elba** [厄尔巴岛].

The next year he returned to Paris and again **seized power** [夺取政权], but this success was **short-lived** [短命的]: the French army's 1815 loss to the **first Duke of Wellington** [第一威灵顿公爵] （1769–1852） at **the Battle of Waterloo** [滑铁卢之战] finished Napoleon **for good** [永远地].

He **was sent into exile** [流放] on the island of **St. Helena**[2] [圣赫勒拿岛], where he died in 1821.

He is remembered as the man who **brought the French Revolution to a close** [结束法国大革命] and as **a military genius** [军事天才]. His system of law, **the Code Napoléon** [《拿破仑法典》], gave the poor people of France some of the rights they had demanded in the revolution. The Code was also welcomed in many of the lands he invaded.

---

1 French general, first consul （1799–1804）, and emperor of the French （1804–1814）, one of the most celebrated personages in the history of the West.

2 圣赫勒拿岛，位于大西洋中，现属英国。1815 年拿破仑被流放到该岛，并与 1821 年死于岛上。

Napoleon

Impossible is a word to be found only in the dictionary of fools.

Never interrupt your enemy when he is making a mistake.

Religion is excellent stuff for keeping common people quiet. Religion is what keeps the poor from murdering the rich.

Imagination rules the world.

History is a set of lies agreed upon.

History is written by the winners.

French Revolution

A watershed event in modern European history [现代欧洲历史分水岭], the French Revolution began in 1789 and ended in the late 1790s when **_Napoleon Bonaparte stepped down_** [拿破仑下台].

During this period, French citizens **_razed and redesigned their country's political landscape_** [将国家的政坛夷为平地，并重建], **_uprooting_** [连根拔除] centuries-old institutions such as **_absolute monarchy_** [君主专制] and the **_feudal system_** [封建体系].

As the 18th century drew to a close [十八世纪接近尾声], **_France's costly involvement in the American Revolution_** [法国参与美国独立的高昂代价] and **_extravagant spending_** [奢侈的消费] by King Louis XVI[1] [路易十六]（1754–1793）and **_his predecessor had left the country on the brink of bankruptcy_** [他的继任者将国家推向破产的边缘].

Not only were the **_royal coffers depleted_** [皇家国库亏空], but **_two decades of poor cereal harvests_** [二十余年谷物收成不佳], drought, **_cattle disease_** [家畜疾病] and **_skyrocketing bread prices_** [面包价格暴涨] had **_kindled unrest among peasants and the urban poor_** [点燃农民和城市贫民的动乱].

Many **_expressed their desperation and resentment toward a regime_** [表达对这个政权的绝望和愤恨] that **_imposed heavy taxes_** [征收重税] yet **_failed to provide relief_** [没有提供救济] by **_rioting_** [暴动], **_looting_** [抢劫] and **_striking_** [罢工].

On June 17, with talks over procedure stalled, the **_Third Estate_**[2] [第三等级] met alone and formally adopted the title of **_National Assembly_** [国民议会]; three days later, they met

---

1　路易十六（Louis XVI，1754–1793），是法国波旁王朝（House of Bourbon）的国王，1793 年 1 月 21 日被送上断头台。

2　三级会议，开始于 1789 年的法国，由三个等级构成：教会、贵族和其余民众。1789 年 5 至 6 月间，第三等级对自己的代表力有异议而解散三级会议，自行组织国民议会，引发法国大革命。

in a nearby indoor tennis court and took the so-called **_Tennis Court Oath_** [网球厅宣誓], vowing not to disperse until **_constitutional reform_** [宪法改革] had been achieved.

Though enthusiastic about the recent **_breakdown of royal power_** [王权瓦解], **_Parisians grew panicky_** [巴黎人变得惶恐不安] as **_rumors of an impending military coup began to circulate_** [有关即将发生军事政变的流言四起].

An **_insurgency culminated_** [叛乱活动达到高潮] on July 14 when **_rioters stormed the Bastille fortress_** [愤怒的民众攻入巴士底狱] **_in an attempt to secure gunpowder and weapons_** [试图获得枪支弹药]; many consider this event, now commemorated in France as a national holiday, as the start of the French Revolution.

The **_wave of revolutionary fervor_** [革命的热浪] and **_widespread hysteria_** [弥漫的歇斯底里] quickly **_swept the country_** [席卷全国].

Although it failed to achieve all of its goals and at times **_degenerated into a chaotic bloodbath_** [退化成混乱的大屠杀], the movement played a critical role in shaping modern nations by showing the world **_the power inherent in the will of the people_** [权利掌握在人民的手中].

Like the **_American Revolution_** [美国革命] before it, the French Revolution was influenced by **_Enlightenment ideals_** [启蒙运动的理念], particularly the concepts of popular **_sovereignty_** [主权] and **_inalienable rights_** [不可剥夺权利].

改写 | Rewrite the Story | in Your Own Words

林肯
ABRAHAM LINCOLN[1] (1809–1865)

解放黑奴
The 16th US president

Born in a log cabin on a farm in Kentucky [出生在肯塔基州一座农场的小木屋], he rose to become the 16th president of the USA. Lincoln, ***the son of an illiterate farmer*** [不识字农民的儿子], ***was educated in primitive backwoods schools*** [在落后偏远山区学校接受教育].

Lincoln ***was largely self-educated*** [大部分是靠自学]. He worked as a farmhand [农场工人] till he was 19, then ***signed on*** [签约雇工] a Mississippi river flatboat as a ***deckhand*** [甲板水手]. There he ***witnessed southern slavery first hand*** [直接目睹南方奴隶现状].

In 1836, he ***qualified as a lawyer*** [获得律师资格] and went to work in ***a law practice*** [律师事务所] in Springfield, Illinois. In 1846 he ***was elected to Congress*** [成为联邦众议员], representing the ***Whig Party***[2] [辉格党] for a term. In 1856, he ***joined the new Republican Party*** [加入共和党] and in 1860 he was asked to run as their ***presidential candidate*** [总统候选人].

In the presidential campaign, Lincoln made his ***opposition to slavery*** [反对农奴制度] very clear. ***His victory provoked a crisis*** [他的胜利引发一场危机], with many southerners fearing that he would attempt to ***abolish slavery in the South*** [在南方废除奴隶制度].

Eleven southern states left the Union to form the ***Confederate States of America***[3] [美利坚联盟国], also known as the ***Confederacy*** [南部邦联]. Four more joined later. Lincoln vowed to preserve the Union even if it meant war.

Fighting broke out [战斗爆发] in April 1861. Lincoln always defined the Civil War as a struggle to save the Union, but in January 1863 he nonetheless issued the ***Emancipation Proclamation*** [《解放奴隶宣言》], which ***freed all slaves*** [释放所有奴隶] in areas still under Confederate control. This was an important ***symbolic gesture*** [标志性的姿态] that identified the Union's struggle as a war to end slavery.

In the effort to win the war, Lincoln ***assumed more power*** [承担更大权力] than any president before him, ***declaring martial law*** [宣布戒严] and ***suspending legal rights*** [暂停合法权益]. He had difficulty finding effective generals [有力的将军] to lead the Union armies until the ***appointment*** [任命] of Ulysses S. Grant[4] as ***overall commander*** [总司令] in 1864.

On 19 November 1863, Lincoln delivered his famous ***Gettysburg Address***[5] [《葛底斯堡演说》] at the ***dedication of a cemetery*** [公墓揭幕致辞] at the site of the ***Battle of Gettysburg***[6]

---

1 16th president of the United States (1861–1865), who preserved the Union during the American Civil War and brought about the emancipation of the slaves.

2 辉格党(Whig Party)，美国政党，自 1833 年至 1856 年间运作。

3 美利坚联盟国(1861–1865)，由 11 个美国南方蓄奴州宣布从美利坚合众国分裂而出的政权。

4 尤利西斯•辛普森•格兰特(1822–1885)，1843 年于西点军校(陆军军官学校，英文全称 The United States Military Academy at West Point)毕业，1864 年起被任命为南北战争联邦军总司令，美国第 18 任总统。

5 《葛底斯堡演说》，林肯总统最著名的演说，其中最著名的一段是："that this nation, under God, shall have a new birth of freedom — and that government of the people, by the people, for the people, shall not perish from the earth."

6 葛底斯堡战役(1863 年 7 月 1 日至 7 月 3 日)，在宾夕法尼亚葛底斯堡及其附近地区进行，是美国内战中最血腥的一场战斗，经常被引以为美国内战的转折点。

政治与权力 POLITICS AND POWER

Chapter 5

[葛底斯堡战役], a decisive Union victory that had taken place earlier in the year.

On 9 April 1865, the Confederate general **_Robert Edward Lee_**[1] [南部邦联总司令罗伯特•李] surrendered, effectively ending the war. It had lasted for more than four years and 600,000 Americans had died. Less than a week later, Lincoln was shot while attending a performance at Ford's Theatre in Washington DC and died the next morning, 15 April 1865. His assassin, John Wilkes Booth[2], was a strong **_supporter of the Confederacy_** [南部邦联的支持者].

Napoleon

...that government of the people, by the people, for the people, shall not perish from the earth.

It is better to remain silent and be thought a fool than to open one's mouth and remove all doubt.

America will never be destroyed from the outside. If we falter and lose our freedoms, it will be because we destroyed ourselves.

The best way to destroy an enemy is to make him a friend.

Nearly all men can stand adversity, but if you want to test a man's character, give him power.

If you once forfeit the confidence of your fellow citizens, you can never regain their respect and esteem. It is true that you may fool all of the people some of the time; you can even fool some of the people all of the time; but you can't fool all of the people all of the time.

American Civil War

The American Civil War started in April 1861. The South **_claimed the right_** [声称有权] to leave the United States, also called the Union, and form its own Confederacy. President Lincoln led the Northern states. He **_was determined to stop the rebellion_** [决心阻止叛乱] and **_keep the country united_** [保持国家统一].

The North had more people, more **_raw materials_** [原材料] for **_producing war supplies_** [生产军备], and a better **_railway system_** [铁路系统]. The South had more **_experienced military leaders_** [有经验的军队指挥官] and **_better knowledge of the battlefields_** [更了解战场] because most of the war was fought in the South.

The war lasted four years. Tens of thousands of soldiers fought on land and sea.

September 17, 1862, was **_the bloodiest day of the war_** [战争最血腥的一天]—**_Maryland Campaign_** [马里兰会战]. The two armies met at Antietam Creek in Maryland. Gen. Robert

1 罗伯特•爱德华•李(Robert Edward Lee, 1807–1870)，美国职业军人，南北战争期间联盟国最出色的将军，联盟国军队总司令。

2 约翰•威尔克斯•布斯(John Wilkes Booth, 1838–1865)，美国戏剧演员，于 1865 年 4 月 14 日刺杀了林肯总统。

E. Lee and his Confederate Army failed to **_force back_** [逼退] the Union troops led by Gen. George McClellan.

Lee escaped with his army. **_The battle was not decisive_** [战斗不分胜负], but it was politically important. Britain and France had planned to recognize the Confederacy, but they delayed. The South never received the help it **_desperately needed_** [迫切需要的].

Later in 1862, President Lincoln issued a preliminary **_Emancipation Proclamation_** [《解放黑奴宣言》] that freed all slaves in the Confederate states. It also **_allowed African Americans into the Union Army_** [允许黑人参军]. The North fought to keep the Union together and to end slavery.

In Virginia in April 1865, Gen. Lee surrendered to Union Gen. Ulysses S. Grant. The Civil War was over.

改写 | Rewrite the Story | in Your Own Words

丘吉尔

SIR WINSTON CHURCHILL[1] （1874–1965）

He is remembered above all for his ***inspiring leadership during World War II*** [二战鼓舞人心的领导], of what was then the ***British Empire*** [大英帝国], against ***the Nazi onslaught of Adolf Hitler*** [纳粹希特勒的进攻].

After the ***fall of France*** [法国陷落] in 1940, it was Churchill who ***rallied the British people to resist alone*** [号召英国国民独自抵抗]. "I have nothing to offer but blood, toil, tears and sweat," he told his people.

Though he ***was born into a life of privilege*** [生来享有特权], he ***dedicated himself to public service*** [献身公共事业]. His legacy is a complicated one—he was an ***idealist*** [理想主义者] and a ***pragmatist*** [现实主义者]; an ***orator*** [演说家] and a soldier; an advocate of ***progressive social reforms*** [支持进步的社会改革] and ***an unapologetic elitist*** [不愿道歉的精英]; ***a defender of democracy*** [民主政治的拥护者] as well as of ***Britain's fading empire*** [衰落的英帝国]—but for many people in Great Britain and elsewhere, Winston Churchill is simply a hero.

Churchill's outstanding political virtue, which never deserted him, was his courage. His daring ***escape from a Boer prison camp*** [从布尔人监狱越狱成功] in 1899 ***made him a national hero*** [成为国家英雄] and ***ushered him into the House of Commons*** [带领他进入下议院], where his career spanned 60 years.

When World War II broke out in 1939, Churchill became ***first lord of the Admiralty*** [第一海军大臣]. In May 1940, ***Neville Chamberlain***[2] [张伯伦] ***resigned as prime minister*** [辞去总理职务] and Churchill took his place.

His refusal to surrender to Nazi Germany [拒绝向纳粹德国投降] inspired the country. He worked ***tirelessly*** [不知疲倦地] throughout the war, ***building strong relations with US President Roosevelt***[3] [和美国总统罗斯福建立强有力的关系] while ***maintaining a sometimes difficult alliance with the Soviet Union*** [和苏联保持时而艰难的同盟关系].

Sir Winston Churchill ***led Great Britain from the peril of subjugation by the Nazi tyranny to victory*** [带领英国从被纳粹征服的险境中走向胜利]; and during that last four years of his active political life he directed his country's efforts to maintain peace with honor, to resist another tyranny, and to ***avert a war more terrible than the last*** [避免比二战更可怕的战争].

In his few leisure moments, Churchill became an accomplished ***watercolorist*** [水粉画家]. "If it weren't for painting ***I couldn't bear the strain of things*** [不能忍受工作的压力]," he declared. He also ***wrote voluminously on history*** [历史方面著述颇丰], and published an

---

1 British statesman, orator, and author who served as prime minister（1940–1945, 1951–1955）rallied the British people during World War II and led his country from the brink of defeat to victory.

2 亚瑟•内维尔•张伯伦（1869–1940），英国保守党政治家，1937 年到 1940 年任英国首相。他由于在第二次世界大战前夕对希特勒之纳粹德国实行绥靖政策（Appeasement）而倍受谴责。

3 富兰克林•罗斯福（Franklin Delano Roosevelt，1882–1945），常简写作 FDR，第 32 任美国总统，自 1933 年至 1945 年间，连续出任四届美国总统，是 20 世纪世界经济危机和世界大战的中心人物之一。

unsuccessful novel. He ***was awarded the Nobel Prize for literature*** [获得诺贝尔文学奖] in 1953.

Quotes by Churchill

We make a living by what we get, but we make a life by what we give.

A pessimist sees the difficulty in every opportunity; an optimist sees the opportunity in every difficulty.

Attitude is a little thing that makes a big difference.

Courage is rightly esteemed the first of human qualities... because it is the quality which guarantees all others.

Courage is what it takes to stand up and speak; courage is also what it takes to sit down and listen.

Everyone has his day and some days last longer than others.

History is written by the victors.

I am fond of pigs. Dogs look up to us. Cats look down on us. Pigs treat us as equals.

改写 Rewrite the Story | in Your Own Words

罗斯福

FRANKLIN D. ROOSEVELT[1] （1882–1945）

Roosevelt was the ***only US president elected to office four times*** [唯一连任四届的总统] and led his country through two of the greatest crises of the 20th century—the ***Great Depression*** [大萧条] and World War Two.

In 1910, Roosevelt ***was elected to the New York Senate*** [被推选为纽约州参议员], where he quickly ***came to national attention*** [受到全国关注] as ***a rising Democratic politician*** [一颗冉冉升起的民主党新星].

From 1913 to 1920—which included the years of World War Ⅰ—Roosevelt was ***assistant secretary of the navy*** [海军助理部长], where he ***achieved a reputation*** [赢得声誉] as a capable young administrator.

In 1921, Roosevelt suddenly ***fell ill with polio*** [因脊髓灰质炎病倒] and was left ***unable to walk without braces or a cane*** [不能独立行走]. ***It seemed to signal the end of his political career*** [这似乎标志着他政治生涯的结束], but through his determination and the support of his wife, who often acted as his ***substitute*** [代理人] at political meetings, he returned to work.

In 1928, Roosevelt ***was elected governor of New York*** [被选举为纽约州州长] and in 1932 became the ***Democratic nominee for president*** [民主党总统候选人], ***winning by a landslide*** [以绝对优势赢得选举].

He came to power when the Great Depression was at its worst. He ushered in the "***New Deal***[2]" [罗斯福新政] program （1933–1938） to ***provide relief for the unemployed*** [缓解失业], and then jobs, as well as attempting to ***reform and strengthen the American economy*** [改革并加强美国经济].

Roosevelt won a second term in 1936 and ***an unprecedented third term*** [史无前例的第三届] in 1940. While initially keeping America out of World War II, he ***provided financial assistance and equipment to Britain and its allies*** [为英国及其盟友提供经济和装备方面的援助].

The Japanese attacked on Pearl Harbor [日本偷袭珍珠港] brought America into the war and Roosevelt ***took the lead in establishing a grand alliance*** [领导建立强大联盟] among the countries ***fighting the Axis powers*** [抵抗轴心国].

He also devoted time to the ***planning of the post-war workload*** [计划战后工作], particularly the ***establishment of the United Nations*** [建立联合国]. Roosevelt ***died in office*** [在任上逝世] on 12 April 1945, less than a month before ***Germany's unconditional surrender*** [德国无条件投降].

---

1 32nd president of the United States （1933–1945）. The only president elected to the office four times, Roosevelt led the United States through two of the greatest crises of the 20th century: the Great Depression and World War II.

2 罗斯福新政（The New Deal），1933 年富兰克林•罗斯福就任美国总统后所实行的一系列经济政策，其核心是三个 R: 救济（Relief）、改革（Reform）和复兴（Recovery），因此有时也被称为三 R 新政。

Quotes by F. D. R.

The only thing we have to fear is fear itself.

Men are not prisoners of fate, but only prisoners of their own minds.

Happiness lies in the joy of achievement and the thrill of creative effort.

The only limit to our realization of tomorrow will be our doubts of today. Let us move forward with strong and active faith.

We cannot always build the future for our youth, but we can build our youth for the future.

I'm not the smartest fellow in the world, but I can sure pick smart colleagues.

Great Depression

The Great Depression [大萧条] (1929–1939) was **the deepest and longest-lasting economic downturn** [最深刻、最持久的经济低迷] in the history of the **Western industrialized world** [西方工业世界]. In the United States, the Great Depression began soon after the **stock market crash** [股票市场崩溃] of October 1929, which **sent Wall Street into a panic** [让华尔街陷入极度恐慌] and wiped out millions of investors.

After nearly **a decade of optimism and prosperity** [十年的乐观与繁荣过后], the United States **was thrown into the abyss of despair** [被抛入绝望的深渊] on Black Tuesday, October 29, 1929, the day the stock market crashed and the official beginning of the Great Depression.

As **stock prices plummeted** [股价暴跌] **with no hope of recovery** [没有恢复的信心], panic struck. **Masses and masses of people tried to sell their stock** [大量投资者试图抛售股票], but no one was buying. The stock market, which had appeared to be the surest way to become rich, quickly became the **path to bankruptcy** [破产的捷径].

Over the next several years, **consumer spending and investment dropped** [消费与投资双双下降], **causing steep declines in industrial output** [导致工业产出直线下降] and **rising levels of unemployment** [失业率上升] as **companies laid off workers** [公司裁员]. By 1933, when the Great Depression reached its nadir, some 13 to 15 million Americans were unemployed and nearly half of the country's banks had failed.

Roosevelt **took immediate action to address the country's economic woes** [立即采取措施解决国家经济困难], first announcing a four-day "bank holiday" during which all banks would close so that Congress could **pass reform legislation** [通过改革法案] and reopen those banks determined to be sound.

He also began **addressing the public directly over the radio in a series of talks** [用一

系列广播直接对话公众], and these so-called "***fireside chats*** [炉边谈话]" ***went a long way towards restoring public confidence*** [花很长的时间恢复公众信心].

During Roosevelt's first 100 days in office, his administration ***passed legislation*** [通过法令] that ***aimed to stabilize industrial and agricultural production*** [旨在稳定工业农业生产], ***create jobs*** [创造工作岗位] and ***stimulate economic recovery*** [刺激经济恢复].

In addition, Roosevelt sought to reform the financial system, creating the Federal Deposit Insurance Corporation[1] （FDIC） to ***protect depositors' accounts*** [保护存款人账户] and the Securities and Exchange Commission[2] （SEC） to regulate the stock market and prevent abuses of the kind that led to the 1929 crash.

Though ***the relief and reform measures put into place*** [救济和改革的办法都已经到位] by President Franklin D. Roosevelt helped lessen the worst effects of the Great Depression in the 1930s, the ***economy would not fully turn around*** [经济没有完全好转] until after 1939, when ***World War II kicked American industry into high gear*** [二战推动美国工业高速运转].

改写 **Rewrite the Story** | **in Your Own Words**

---

1 美国联邦存款保险公司，简称 FDIC，是一个在大萧条时期由美国联邦政府创办，为商业银行储蓄客户提供保险的公司。

2 美国证券交易委员会，简称 SEC，是直属美国联邦政府的独立准司法机构，负责美国的证券监督和管理工作，是美国证券行业的最高机构。

希特勒
ADOLF HITLER[1] （1889–1945）

一个时代的魔咒
Dictator of Germany

Few men in the world history and ***none in modern times have been the cause of human suffering on so large as scale as Hitler*** [在现代没有人比希特勒给人类造成更大规模的苦难]. If history judges to be greatest those who fill most of her pages, Hitler was a very great man; and the house-painter who became for a while master of Europe ***cannot be denied the most remarkable talents*** [他的能力不能被否认].

He found Germans depressed, bewildered, aimless [发现德国人沮丧、困惑、漫无目的]. After five years in office, he had ***united the German race in a single Reich*** [统一德国种族成一个德意志国家], ***abolished regional diversities of administration*** [取消行政区各自为政的管理体制], and ***got rid of unemployment*** [消除失业]. But ***these achievements were merely instruments of an overwhelming lust for power*** [这些成就仅仅是对权利无限渴望的工具而已].

Nazi domination over Germany was a ***stepping stone*** [垫脚石] towards the domination of Nazi Germany over the world. The process was continuous, and the methods were the same.

Hitler ***effected the triumph of the Nazi Party*** [实现纳粹党的胜利] in Germany ***by a mixture of deceit and violence*** [结合欺瞒和暴力]; he then ***employed the same devices to destroy other nations*** [又使用相同方法征服其他国家]. From the time he became master of Germany he ***made lies, cruelty, and terror his principal means*** [主要使用谎言、暴力和恐怖等方法] to ***achieve his ends*** [达到他的目的].

Hitler was ***unimpressive*** [难留下印象的] to ***meet on informal occasions*** [平时见面], but became transformed when he ***was face to face with a crowd*** [面对人群], ***especially if it was an audience of his followers*** [特别当听众都是他的追随者]. He would speak to them like a man ***possessed*** [着魔的] and give the appearance of ***utter exhaustion*** [完全力竭] when his speech was over.

His father was a ***customs official*** [海关官员]. Hitler left school at 16 and ***struggled to make a living*** [挣扎地维持生活] as a painter in Vienna. Before embarking on a political career [开始政治生涯] in September 1919 at the age of thirty, Adolf Hitler had been a ***nonentity*** [一文不名]. ***With no formal qualifications*** [没有正式的文凭资格], he had ***become an aimless drifter*** [成为游手好闲的人] and failed artist before ***joining the army*** [参军] on the outbreak of war in August 1914.

In 1919, he ***joined the fascist German Workers' Party***[2] [加入法西斯德国工人党]（DAP）. By 1921 he was ***the unquestioned leader*** [毋庸置疑的领袖] of what was now the ***National Socialist German Workers' Party*** [国家社会主义德国工人党]（NSDAP or Nazi Party）.

In 1923, Hitler ***attempted an unsuccessful armed uprising in Munich*** [在慕尼黑发动了一场不成功的武装起义] and ***was imprisoned*** [被关进监狱] for nine months, during which time he dictated his book "***Mein Kampf*** [《我的奋斗》]" ***outlining his political ideology*** [勾勒出他的政治理念].

---

1 Leader of the National Socialist（Nazi）Party（from 1920/21）and chancellor（Kanzler）and Führer of Germany（1933–1945）.

2 德国工人党，后发展为纳粹党（Nazi Party），即（民族）国家社会主义德国工人党（The National Socialist German Workers' Party）。

On his release [出狱后] he began to ***rebuild the Nazi Party*** [着手重建纳粹党] and ***used new techniques of mass communication*** [使用大众传播的新技术], ***backed up with violence*** [暴力支持], to ***get his message across*** [传播他的信息].

Against a background of economic depression and political turmoil [在经济萧条和政治动荡的大背景下], the Nazis grew stronger and in the 1932 elections became the ***largest party in the German parliament*** [德国国会最大党派].

In January 1933, Hitler became ***chancellor of a coalition government*** [德国联合政府总理]. He quickly ***took dictatorial powers*** [开始独裁统治] and began to ***institute anti-Jewish laws*** [制定反犹太法律].

He also began the process of German ***militarization*** [军事化] and ***territorial expansion*** [领土扩张] that would ***eventually lead to World War II*** [最终导致二战爆发]. He ***allied with Italy and later Japan to create the Axis***[1] [和意大利及日本结盟形成轴心国].

Hitler's ***invasion of Poland*** [侵略波兰] in September 1939 began World War II. After military successes in ***Denmark*** [丹麦], ***Norway*** [挪威] and Western Europe, but after ***failing to subdue Britain*** [征服英国失败] in 1941, Hitler ***ordered the invasion of the Soviet Union*** [下令侵略苏联].

The Jewish populations of the countries conquered by the Nazis ***were rounded up and killed*** [被围捕后杀害]. Millions of others whom the Nazis considered racially inferior were also killed or worked to death.

In December 1941, Hitler ***declared war on the United States*** [对美宣战]. ***The war on the eastern front*** [东线战事] drained Germany's resources [耗尽德国资源] and in June 1944, ***the British and Americans landed in France*** [英美联军在法国登陆]. With Soviet troops poised to take the German capital, Hitler ***committed suicide in his bunker in Berlin*** [在柏林地下碉堡自杀] on 30 April 1945.

 Hitler

If you win, you need not have to explain...If you lose, you should not be there to explain!

If you tell a big enough lie and tell it frequently enough, it will be believed.

It is not truth that matters, but victory.

Those who want to live, let them fight, and those who do not want to fight in this world of eternal struggle do not deserve to live.

What good fortune for governments that the people do not think.

---

1 轴心国，指在第二次世界大战中结成的战争联盟，包括纳粹德国、大日本帝国和意大利王国等国家。

World War II

In the early morning hours of September 1, 1939, the **_German armies marched into Poland_** [德军进攻波兰]. On September 3 the British and French surprised Hitler by **_declaring war on Germany_** [对德宣战], **_but they had no plans for rendering active assistance to the Poles_** [但是没有计划给波兰提供积极援助].

Except **_the British navy imposed a blockade at sea_** [英国海军在海上给德军以还击], so little was going on after the first week in October 1939. **_French strategy was defensive_** [法国的策略是防守], based on **_holding the heavily fortified Maginot line_**[1] [荷枪实弹地躲在马其诺防线后].

Unfortunately, the Maginot line covered the French-German frontier, but not the **_French-Belgian frontier_** [法国比利时边界]. Thus the Germans in May 1940 **_outflanked the line_** [从侧翼包围马其诺防线]. Having **_made a breakthrough with their tanks and planes_** [利用坦克飞机火力突破], they **_continued around to the rear of the line_** [继续绕行到防线后方], **_making it useless_** [让其毫无用武之地].

On December 7, 1941, Japanese **_carrier-based airplanes_** [飞机从航空母舰起飞] **_struck Pearl Harbor_**[2] [袭击珍珠港] on **_Oahu Island_** [瓦胡岛], Hawaii.

In the **_aerial attack_** [空袭] lasting less than two hours, they **_sank_** [击沉] or **_seriously damaged_** [严重损毁] eight **_battleships_** [战舰] and 13 other **_naval vessels_** [海军舰艇]. The Japanese attack brought the United States into the war on December 8, 1941.

Battle of Midway [中途岛之战] was fought in June 1942 near the Midway Islands by Japanese and US **_aircraft carriers_** [航空母舰]. **_It gave the United States sea power over the Japanese_** [美国夺走日本制海权].

On June 6, 1944, about 120,000 **_Allied troops_** [联军] landed at five beach locations along the coast of the **_French province of Normandy_** [法国诺曼底] after **_crossing the English Channel_** [横渡英吉利海峡] from bases in southern England.

D-Day[3] Invasion or Invasion of Normandy represented a **_major turning point_** [转折点] in World War II. Many historians consider the D-Day invasion the greatest military achievement of the 20th century.

In August 1945, US planes dropped two atom bombs on **_Hiroshima_** [广岛] (On August 6, 1945) and **_Nagasaki_** [长崎] (On August 9, 1945), Japan. On August 14, 1945, **_Japan announced its surrender_** [日本宣布投降].

政治与权力 POLITICS AND POWER

Chapter 5

---

1 马奇诺防线，时任法国陆军部长的马奇诺（1877–1932）从 1929 年起开始建造，1940 年基本建成。防线由钢筋混凝土建造而成，十分坚固。

2 珍珠港，位于美国夏威夷州瓦胡岛上的海港，位于该州首府檀香山西方。珍珠港港区与邻近岛屿上大部分的设施都属于美国海军所有，作为深水军港使用，也是美国海军太平洋舰队的总部所在地。

3 D 日（D-Day），"D" 在英语中代表 "日（date）"，在军事术语中经常作为表示一次作战或行动发起的那天。最著名的 D 日是 1944 年 6 月 6 日的诺曼底战役打响之日。

里根

RONALD REAGAN[1] （1911–2004）

Ronald Reagan manifestly ***lived the American dream*** [实现美国梦] in which he so ***fervently*** [热诚地] believed. He ***rose from the humblest origins*** [出身卑微] to become a ***minor Hollywood star*** [二线好莱坞影星], ***Governor of California*** [加州州长] for two terms, and finally America's fortieth President.

As President, he will be primarily remembered for ***hastening the end of the Cold War*** [加速冷战的结束]—or even, ***some claim*** [有人称], winning it. He did this by ordering the largest ***peacetime military build-up*** [和平时期军事发展] in United States history and by the development of the "***Star Wars***[2] [星球大战计划]" program, which ***was designed to*** [设计用来] ***shield America from incoming missiles*** [保护美国不受来袭导弹侵害].

The policy of "peace through strength" made clear to ***an economically faltering Soviet Union*** [经济方面步履蹒跚的苏联] that the ***arms race was unwinnable*** [军备竞争无法胜利], and ***two crucial nuclear arms reduction treaties ensued*** [两个重要的削减核武器条约紧随其后]. By the time Regan left office, the threat of nuclear war between the ***West and the Communist bloc*** [西方和社会主义阵营] had ***greatly diminished*** [大幅减弱].

Domestically, Reagan's two great achievements were to ***restore America's pride and confidence*** [恢复美国的自豪与自信] after ***Vietnam War*** [越南战争], ***Watergate Scandal*** [水门事件], and fundamentally to change the terms of the political debate by advancing what was, in 1980, the almost ***heretical notion*** [怪异的主张] that government was part of problem, not the solution.

While Reagan remained a popular president, he never fully recovered his former levels of support following the ***Iran-contra scandal***[3] [伊朗门事件] of 1986.

In 1989, Reagan ***stood down*** [退位] and ***was succeeded by his vice president*** [由副总统继任], ***George Bush Senior*** [老布什], for whom Reagan campaigned. In 1994, Reagan announced that he had ***Alzheimer's disease*** [老年痴呆症] and died of a related illness on 5 June, 2004.

Reagan

A people free to choose will always choose peace.

---

1 40th president of the United States （1981–1989）, noted for his conservative Republicanism, his fervent anticommunism, and his appealing personal style, characterized by a jaunty affability and folksy charm.

2 反弹道导弹防御系统之战略防御计划（Strategic Defense Initiative），简称 "星球大战"，计划的目的是以各种手段攻击敌方的外太空的洲际战略导弹和外太空航天器，以防止敌对国家对美国及其盟国发动的核打击。

3 伊朗门事件，发生在美国 20 世纪 80 年代中期的政治丑闻，美国里根政府向伊朗秘密出售武器一事被揭露后而造成严重政治危机事件。

政治与权力 POLITICS AND POWER

Chapter 5

Government does not solve problems; it subsidizes them.

Above all, we must realize that no arsenal, or no weapon in the arsenals of the world, is so formidable as the will and moral courage of free men and women. It is a weapon our adversaries in today's world do not have.

Freedom is never more than one generation away from extinction. We didn't pass it to our children in the bloodstream. It must be fought for, protected, and handed on for them to do the same.

It has been said that politics is the second oldest profession. I have learned that it bears a striking resemblance to the first.

Government's first duty is to protect the people, not run their lives.

Information is the oxygen of the modern age. It seeps through the walls topped by barbed wire, it wafts across the electrified borders.

Cold War

During World War II, the **_United States and the Soviet Union fought together as allies against the Axis powers_** [美国和苏联建立同盟共同抵抗轴心国]. However, the relationship between the two nations was a tense one.

Americans **_had long been wary of_** [一直都在警惕] **_Soviet communism_** [苏联共产主义] and concerned about **_Russian leader's tyrannical, blood-thirsty rule_** [俄罗斯领导残暴、嗜血的统治] of his own country.

For their part, the Soviets **_resented_** [憎恨] the Americans' decades-long refusal to treat the USSR (Union of Soviet Socialist Republics) as **_a legitimate part of the international community_** [国际社会合法的一部分] as well as their **_delayed entry into World War II_** [推迟介入二战], which resulted in the deaths of tens of millions of Russians.

After the war ended, **_these grievances ripened into an overwhelming sense of mutual distrust and enmity_** [积怨发酵成强烈的不信任和敌对]. **_In such a hostile atmosphere_** [在这样的敌对气氛中], no single party was entirely to blame for the Cold War; in fact, **_some historians believe it was inevitable_** [一些历史学家相信冷战不可避免].

American officials encouraged the **_development of atomic weapons_** [开发核武器] like the ones that had ended World War II. Thus began **_a deadly "arms race_** [可怕的军备竞赛]."

In 1949, the Soviets tested an atom bomb of their own. In response, **_President Truman_**[1] [杜鲁门总统] announced that the United States would build an **_even more destructive atomic weapon_** [更具毁灭性的核武器]: the **_hydrogen bomb_** [氢弹], or "superbomb."

The **_ever-present threat of nuclear annihilation_** [挥之不去的核武灭绝性威胁] **_had a great impact on domestic life_** [给人们生活带来巨大影响] as well. People **_built bomb shelters in their backyards_** [在自家后院修建炸弹掩体]. They **_practiced attack drills_** [进

1 杜鲁门 (Harry S. Truman, 1884–1972), 美国民主党政治家, 第 34 任副总统 (1945 年)。

行攻击演习] in schools and other public places.

Space exploration [太空探索] served as ***another dramatic arena for Cold War competition*** [冷战竞赛的舞台]. On October 4, 1957, a Soviet ***R-7 intercontinental ballistic missile launched Sputnik*** [R-7 洲际导弹发射人造卫星], ***the world's first artificial satellite*** [世界第一颗人造卫星] and the first man-made object to be placed into the ***Earth's orbit*** [地球轨道].

The Soviets ***were one step ahead*** [领先一步], launching the first man into space in April 1961. Neil Armstrong of NASA's Apollo 11 mission, ***became the first man to set foot on the moon*** [成为登月第一人], effectively winning the Space Race for the Americans.

In November 1989, the ***Berlin Wall*** [柏林墙]—***the most visible symbol of the decades-long Cold War*** [持续数十年冷战的最显眼标志]—was finally destroyed. By 1991, the ***Soviet Union itself had fallen apart*** [苏联自行解体]. The Cold War was over.

改写 | Rewrite the Story | in Your Own Words

尼克松

RICHARD NIXON[1] （1913–1994）

Reconciliation [调和] was the first goal set by President Richard M. Nixon. The Nation ***was painfully divided*** [被痛苦地分裂], with ***turbulence*** [骚乱] in the cities and ***war overseas*** [海外战争].

During his ***Presidency*** [总统职位], Nixon ***succeeded in*** [成功] ***ending American fighting in Vietnam*** [结束越战] and ***improving relations with the U.S.S.R. and China*** [改善美国和中国及苏联的关系].

But the ***Watergate scandal*** [水门事件] ***ultimately led to his resignation*** [最终导致他的下台]. Richard Nixon was the only president in the history of US to be forced to resign in order to ***avoid impeachment*** [避免弹劾].

During the 1972 ***election campaign*** [竞选] there was ***a break-in at the offices of the Democratic Party's national headquarters*** [私闯民主党全国总部] in the Watergate complex in Washington D.C.. Five men connected with Nixon's campaign team ***were arrested*** [被捕].

Evidence of a cover-up [掩盖事实的证据] ***was gradually uncovered*** [被逐渐揭露] and ***President Nixon himself was implicated*** [尼克松总统自己也受到牵连]. On 8 August, 1974, following months of a growing sense of scandal, he announced his resignation. ***Vice President Gerald Ford was sworn in as president*** [副总统福特宣誓就职总统].

Yet the ***disgrace*** [羞耻] of Watergate ***masked*** [掩盖] some real and lasting achievements as a ***statesman*** [政治家]. He ***had a sure touch in foreign affairs*** [处理外交事务沉着冷静]. He achieved, for instance, ***a realistic Far East policy*** [务实的远东政策] by ***reaching an understanding with China*** [和中国达成和解]. And he evacuated his country, ***with as much dignity as was possible*** [以极大的尊严], from ***the quagmire of the Vietnam War***[2] [越战泥潭].

Nevertheless, the ***damage the sheer sleaze of his methods inflicted on standards of American public life was enormous*** [尼克松低劣手段对美国民主生活造成破坏极大], and the ***modern presidency was never to be looked upon in quite the same reverent light again*** [现代总统再也没有受到此前的尊敬].

It was Nixon who ***opened the floodgates for the spirit of public skepticism*** [为公众怀疑精神打开闸门], which today appears to ***characterize the American political process*** [美国政治特色].

---

1 37th president of the United States（1969–1974）, who, faced with almost certain impeachment for his role in the Watergate Scandal, became the first American president to resign from office.

2 （美国的）越南战争（1961-1973）, 简称越战, 为南越（越南共和国）及美国对抗共产主义的北越（越南民主共和国）及"越南南方民族解放阵线"（又称越共）的一场战争。

Nixon

Remember, always give your best. Never get discouraged. Never be petty. Always remember, others may hate you. But those who hate you don't win unless you hate them. And then you destroy yourself.

Any change is resisted because bureaucrats have a vested interest in the chaos in which they exist.

The Chinese use two brush strokes to write the word "crisis" One brush stroke stands for danger; the other for opportunity. In a crisis, be aware of the danger, but recognize the opportunity.

改写 | Rewrite the Story | in Your Own Words

肯尼迪

JOHN F. KENNEDY[1] (1917–1963)

He was the youngest man ever to be elected to the White House [他是入主白宫最年轻的总统]. He was the first President born in the 20th century; the first ***Roman Catholic*** [罗马天主教], and the first of ***purely Irish descent*** [正宗爱尔兰人后代].

He had many of the qualities necessary to achieve greatness in the White House— ***a cool and practical judgment*** [冷静而实用的判断]; ***a penetrating intellect*** [有洞察力的智者]; and ***a keen and ruthless political sense*** [敏锐而无情的政治触觉]. All these gifts were combined with ***enormous driving energy*** [巨大动力].

President Kennedy's years in office ***will always be marked with distinction*** [处处可圈可点], above all for his ***handling of the Cuban crisis***[2] [处理古巴危机]. It was then that he ***took the supreme risk*** [冒着极大风险], told the American people, and indeed the free world, what had to be faced, and ***firmly blocked the advancing convoy*** [坚决制止继续护送任务] which was ***bringing the medium-range rockets to sites in Cuba*** [运送中级导弹到古巴], from which they would profoundly have ***altered the strategic balance of power*** [改变权力战略平衡].

The decisiveness of US policy [美国果断的政策] at this time not only won President Kennedy ***an abiding place*** [持久的位置] among the great Presidents of the US but ***leading to an easing of the cold war*** [导致冷战缓和], may well ***be regarded as one of the real turning-points in history*** [被认为是历史转折点之一].

Domestically [国内方面], Kennedy ***oversaw the desegregation*** [监督废除种族隔离政策] of the University of Mississippi in 1962, and of the University of Alabama the following year - ***despite the opposition to this policy of each state's political establishment*** [尽管与各州政府制度相悖].

Kennedy ***was assassinated*** [被行刺] on 22 November 1963 in Dallas [达拉斯], Texas. According to the Warren Commission[3] established to investigate the assassination, ***a lone gunman*** [唯一枪手], Lee Harvey Oswald, killed the president, but ***there has been consistent speculation ever since*** [推测持续不断] that ***Kennedy's death was the result of a conspiracy*** [肯尼迪之死是阴谋的结果].

---

1 35th president of the United States (1961–1963), who faced a number of foreign crises, especially in Cuba and Berlin, but managed to secure such achievements as the Nuclear Test-Ban Treaty and the Alliance for Progress. He was assassinated while riding in a motorcade in Dallas.

2 古巴导弹危机，是 1962 年冷战时期在美国、苏联与古巴之间爆发的一场极其严重的政治、军事危机。事件爆发的直接原因是苏联在古巴部署导弹。

3 沃伦委员会，成立于 1963 年 11 月 29 日，以调查美国前总统约翰·肯尼迪遇刺事件。

Kennedy

And so, my fellow Americans, ask not what your country can do for you, ask what you can do for your country. My fellow citizens of the world: ask not what America will do for you, but what together we can do for the freedom of man.

Change is the law of life. And those who look only to the past or present are certain to miss the future.

If we cannot end now our differences, at least we can help make the world safe for diversity.

Let us never negotiate out of fear but let us never fear to negotiate.

Now the trumpet summons us again—not as a call to bear arms, though arms we need; not as a call to battle, though embattled we are; but a call to bear the burden of a long twilight struggle, year in and year out, 'rejoicing in hope, patient in tribulation', a struggle against the common enemies of man: tyranny, poverty, disease and war itself.

The complacent, the self-indulgent, the soft societies are about to be swept away with the debris of history.

改写 | Rewrite the Story | in Your Own Words |

政治与权力 POLITICS AND POWER

Chapter 5

Notes

Chapter 6

社会与变革

SOCIETY AND REFORM

本 章 目 录

圣女贞德

JOAN OF ARC[1] (1412–1431)

法国民族英雄
A national heroine

On 30 May 1431, a farmer's daughter, **_sentenced to death as a relapsed heretic_** [因异端被判处死刑], **_was burnt in the Old Market Place[2] at Rouen_** [在鲁昂的老集市广场执行火刑]. By 1910 **_it was reckoned_** [据估算] that there were some 20,000 statues of Joan of Arc in France.

At around the age of 17 she believed that she **_had received visions from God_** [得到上帝的启示] that she could **_lead the French to victory_** [引导法国走向胜利]; in 1429 **_she was sent to relieve the siege of Orléans_**[3] [派去奥尔良解围], and her success was remarkable.

She played a part in a number of other battles, but **_was captured_** [被擒] at Compiègne[4] in 1430, **_tried and convicted of heresy_** [被判异端] by the English in 1431 and **_burnt at the stake_** [在火刑柱上烧死] at Rouen. Her bones have never been found, as after her death, **_they were apparently burnt twice over_** [骨灰被再次焚烧] and the **_ashes thrown into the Seine_** [骨灰撒向塞纳河] to **_prevent the collection of any relics_** [防止遗骸被搜集].

In 1455, **_her case was reopened_** [案件被重判] and the **_Pope, Callixtus III_**[5] [教皇嘉礼三世] **_overturned the original verdict_** [推翻最初判决]. But her **_beautification_** [美化] had to wait until 1909.

It is hardly surprising then that in 1920 the **_Vatican_** [梵蒂冈], **_yielding to this monumental pressure_** [迫于压力], decided to **_recognize her as a saint_** [被封圣]. The date of Joan's **_canonization_** [封圣] **_is an indication of_** [说明] **_her appeal to the nationalist sentiment_** [对民族主义情绪的感染力] so characteristic of the nineteenth century.

Joan of Arc **_achieved a remarkable achievement_** [取得不平凡的成就] in her short life of 19 years. In particular she **_embodied religious devotion with great bravery and humility_** [体现宗教的虔诚与极大的勇气和谦卑], **_and she helped change the course of French history_** [她帮助改写了法国的历史].

Joan of Arc

One life is all we have and we live it as we believe in living it. But to sacrifice what you are and to live without belief, that is a fate more terrible than dying.

---

1 National heroine of France, a peasant girl who, believing that she was acting under divine guidance, led the French army in a momentous victory at Orléans that repulsed an English attempt to conquer France during the Hundred Years' War.

2 法国鲁昂一个古老的广场，1979 年兴建了圣女贞德教堂。

3 奥尔良之围（1428 年 10 月–1429 年 5 月），英国军队对法国城市奥尔良的围攻战。围攻战被法国民族英雄圣女贞德率领军队解除，这场战役成为英法百年战争（Hundred Years' War）中一个重大的也是最后的转折点，为法国最终取得胜利奠定了基础。

4 贡比涅（Compiègne），距离首都巴黎约 80 公里，是瓦兹省的首府。

5 教皇嘉礼三世（1378–1458），又译卡利克斯特三世，1455–1458 年在位。

I am not afraid..... I was born to do this.

Every man gives his life for what he believes ... one life is all we have to live and we live it according to what we believe.

改写 | **Rewrite the Story** | **in Your Own Words**

马丁·路德
MARTIN LUTHER[1] （1483-1546）

It is not often that one individual has had a profound impact on the course of history
[一个人对历史产生深刻影响的情况不常见], but Martin Luther is certainly one such person. More than any other individual, he was the initiator of the ***Protestant Reformation***[2] [宗教改革], though he was not the first ***religious rebel within the Roman Catholic church*** [罗马天主教内部叛乱].

John Wycliffe[3] in England survived his difficulties, but years ***after his death his body was disinterred and burnt*** [死后尸体被掘出后焚烧]. Jan Huss[4] in ***Prague*** [布拉格], ***less fortune*** [没那么幸运], ***was burned at the stake for his views*** [因异端被执行火刑].

By contrast, Martin Luther survived very successfully, and ***founded the largest Protestant denomination*** [成立最大的新教教派] following his ***break with the Church of Rome*** [和罗马教堂决裂].

Luther ***was born of peasant stock*** [出生于农民人家] in the German town of Eisleben[5]. His father was able to give his son a good education in law. After ***a terrifying experience*** [一次让人毛骨悚然的经历] in which he ***was struck by lightning*** [被雷电击中], ***crying out in terror*** [恐惧地叫喊]: "St. Anne[6], help me! I will become a monk!" Martin ***entered the Augustinian order*** [进入奥古斯丁修道会].

In 1510 he visited Rome on behalf of a number of Augustinian monasteries, and ***was appalled by the corruption he found there*** [惊愕于当地的腐败].

Luther became increasingly angry about the clergy selling "***indulgences***" [赎罪券], which promised ***remission from punishments for sin*** [免除罪恶的惩罚], either for someone still living or for one who had died and was believed to be in ***purgatory*** [炼狱]. On 31 October 1517, he published his "***95 Theses***[7]" [《九十五条论纲》], ***attacking papal abuses and the sale of indulgences*** [攻击罗马教皇暴行及贩卖赎罪券].

Luther had come to believe that Christians are saved through faith and not through their own efforts. This ***turned him against many of the major teachings of the Catholic Church*** [反对罗马教堂的教义]. From 1519 to 1520, he ***wrote a series of pamphlets*** [写了一系列小册子] developing his ideas. Thanks to the printing press, Luther's "95 Theses" and his other writings ***spread quickly through Europe*** [在欧洲迅速传播].

In January 1521, Luther ***was excommunicated*** [被逐出教会]. Later, Luther ***became***

---

1 German theologian and religious reformer who was the catalyst of the 16th-century Protestant Reformation.

2 宗教改革，是基督宗教在 16 世纪至 17 世纪进行的一次改革。

3 约翰·威克里夫（John Wycliffe，1328-1384），出生于英国，欧洲宗教改革的先驱。

4 扬·胡斯（Jan Hus，1369?-1415），捷克宗教思想家、哲学家、改革家，以献身教会改革和捷克民族主义而留名于世。

5 艾斯莱本（Eisleben），德国萨克森-安哈尔特州的一个城镇，宗教改革领袖马丁·路德出生和去世的地方。

6 圣安妮（Saint Anne，或 Saint Ann），也译为圣安娜（Saint Anna），传统上认定这是圣母马利亚之母，耶稣外祖母的名字。

7 《九十五条论纲》，即"关于赎罪券的意义及效果的见解"，是马丁·路德于 1517 年 10 月 31 日张贴在德国维滕贝格城堡教堂（All Saints' Church, Wittenberg）大门上的辩论提纲，现在普遍被认为是新教的宗教改革运动之始。

involved in the controversy [卷入争论] surrounding the **Peasants War** [德国农民战争] （1524–1526）, the leaders of which had used Luther's arguments to **justify their revolt** [使他们的反叛合法化]. He **rejected their demands** [拒绝要求] and **upheld the right of the authorities to suppress the revolt** [支持当局镇压反叛], which **lost him many supporters** [使他失去很多追随者].

In 1534, Luther **published a complete translation of the bible into German** [出版德文版全套圣经], underlining his belief that people should be able to read it in their own language. **The translation contributed significantly to the spread and development of the German language** [译本极大地推动了德语的传播和发展].

Martin Luther

Everything that is done in this world is done by hope.

If you want to change the world, pick up your pen and write.

An unjust law, is no law at all.

改写 | Rewrite the Story | in Your Own Words

南丁格尔

FLORENCE NIGHTINGALE[1] (1820–1910)

提灯女神
The lady with the lamp

The most famous women in the world…a nurse? ***In these days of pop and sports superstars*** [如今流行乐和体育明星大行其道], that ***seems a highly unlikely situation*** [看似不太可能的情况]. Yet it was the case. ***The daughter of well-to-do parents*** [富裕家庭的女儿], Florence Nightingale ***sparked a revolution in health care*** [点燃了一场医疗护理的革命].

Nursing, which before her time ***was considered*** [被认为] ***low-grade unskilled labor*** [非技术低等工种], ***became a respected profession*** [受尊敬的职业] ***because of her efforts*** [由于她的努力]. Back in 1830s England, nursing wasn't a ***vocation*** [职业] for ***respectable*** [可敬的] women.

Florence Nightingale was born in 1820 to ***a wealthy family*** [富裕家庭]. She decided ***in her teens*** [在少女时代] to become a nurse. At that time, most nurses ***were from poor families*** [出身贫苦人家] and had little or no training.

The Crimean War [克里米亚战争] broke out in 1854. The hospital at the front was in terrible condition: ***unsanitary*** [不卫生的], disorganized, and ***lacking basic medical equipment*** [缺乏基本医疗设备]. She took 38 nurses, and they, together cared for ***the sick*** [护理病人] and ***wounded British soldiers*** [受伤的英国士兵], and ***saved thousands of lives*** [拯救数以千计的生命]. In just a few months, the ***death rate fell from*** [死亡率下降] about 40 percent to only 2 percent.

The soldiers ***adored*** [仰慕] her and called her the "the lady with the lamp" because she ***inspected every ward personally late at night*** [深夜亲自检查每间病房]. "The lady with the lamp" is a positive image of nursing ***in the modern era*** [在现代].

Her ***success in*** [成功] improving nursing care ***brought her great fame*** [带来美誉]. She returned to England as a ***heroine*** [女英雄] and went on to establish the Nightingale Training School for nurses. There she trained her nurses to ***provide possible best scientific care*** [尽力提供最科学的医疗护理].

She ***established nursing as a profession*** [让护士成为一类职业]. She ***used her reputation to*** [用她的影响力] ***improve hospital care*** [改善医疗护理] throughout England. Nightingale never married, dedicating herself to the reform of British army medical services and establishment of proper hospital facilities in the US.

She founded the Nightingale School of Nurses in London, the first of its kind in the world. ***Her efforts never slackened*** [她的努力从未松懈], even after ***rejected the honors and adulation showered upon her*** [拒绝汹涌而至的荣誉和赞誉].

---

1 Foundational philosopher of modern nursing, statistician, and social reformer. Nightingale was put in charge of nursing British and allied soldiers in Turkey during the Crimean War.

Nightingale

I attribute my success to this—I never gave or took any excuse.

To understand God's thoughts we must study statistics, for these are the measure of his purpose.

The very first requirement in a hospital is that it should do the sick no harm.

改写 **Rewrite the Story** | **in Your Own Words**

甘地
MAHATMA GANDHI[1] (1869-1948)

印度圣雄
The leader of the Indian nationalist movement

Gandhi was probably ***the most influential figure*** [最有影响力的人物] India has produced for generations. He judged all activities, whether of the State or of the individual, by ***their conformity to the doctrine of non-violence*** [是否符合非暴力的教义], which he held to ***be the panacea of all human ills*** [人类所有苦难的万能药], political, social, and economic.

To this day millions ***over the world*** [全世界] look to his example in the continuing ***fight against injustice and oppression*** [不断抗击不公平和压迫]. ***To achieve independence for India*** [为争取印度独立], Gandhi took on the ***mighty British Empire*** [强大的大英帝国], and was able to ***force the imperial power to withdraw*** [迫使帝国退缩] with vast support within and outside India, still ***retaining its friendship and good will*** [保持着友谊和善意].

In all parts of the world, many regarded the '***Mahatma***' [圣雄] ('great soul') as both a great moral teacher and a great Indian ***patriot*** [爱国者]. He set out to ***promote national consciousness*** [促进国家意识], and to defend the ancient Indian ideals of poverty and simplicity against the ***inroads of modern industrialism*** [现代工业侵害].

Gandhi ***was born into a well-to-do merchant caste family*** [生在有社会地位的富裕家庭]. At 19, Gandhi went off to London to study law. He ***obtained his law degree*** [获得法律学位], but ***abandoned his social-climbing ambitions*** [放弃追权逐贵的野心]. He returned to India and ***set up a successful law practice*** [成功地开始自己的律师事务]. Offered a year's contract in South Africa, he ***accepted with alacrity*** [欣然接受].

Barely had he arrived when he ***found himself up against white racism*** [深陷白人种族主义]. He ***was ejected from his first-class compartment on a train*** [从火车头等车厢中被驱逐] and ***beaten when he boarded a state coach*** [上长途汽车后被打]. Gandhi soon ***relinquished his law practice*** [放弃法律事务] to work for ***civil rights in South Africa*** [南非人权]. Gandhi left South Africa in 1914, the year in which ***World War I broke out*** [一战爆发].

Influenced primarily by Hinduism [深受印度教影响], but also by elements of ***Jainism***[2] [耆那教] and ***Christianity*** [基督教] as well as writers including ***Tolstoy***[3] [托尔斯泰] and ***Thoreau***[4] [梭罗], Gandhi developed the ***satyagraha*** [非暴力不合作主义] ("devotion to truth"), ***a new non-violent way to redress wrongs*** [一种非暴力的方法来改正错误].

---

1 Leader of the Indian nationalist movement against British rule, considered to be the father of his country. He is internationally esteemed for his doctrine of nonviolent protest to achieve political and social progress.

2 耆那教，是起源于古印度的古老宗教之一，有其独立的信仰和哲学。创始人为筏陀摩那(Vardhamana，公元前 599 年-公元前 527 年)，他早于佛教的始创人释迦牟尼出生。

3 列夫•托尔斯泰(Leo Tolstoy，1828–1910)俄国著名小说家，《战争与和平》(***War and Peace***)和《安娜•卡列尼娜》(***Anna Karenina***)是他创作的两部经典长篇小说。

4 亨利•大卫•梭罗(Henry David Thoreau，1817–1862)，美国作家、哲学家，著有散文集《瓦尔登湖》(***Walden***)和论文《论公民的不服从权利》(***Civil Disobedience***)。

In 1919, British plans to intern people suspected of sedition—the ***Rowlatt Acts***[1] [《罗拉特法案》]—prompted Gandhi to announce a new satyagraha which attracted millions of followers. A demonstration against the acts resulted in the Amritsar Massacre[2] by British troops.

By 1920, Gandhi was ***a dominant figure in Indian politics*** [印度政坛风云人物]. He transformed the ***Indian National Congress*** [印度国民大会党], and his program of peaceful non-cooperation with the British included **boycotts of British goods and institutions** [抵制英国货和法律], leading to arrests of thousands.

In 1922, Gandhi himself ***was sentenced to six years' imprisonment*** [被判六年监禁]. In 1930, Gandhi proclaimed a new campaign of civil disobedience ***in protest at a tax on salt*** [抗议对食盐征税], leading thousands on a "March to the Sea[3]" to ***symbolically make their own salt from seawater*** [象征性地用海水晒盐].

In 1945, the British government began negotiations which ***culminated in*** [结束于] the ***Mountbatten Plan***[4] [《蒙巴顿方案》] of June 1947, and the ***formation of the two new independent states of India and Pakistan*** [成立印度和巴基斯坦两个独立的国家], divided along religious lines.

Gandhi is widely considered the father of his country. His doctrine of ***non-violent protest*** [非暴力的抗议] to achieve political and social progress has been hugely influential. Gandhi's ideals live on as personified, for example, in ***Martin Luther King*** [马丁路德金] and ***Nelson Mandela*** [曼德拉].

Q by Quotes Gandhi

Be the change that you wish to see in the world.

Live as if you were to die tomorrow. Learn as if you were to live forever.

An eye for an eye will only make the whole world blind.

Happiness is when what you think, what you say, and what you do are in harmony.

First they ignore you, then they ridicule you, then they fight you, and then you win.

When I despair, I remember that all through history the way of truth and love have always won. There have been tyrants and murderers, and for a time, they can seem invincible, but in the end, they always fall. Think of it—always.

Where there is love there is life.

---

1 罗拉特法案，英属印度政府于 1919 年 3 月通过的一项法案，其目的是针对第一次世界大战期间可能出现社会动荡或颠覆政府的不确定因素下实行紧急状态。

2 阿姆利则屠杀，又称为札连瓦拉园屠杀，是 1919 年 4 月 13 日发生在印度北部城市阿姆利则的札连瓦拉园，英国军队对 5 万余示威抗议的印度人民开枪杀人事件。

3 食盐进军，发生于 1930 年，为印度国父甘地领导的"非暴力不合作运动"之一。

4 蒙巴顿方案，也称印度独立法案，法案主要内容是英国政府以宗教信仰作为划分国家的原则依据，将印度分割成印度和巴基斯坦两个国家。

The weak can never forgive. Forgiveness is the attribute of the strong.

Non-violence is the greatest force at the disposal of mankind. It is mightier than the mightiest weapon of destruction devised by the ingenuity of man.

Increase of material comforts, it may be generally laid down, does not in any way whatsoever conduce to moral growth.

Caste System

The traditional **_caste system_**[1] [种姓制度] of India developed more than 3000 years ago. Hindu thought has long recognized four major occupational groupings.

☐ In the first group are **_priests_** [僧侣], scholars, and others who **_represent knowledge and spirituality_** [代表着知识和信仰]. People in this group are called brāhmanas, or **_Brahmans_** [婆罗门].

☐ Those in the second group, called **_kshatriyas_** [刹帝利], are represented by kings, **_warriors_** [勇士], **_government bureaucrats_** [官僚], and others who **_represent power_** [代表着权利].

☐ Those in the third group, called **_vaishyas_** [吠舍], are represented by farmers, **_merchants_** [商人], and other **_skilled workers_** [工匠].

☐ Those in the fourth group, called **_shūdras_** [首陀罗], are represented by unskilled workers.

☐ A group sometimes known as **_untouchables_** [贱民] has at times **_constituted a subcategory_** [组成一个子类别] within the shūdra class, sometimes referred to as [被称作] a fifth group.

Many of the poor in India were victims of **_Hindu caste system_** [印度种姓制度]. Most of India's population practices **_Hinduism_** [印度教], a religion whose followers worship several gods and believe in **_reincarnation_** [轮回转世], or **_continual rebirth_** [再生].

Hindus believe that people are born into their "place" in society, and that **_place determines occupation and marriage_** [社会地位决定职业和婚嫁]. Higher castes were assured good jobs and comfortable lives. Even lower than the lowest caste, the "**_Untouchable_** [贱民]" **_lived in poverty_** [生活贫困] and **_worked in the most menial jobs_** [从事最卑微的活计].

Hindus could not change their castes, so lower caste members and untouchables could not hope for a better life for themselves and their children. Only in their next life could they **_hope to be in a higher caste_** [只能期待来世有更高的社会地位].

---

1 种姓制度（caste system in India），是印度与其他南亚地区普遍存在的社会体系。

海伦·凯勒
HELEN KELLER[1] (1880–1968)

"给我三天光明"
An inspiration for people with disabilities

Helen Keller was one of the most famous **handicapped persons** [残疾人] in the world. At the age of 19 months, Helen **was stricken with severe fever** [因严重高烧而病倒], which left her deaf and blind and **barely able to communicate** [几乎无法交流]. At that time, people who were both deaf and blind **were classified in law as idiots** [根据法律被分类为智障].

At the age of six, Keller's parents chose Anne Mansfield Sullivan (1866–1936) (later Macy) as a teacher of Keller. Thus **began a great association** [开始一段伟大的友谊] that lasted until Sullivan's death in 1936.

Sullivan's first task was to **break through the barrier of darkness and silence that surrounded the child** [打破凯勒无光无声的世界]. By means of a **finger alphabet** [手语], Sullivan **"spelled" onto the palm of Keller's hand the names of familiar things** [在凯勒掌心上拼写一些常见事物的名字].

The first big achievement came when Sullivan **pumped water from a well** [从井里抽水] onto Keller's hand and **spelled out the word for water** [拼写出"水"的英文单词], and Keller suddenly **grasped** [领会] that everything has its own name. Two years later she was reading and writing fluently using the **Braille system**[2] [布莱叶盲字].

When Keller was ten, she **begged to relearn how to speak** [请求重新学习说话]. At first this seemed impossible, but Sullivan discovered that Keller could learn sounds by placing her fingers on her teacher's **larynx** [咽喉] and **sensing the vibrations** [感觉振动].

In 1900 Keller entered **Radcliffe College**[3] [拉德克利夫学院], where Anne Sullivan "spelled" the lectures into her hand. Four years later Keller graduated with honors and decided to **devote her life to helping the blind and deaf** [用毕生精力帮助盲人和聋人].

Through her essays and articles in major magazines and newspapers, Keller explained the **problems encountered** [遇到的问题] by people who are deaf and blind and the **responsibilities of society** [社会责任]. Keller also traveled and lectured throughout the world.

Helen Keller

Life is a daring adventure or nothing at all.

---

1 American author and educator who was blind and deaf. Her education and training represent an extraordinary accomplishment in the education of persons with these disabilities.

2 路易·布莱叶（Louis Braille，1809–1852），世界通用布莱叶点盲文发明者。

3 拉德克利夫学院（Radcliffe College），曾是位于美国马萨诸塞州剑桥的一个女子文理学院，创建于 1879 年，1999 年全面整合到哈佛大学。

I would rather walk with a friend in the dark, than alone in the light.

When one door of happiness closes, another opens; but often we look so long at the closed door that we do not see the one which has been opened for us.

Character cannot be developed in ease and quiet. Only through experience of trial and suffering can the soul be strengthened, vision cleared, ambition inspired, and success achieved.

Keep your face to the sun and you will never see the shadows.

It would be an excellent rule to live each day as if we should die tomorrow. Such an attitude would emphasize sharply the values of life. We should live each day with gentleness, vigor and a keenness of appreciation which are often lost when time stretches before us in the constant panorama of more days and months and years to come.

Only the deaf appreciate hearing, only the blind realize the manifold blessings that lie in sight.

改写 | Rewrite the Story | in Your Own Words

白求恩

NORMAN BETHUNE[1] （1890–1939）

Which Canadian doctor is far more famous in China than in his own country? The answer is Dr. Norman, who was born in Gravenhurst[2], **_Ontario_** [安大略].

Rather than enter university immediately after **_graduating with honors from high school_** [从高中荣誉毕业], Bethune **_took work as a lumberjack_** [开始伐木工作]. **_The idea of studying medicine took hold in his mind_** [学医的主意在他脑中一直萦绕不去] and he **_enrolled at the University of Toronto_** [报读了多伦多大学].

All of this came to an abrupt end [所有这一切戛然而止] **_with the outbreak of World War I_** [随着一战爆发] in 1914. Bethune joined the Field Ambulance Medical Corps [战地医疗军团] and sailed for France in February 1915. He was working as a **_stretcher-bearer_** [担架手] in Ypres[3], **_Belgium_** [比利时], when **_a shrapnel shell exploded close to him_** [一弹壳在他身边炸开] and **_pieces of it pierced his leg_** [弹壳碎片刺穿了他的腿].

When Bethune returned to Canada, he **_resumed his medical studies_** [继续医疗学习] and **_completed his Bachelor of Medicine_** [完成医学学士] in December 1916.

In 1937, the **_Japanese invaded China_** [日本侵略中国] and Bethune saw this as another **_battle against fascism_** [反法西斯战争] and he was determined to help.

He **_gathered together a medical team_** [组织一支医疗队] and left Canada to join the **_8th Route Army_** [八路军]. He **_worked long hard days under the most rudimentary conditions_** [在艰苦的条件下长时间工作] and quickly became known as **_a skilled surgeon_** [技术丰富的外科医生] and a dedicated teacher.

In October 1939, the Japanese **_launched another attack_** [发起另一轮进攻]. Dr. Bethune and his team **_rushed to the front_** [赶赴前线] where the **_worst fighting was unfolding_** [激烈的战斗正在展开] and worked long hours caring for the wounded [伤员]. While he **_was operating on a soldier_** [给士兵做手术], Bethune cut his finger. Probably due to his weakened state, he **_contracted blood poisoning_** [感染败血病] and died of his wounds on November 12, 1939.

Dr. Bethune's death shocked the Chinese nation. Chinese **_Chairman Mao Zedong wrote a tribute titled "In Memory of Norman Bethune,"_** [毛泽东主席撰文《纪念白求恩》悼念他] in which he praised the doctor for his **_selflessness and dedication_** [无私和奉献] to the Chinese people. To this day, his memory is honored in China.

Norman Bethune University of Medical Sciences [白求恩医科大学], founded in Changchun, Jilin and **_later merged into Jilin University_** [后并入吉林大学] as Norman Bethune College of Medicine, **_is named after him_** [以他的名字命名].

---

1 Canadian surgeon and political activist.

2 格雷文赫斯特镇，位于加拿大安大略省（Ontario）中部。

3 伊佩尔，是世界上第一次被使用化学武器的地方。

德雷莎修女
MOTHER TERESA[1] (1910–1997)

More than anyone else of her time, Mother Teresa came to be regarded by millions as the ***embodiment of human goodness*** [人类美德的化身]. By her compassion, humility, and, it has also to be said, ***shrewd eye for publicity*** [宣传方面精明的眼力], she ***raised public concern for*** [引起公众关注] the destitute [赤贫者]; by ***devoting herself with single-minded vigor to the relief of human suffering*** [把自己毕生精力献给减轻人类痛苦的事业上], she ***galvanized individuals*** [激励每一个人], both believers and non-believers, and even governments into action.

Mother Teresa's ***simplicity of purpose and approach*** [目的和方法的简单性] ***hid a formidable personality*** [掩藏着强大的个性] and a determined strength of character [果决的性格]. Despite ***a seemingly frail stature*** [身子骨看起来弱不禁风], she was physically strong and ***exercised a sometimes stern, unbending authority*** [有时行使着严峻不屈的权威] over her ***followers*** [信徒].

By the time she ***was in senior high school*** [在她读高中时], she had decided to ***devote herself to God*** [投身于上帝的事业] and ***follow his will*** [追随上帝的召唤]. She ***joined a convent*** [加入一所修道院], and her work took her into India's worst ***slums*** [贫民窟].

Here, she eventually became the ***world-renowned*** [举世皆知的] and ***beloved*** [受人爱戴的] Mother Teresa, who worked among the world's poorest people, ***carrying out her mission of charity*** [完成自己博爱的使命] ***in the name of God*** [以上帝的名义].

Mother Teresa was born in ***Skopje***[2] [斯科普里]. At the age of 12, she decided to become a nun. At the age of 18, she joined the ***Order of the Sisters of Our Lady of Loreto in Ireland*** [爱尔兰罗蕾托女修道院]. After training in Dublin for a few months, she went to India.

In 1948 she ***was granted permission*** [获准] to leave the convent and work as an independent nun. That year she founded the ***Missionaries of Charity*** [仁爱传教修女会], a religious order to help the sick and ***destitute*** [贫苦的].

Mother Teresa was pleased to receive ***new novices*** [见习修女] as long as they ***met her strict requirements*** [满足严格要求]. They had to live ***without income*** [没有收入], ***personal possessions*** [个人财产], or ***lives outside the order*** [修道会之外的生活].

Their ***worldly possessions*** [私人物品] ***consisted of*** [包括] three ***saris*** [纱丽], a ***rosary*** [祈祷用的念珠], ***a Bible***, a copy of the ***order's constitution*** [修道会的章程], and ***a bucket for washing*** [洗漱用的木桶]. They were not allowed to accept anything, not even a cup of tea or a glass of water from anyone.

Mother Teresa expected her nuns to ***serve the poor willingly and happily*** [心甘情愿地、开

---

1 Founder of the Order of the Missionaries of Charity, a Roman Catholic congregation of women dedicated to the poor, particularly to the destitute of India. She was the recipient of numerous honours, including the 1979 Nobel Prize for Peace.

2 斯科普里，前南斯拉夫的一个城市。

开心心地为穷人服务] and be always **_with a smile on their faces_** [面带笑容] as herself had been doing for several years.

She wanted them to **_wash sores_** [溃烂伤口] and wounds, **_change bedpans_** [更换便盆], and **_mop up urine and vomit_** [擦净尿液和呕吐物] with the same respect and reverence as if they **_were praying to God_** [向上帝祷告].

The poor lay dying in the gutters [穷人躺在臭水沟，奄奄一息], **_alone and rejected_** [孤独无助], **_rats gnawing on their bodies_** [老鼠咬着他们的身体]. Mother Teresa and the nuns walked through the streets and picked up the dying. They washed and fed them and put them in beds. Mother Teresa helped to serve the poor with love and give the poor a place to **_die with dignity_** [有尊严的逝去].

Almost 50 years later, the Missionaries of Charity have grown from 12 sisters in India to over 3000 in 517 missions throughout 100 countries worldwide. For her **_humanitarian work_** [人道主义工作] she **_won the Nobel Peace Prize_** [获得诺贝尔和平奖] in 1979.

During a visit to London in 1988, she visited both **_Downing Street_**[1] [唐宁街] and the **_homeless of the capital_** [首都无家可归的人]; she praised **_Margaret Thatcher_** [撒切尔夫人] for supporting her sentiments, but when no progress was made against the homelessness problem, she **_spoke out against the Government's inaction_** [大胆地指出政府的无作为].

 Mother Teresa

If you judge people, you have no time to love them.

Not all of us can do great things. But we can do small things with great love.

People are often unreasonable, illogical, and self-centered; Forgive them anyway.

What you spend years of building, someone could destroy overnight; Build anyway.

Love until it hurts. Real love is always painful and hurts; then it is real and pure.

Yesterday is gone. Tomorrow has not yet come. We have only today. Let us begin.

The hunger for love is much more difficult to remove than the hunger for bread.

---

1 唐宁街，位于伦敦市中心的白厅，过去 200 年是重要内阁官员的官邸。唐宁街 10 号现在是首相官邸，因此"唐宁街"和"唐宁街 10 号"是英国首相代名词；"唐宁街 11 号"就代表财政大臣或其办公室。

曼德拉

NELSON MANDELA[1] （1918–）

南非国父
First President of new South Africa

Over his 27 years in jail, Nelson Mandela became the **_symbol of an entire people's struggle against injustice_** [成为全人类反抗非正义的标志]. And as his time behind bars grew so did the **_anti-apartheid movement_** [反对种族隔离运动] he helped spur on.

Nelson Mandela **_is one of the world's most revered statesmen_** [最受尊敬的政治家之一], who led the struggle to replace the **_apartheid regime of South Africa_** [南非种族隔离制度] with a **_multi-racial democracy_** [多民族的民主制度].

Jailed for 27 years, he **_emerged to become the country's first black president_** [复出成为该国第一人黑人总统] and to **_play a leading role in_** [扮演重要角色] the **_drive for peace_** [推动和平进程] **_in other spheres of conflict_** [在其他冲突问题上]. He **_won the Nobel Peace Prize_** [获得诺贝尔和平奖] in 1993.

His **_charisma_** [魅力], **_self-deprecating sense of humor_** [谦虚的幽默] and **_lack of bitterness over his harsh treatment_** [对他刻薄待遇少有怨言], as well as his amazing life story, partly explain **_his extraordinary global appeal_** [非凡的世界号召力].

Nelson was a good student and **_qualified with a law degree_** [获得法学学历] in 1942. During his time at University Nelson Mandela **_became increasingly aware of the racial inequality_** [越来越多地注意到种族不平等现象] and injustice faced by non-white people. He **_decided to join the ANC_**[2] [加入非国大] and **_actively take part in the struggle against apartheid_** [积极投入反种族隔离的斗争当中].

In 1956, Nelson Mandela, along with several other members of the ANC **_were arrested and charged with treason_** [被捕而被指控叛国]. **_After a lengthy and protracted court case_** [旷日持久又不断拖延的审判], **_the defendants were finally acquitted_** [被告最后被无罪释放] in 1961.

In 1963, Mandela was again arrested and put on trial for treason. This time the state **_succeeded in convicting of plotting to overthrow the government_** [成功指控他图谋推翻政府]. However, the case **_received considerable international attention_** [受到国际社会的重视] and the apartheid regime of South Africa **_became under the glare of the international community_** [国际社会的关注下].

Mandela's **_death sentence was commuted to life imprisonment_** [死刑被改判终身监禁] and from 1964 to 1981 he **_was incarcerated at Robben Island Prison_**[3] [在罗本岛监狱服刑].

In prison the conditions were intolerable [监狱环境常人难以忍受]; however, Mandela was

---

1 Black nationalist and first black president of South Africa（1994–1999）.

2 南非非洲人国民大会（The African National Congress of South Africa），简称非国大（ANC），于 1912 年成立，自 1994 年 5 月至今是南非最大的政党、执政党。

3 罗本岛，南非开普敦桌湾中一小岛。岛上监狱曾在南非种族隔离时代长期关押包括曼德拉等大批黑人政治犯而闻名，该监狱现已改建成罗本岛博物馆。

with many other political prisoners and ***there was a strong bond of friendship*** [有一种牢固的友谊纽带] which helped to make more bearable prison conditions.

Also, in prison Nelson Mandela ***was highly disciplined*** [生活规律的], he would try and study and ***take part in exercise every day*** [每天参加锻炼]. He later said these years of prison were a period of great learning, even if painful.

During his time in prison, Mandela became increasingly well known throughout the world. Mandela became the ***best known black leader*** [最著名的黑人领袖] and opposition to the apartheid regime. ***Largely unbeknown to Mandela*** [曼德拉本人所不知情的], his continued imprisonment ***led to worldwide pressure for his release*** [来自全球的压力要求释放他].

Eventually Nelson Mandela was released on February 11, 1990. The day ***was huge event*** [重大事件] for South Africa and the world. Following his release there followed ***protracted negotiations*** [旷日持久的谈判]. However, eventually in April 1994, South Africa had its first ***full and fair elections*** [全民公平选举]. The ANC with 65% of the vote were elected and Nelson Mandela became the first President of the new South Africa.

As President, he ***sought to heal the rifts of the past*** [努力弥合历史的创伤]. ***Despite being mistreated*** [尽管被虐待], ***he was magnanimous in his dealing with his oppressors*** [对曾经压迫他的人宽宏大量]. His forgiving and tolerant attitude ***gained the respect*** [获得尊敬] of the whole South African nation and considerably ***eased the transition to a full democracy*** [缓和全面民主化过程].

Since ***stepping down as president*** [总统退位] in 1999, Mandela continues to support a variety of causes, particularly the fight against HIV-Aids. He helped ***secure his country's right to host the 2010 football World Cup*** [确保南非获得 2010 年世界杯的主办权]. On 29 August 2007, ***a permanent statue to Nelson Mandela was unveiled in Parliament Square***[1] [曼德拉的雕像在国会广场揭幕], London.

Mandela

Education is the most powerful weapon which you can use to change the world.

I learned that courage was not the absence of fear, but the triumph over it. The brave man is not he who does not feel afraid, but he who conquers that fear.

It always seems impossible until it's done.

Resentment is like drinking poison and then hoping it will kill your enemies.

---

1 国会广场，位于伦敦威斯敏斯特宫西北的一个广场，这里有著名的政治家雕像。

安妮

ANNE FRANK[1] （1929–1945）

《安妮日记》
A courageous young girl

Anne is known for the diary she wrote while ***hiding from anti-Jewish persecution*** [躲避反犹太迫害] in ***Amsterdam, Netherlands*** [荷兰阿姆斯特丹], during World War II（1939–1945）. Her diary describes with wisdom and humor the ***two arduous years she spent in seclusion*** [两年与世隔绝的艰难生活] before her tragic death at the age of 15. Since it was first published in 1947, ***her diary has appeared in more than 50 languages*** [她的日记被翻译成五十多种语言].

Anne Frank's life ***was short and tragic*** [短暂而又悲惨]. Yet her ***brave spirit*** [勇敢精神] has survived in her diary. She ***wrote this diary*** [写日记] while ***hiding from the Nazis*** [躲避纳粹] during ***World War II*** [第二次世界大战].

Anne Frank's family was ***Jewish*** [犹太人]. In 1933, the Nazi Party ***came to power*** [当权] in Germany. The Nazis blamed Jews for the nation's problems and began a ***campaign against Jews*** [针对犹太人的运动].

Her father ***secretly prepared a hiding place*** [安排藏身之处] by ***sealing off*** [堵住] several rooms at the rear of his Amsterdam ***office building*** [办公楼]. The rooms ***were hidden behind a swinging bookcase*** [隐藏在一个旋转书架的后面]. The Frank family and their friends ***stayed shut away in secret*** [秘密躲藏] for over two years.

Constant fear and loss of freedom ***were hard to bear*** [很难忍受]. For comfort, Anne started to write a diary. She was very good at ***expressing her thoughts and feelings in words*** [用文字表达想法和感情].

Over the course of 25 months, Anne ***recorded her experiences*** [记录下自己的经历] while hiding from German troops. Her diary ***describes the fears and emotional conflicts of people*** [描述人们的恐惧和思想斗争] crowded together ***in secrecy*** [秘密地], as well as ***humorous and joyful moments*** [幽默和快乐的时刻]. These include ***birthday celebrations*** [生日庆祝活动] and Anne's ***first experience with falling in love*** [初恋的经历].

Throughout her time in hiding, Anne maintained her faith in human nature. She wrote, "In spite of everything, I still believe that ***people are really good at heart*** [心地是善良的]."

In 1944, Anne and the others in the group were discovered and arrested by the ***Gestapo***[2] [盖世太保]（***German secret police*** [德国秘密警察]）. Anne was sent to the ***Bergen-Belsen prison camp***[3] [伯根·拜尔森战俘集中营] in Germany. She died at the camp in 1945 at the age of 15, two months before the German Army's surrender.

Anne's father was the only member of the Frank family to ***survive the war*** [幸免于难]. He ***published her diary*** [出版日记] in 1947. Millions of people have visited the family's hiding

---

1 Young Jewish girl whose diary of her family's two years in hiding during the German occupation of the Netherlands became a classic of war literature.

2 秘密国家警察，汉语音译"盖世太保"，由党卫队控制，是纳粹德国时期的秘密警察。

3 伯根·拜尔森集中营，是纳粹德国在德国西北部建立的一座集中营。另一座臭名昭著的集中营是奥斯维辛集中营（Auschwitz Concentration Camp）是纳粹德国时期建立最主要的集中营和灭绝营。

place in Amsterdam [阿姆斯特丹]. Anne Frank's story still **_inspires people to fight against_** [激励人们战斗] all kinds of **_discrimination_** [歧视].

Many of the passages concern [很多章节涉及] Anne's emotional growth and her discoveries about herself, other people, and the beauty of life. She **_dreamed of becoming an author_** [梦想成为一名作家], never realizing that her diary would be read by millions.

Although written in Europe nearly a half-century ago, Anne Frank's diary has **_remained immensely popular throughout the world_** [仍然在全世界深受欢迎]. Anne **_maintains a sense of humor and optimism throughout her ordeal_** [面对折磨保持幽默和乐观].

Anne Frank: The Diary of a Young Girl has **_been adapted both to the stage and to film_** [改编后被搬上舞台荧幕] under the title The Diary of Anne Frank. The adaptations follow the basic ideas of the diary and **_capture the spirit of the young girl_** [刻画一个年轻女孩的精神世界].

Q by Quotes Anne

_____ *I don't think of all the misery, but of the beauty that still remains.*

_____ *No one has ever become poor by giving.*

_____ *Where there's hope, there's life. It fills us with fresh courage and makes us strong again.*

_____ *Human greatness does not lie in wealth or power, but in character and goodness. People are just people, and all people have faults and shortcomings, but all of us are born with a basic goodness.*

改写 Rewrite the Story | in Your Own Words

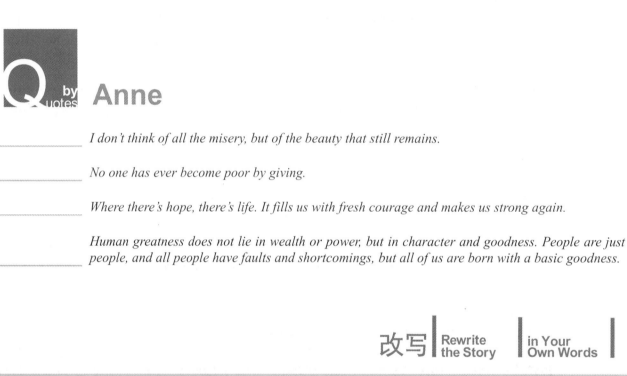

马丁·路德·金
MARTIN LUTHER KING[1] （1929–1968）

"我有一个梦想"
Civil Rights Movement Leader

In the maelstrom of racialistic strife [在种族冲突的大漩涡中], *King's strict adherence to non-violence* [坚持非暴力方法] *won respect for the Negro struggle among millions* [为黑人斗争赢得众人尊重]. The essential dignity of the Negro remained intact: King was 'a kind of *modern Moses*[2] [现代的摩西] who has brought new self-respect to southern Negroes'.

As regards the *ultimate success of the civil rights movement* [民权运动最终获得胜利], King's discipline proved that unlike white extremists, Negroes could *fight for their rights in a civilized way* [以文明的方法为权利而战].

King's non-violence tactics *were based on Gandhi's thinking* [基于甘地的思想]. They *went further* [再进一步]: he *included the Christian element of love* [包含基督教 "爱" 这一元素], realizing the *reconciliation of the Negroes to the whites* [黑人和白人和解] was just as important for his cause *as vice versa* [反之亦然].

Unlike Gandhi, King was *fighting for the rights of a minority* [为少数人的权利而战]. Unlike the Indian leader, King had no easily defined opponent such as an *imperial overload* [帝国压迫]; he had to *conquer the confused racial prejudices* [征服不明就里的种族偏见] and fears of a white, dominant race.

In a world racked by terrorism and violence [在这个被恐怖主义和暴力折磨的世界], it is appropriate that we *commemorate* [纪念] the Martin Luther King Jr.'s *message of love and nonviolence* [爱和非暴力的启示].

It is also fitting that while *remembering his relentless fight for equality and justice* [纪念他为公平正义不屈不挠的斗争], we *mull the wellsprings of his philosophy* [思考他智慧的源泉] that *changed the face of this nation* [改变这个国家的面貌].

By chance King had his first opportunity to *test his newfound theories* [检验他刚刚找到的理论] of love and nonviolence. Following the well-known *Montgomery bus incident* [蒙哥马利罢乘公车运动], in which Rosa Parks[3] was arrested for refusing to give up her seat to a white man, King helped *organize within 24 hours a complete boycott of the buses* [组织 24 小时抵制公车运动], which lasted for more than a year until, on Nov. 13, 1956, the *U.S. Supreme Court* [美国高等法院] *ruled that segregation on public buses was unconstitutional* [裁决在公车上设隔离这一行为违反宪法], vindicating his cause, and more important, the philosophy behind it.

The Montgomery campaign had not only united his people but also *stirred the conscience of*

---

1 Baptist minister and social activist who led the civil rights movement in the United States from the mid-1950s until his death by assassination in 1968. His leadership was fundamental to that movement's success in ending the legal segregation of African Americans in the South and other parts of the United States.

2 摩西，按照出埃及记的记载，摩西受耶和华之命，率领被奴役的希伯来人逃离古埃及前往一块富饶的应许之地。

3 罗莎·帕克斯（Rosa Louise McCauley Parks，1913–2005），美国黑人民权行动主义者，美国国会后来称她为 "现代民权运动之母"。在 1955 年 12 月 1 日，帕克斯因拒绝听从公车司机詹姆斯·布莱克（James Blake）的命令，让位给一名白人乘客而成名。这起非暴力反抗的行为引发联合抵制蒙哥马利公车运动。

the country [激起一个国家的良知]. From then on, ***the civil rights movement gained momentum*** [民权运动势头更猛] ***under his leadership*** [在他的领导下], leading from one victory to another.

King's "I Have a Dream" speech was given in front of the ***Lincoln Memorial***[1] [林肯纪念堂] during the 1963 ***March on Washington for Jobs and Freedom***[2] [《为工作和自由向华盛顿进军》]. It is regarded, along with Abraham Lincoln's ***Gettysburg Address***[3] [《葛底斯堡演说》] and Franklin D. Roosevelt's ***Infamy Speech***[4] [《国耻日演说》], as one of the finest speeches in the history of American oratory.

In 1964, King ***became the youngest person to receive the Nobel Peace Prize*** [诺贝尔和平奖最年轻得主] for his work to end racial segregation and racial discrimination through civil disobedience and other nonviolent means.

Martin Luther King

I have a dream that my four little children will one day live in a nation where they will not be judged by the color of their skin, but by the content of their character.
I have a dream that one day every valley shall be exalted, every hill and mountain shall be made low, the rough places will be made straight and the glory of the Lord shall be revealed and all flesh shall see it together.
I have a dream that one day on the red hills of Georgia, the sons of former slaves and the sons of former slave owners will be able to sit together at the table of brotherhood.

A genuine leader is not a searcher for consensus but a molder of consensus.

At the center of non-violence stands the principle of love.

Darkness cannot drive out darkness; only light can do that. Hate cannot drive out hate; only love can do that.

Discrimination is a hellhound that gnaws at Negroes in every waking moment of their lives to remind them that the lie of their inferiority is accepted as truth in the society dominating them.

Human progress is neither automatic nor inevitable... Every step toward the goal of justice requires sacrifice, suffering, and struggle; the tireless exertions and passionate concern of dedicated individuals.

I look to a day when people will not be judged by the color of their skin, but by the content of their character.

---

1 林肯纪念堂（Lincoln Memorial），为纪念美国总统林肯而设立的纪念堂，位于华盛顿特区国家广场西侧。

2 全称是"为工作和自由向华盛顿进军"，也称"向华盛顿的伟大进军"，发生于 1963 年 8 月 28 日，是美国历史上最大的一场人权政治集会。集会中，马丁•路德•金在林肯纪念堂前发表了旨在推动族际和谐的著名演讲"我有一个梦想"。

3 译作《葛底斯堡演说》（Gettysburg Address），1863 年 11 月 19 日，美国内战中葛底斯堡战役结束四个半月后，美国前总统亚伯拉罕•林肯最著名的演说，也是美国历史上被人引用最多的政治性演说之一。

4 译作《国耻日演说》（***Infamy Speech*** 或 ***Day of Infamy Speech***），1941 年 12 月 8 日，罗斯福总统发表演说，宣布对日宣战。

Notes

Chapter 7

艺术与流行
ART AND FASHION

本 章 目 录

达·芬奇

LEONARDO DA VINCI[1] (1452–1519)

Leonardo, a true Renaissance man, was not only ***a magnificent painter*** [伟大的画家], he ***was hugely influential*** [极富影响力] as an artist and sculptor but also ***immensely talented as an engineer, scientist and inventor*** [才华横溢的工程师、科学家、发明家]. He ***excelled at*** [擅长] ***whatever he turned his hand to*** [在他所有触及的领域].

The fame of Da Vinci's surviving paintings has meant that he has been regarded primarily as an artist, but the thousands of ***surviving pages of his notebooks*** [他现存的笔记] reveal the most brilliant of minds.

He wrote and drew on subjects including geology, ***anatomy*** [解剖学]（which he studied in order to paint the human form more accurately）, flight, and optics [光学], often flitting from subject to subject on a single page.

He "invented" the bicycle, airplane, ***helicopter*** [直升机], and ***parachute*** [降落伞] some 500 years ***ahead of their time*** [领先他的时代].

If all this work had been published ***in an intelligible form*** [以易于理解的形式], da Vinci's place as a ***pioneering scientist*** [科学家的先驱] would have ***been beyond dispute*** [不容置疑的]. Yet his true genius was not as a scientist or an artist, but as a combination of the two: an "artist-engineer".

His painting was scientific, ***based on a deep understanding of the workings of the human body*** [基于对人体功能的深刻理解] and ***the physics of light and shade*** [光影的物理研究]. His science was expressed through art, and his drawings and diagrams show what he meant, and how he understood the world to work.

Leonardo, born in Vinci, ***was the illegitimate son of a wealthy Florentine notary*** [一个富有的佛罗伦萨公证员的私生子]. At the age of 16 he ***was apprenticed to a highly successful painter and sculptor*** [师从极负盛名的画家和雕塑家], Andrea del Verrocchio[2]. The pupil ***very quickly surpassed his master*** [学生很快就超越自己的老师] and eventually ***set up his own studio*** [建立自己的工作室].

Charming and handsome, in addition to his other talents, Leonardo ***was much sought after by the wealthy and powerful*** [深受权贵追捧]. He ***designed artillery*** [设计火炮], ***built canals and bridges*** [修水渠，造桥], ***organized huge festivals*** [举行大型庆典], invented machines, ***designed a mechanism*** [设计机构] for flight and parachutes, all the while studying the nature of the universe intensively.

At the same time, he ***continued his artistic endeavors*** [继续自己的艺术创作], which ***influenced a whole generation of painters*** [影响了一整代画家] including ***Rafael*** [拉斐

---

1 Italian painter, draftsman, sculptor, architect, and engineer whose genius, perhaps more than that of any other figure, epitomized the Renaissance humanist ideal.

2 安德烈·德尔·委罗基奥（Andrea del Verrocchio, 1435–1488），意大利画家和雕塑家，达·芬奇等著名画家都是他的学生，他对米开朗基罗也有很大的影响。

尔], ***Michelangelo*** [米开朗基罗] and ***Botticelli***[1] [波提切利].

Mona Lisa[2] [《蒙娜丽莎》] by Leonardo da Vinci is probably the most famous painting in Western art. ***Set against a misty mountain background*** [以薄雾笼罩的远山为背景], ***a young Florentine woman gazes at us with a mysterious smile*** [一位年轻的佛罗伦萨少女注视着人们，嘴角泛起神秘的微笑] that ***has fascinated generations of viewers*** [让一代代的参观者为之倾倒].

The Virgin of the Rocks[3] [《岩间圣母》] depicts the legend of the meeting in the wilderness between the young ***John the Baptist***[4] [施洗约翰] and Jesus returning home from Egypt.

Leonardo's ***Last Supper***[5] [《最后的晚餐》] is among the most famous paintings in the world. The power of its effect comes from the ***striking contrast in the attitudes of the 12 disciples*** [十二个门徒态度的巨大差异] as ***counterposed to*** [对比] Christ.

 by Quotes # Leonardo da Vinci

Simplicity is the ultimate sophistication.

A painter should begin every canvas with a wash of black, because all things in nature are dark except where exposed by the light.

Painting is poetry that is seen rather than felt, and poetry is painting that is felt rather than seen.

Once you have tasted flight, you will forever walk the earth with your eyes turned skyward, for there you have been, and there you will always long to return.

The painter has the Universe in his mind and hands.

改写 | Rewrite the Story | in Your Own Words

1　桑德罗•波提切利(Sandro Botticelli，1445–1510)，欧洲文艺复兴早期意大利佛罗伦萨艺术家。

2　《蒙娜丽莎》，达•芬奇所绘的丽莎•乔宫多的肖像画，现在的拥有者是法国政府，被保存在巴黎卢浮宫。

3　《岩间圣母》，有两副作品，他们的作者都是达•芬奇，这两幅画构图基本相同，一幅现藏于卢浮宫(创作于 1483 年至 1486 年)，另一幅画现藏英国国家美术馆(创作于 1491 年至 1508 年)。

4　天主教汉译作"圣若翰洗者"，基督教新教汉译作"施洗约翰"，伊斯兰教汉译作"叶哈雅"，是耶稣基督的表兄，在耶稣基督开始传福音之前在旷野向犹太人劝勉悔改，并为耶稣基督施洗。

5　《最后的晚餐》，一幅达•芬奇创作的大型壁画，创作在意大利城市米兰的一处天主教建筑——恩宠圣母(Holy Mary of Grace)道明会院食堂墙壁上。

米开朗基罗
MICHELANGELO[1] (1475–1564)

This Renaissance genius ***left behind him a heritage*** [留下遗产] which includes the famous ***sculpture of David*** [大卫雕像] and a ***Pieta*** [圣母怜子雕像] in which Michelangelo portrays himself.

Michelangelo's David [米开朗琪罗的大卫雕像] ***has been naked in the heart of Florence for nearly 5 centuries*** [在佛罗伦萨市中心赤裸裸地站立近五个世纪].

In 1504, he was ***commissioned*** [委托] to create a ***colossal*** [巨大的] ***statue of David*** [大卫雕像] (1501–1504), the ***Hebrew shepherd*** [希伯来牧童] who ***slew a giant called Goliath with a single stone from his slingshot*** [用弹弓射杀名叫歌利亚的巨人].

Four years later he ***was on his back*** [仰卧], ***working in extremely cramped conditions*** [在极为狭促的环境工作], painting a fresco twenty meters above the floor. The ceiling frescoes of ***Sistine Chapel***[2] ***ceiling*** [西斯廷教堂天花板] (1508–1512), commissioned by ***Pope Julius the Second*** [罗马教皇尤利乌斯二世], took Michelangelo four years to complete.

The ceiling ***depicts scenes from the biblical book of Genesis***[3] [描绘《圣经》中《创世纪》的景象], including ***the Creation of Adam*** [《创造亚当》], the Creation of Eve[4] [《创造夏娃》], ***the Temptation and Fall of Adam and Eve*** [《亚当夏娃偷吃禁果》], and ***the Flood*** [《大洪水》]. He also painted the controversial fresco ***Last Judgment*** [《最后的审判》] (1536–1541) on the chapel wall ***above the altar*** [圣坛上方].

He proved himself to be a gifted architect as well by designing ***Saint Peter's basilica*** [圣彼得教堂] before his death in 1564, at the age of 89. ***The cathedral stands today as the symbol of the Roman Catholic Church*** [大教堂时至今日依然是天主教象征].

Michelangelo's best work offers ***a combination of detail and exquisite beauty*** [细节和高雅的结合] that is ***unmatched*** [不可匹敌的]. His attention to the technical aspects of ***human anatomy*** [人体解剖学], especially the ***male nude*** [裸体男性], is brilliant and influential.

Michelangelo's work is also intellectually ***stimulating*** [启发智慧的], ***grounded in*** [根植于] ***mythology*** [神话], religion, and other references. Widely considered the greatest artist of his own time, Michelangelo is still seen as a key to the flowering of ***the Renaissance*** [文艺复兴].

---

1 Italian Renaissance sculptor, painter, architect, and poet who exerted an unparalleled influence on the development of Western art.

2 又译"西斯廷小堂"、"西斯廷礼拜堂",位于梵蒂冈,天主教小堂,以米开朗基罗所绘的《创世纪》穹顶画及壁画《最后的审判》而闻名。

3 译作《创世记》,在犹太人的传说中,《创世记》是由摩西根据耶和华的启示写成的。米开朗基罗的《创世记》壁画共有 9 副,分别为《神分光暗》、《创造日、月、草木》、《神分水陆》、《创造亚当》、《创造夏娃》、《亚当夏娃偷吃禁果》、《诺亚献祭》、《大洪水》和《诺亚醉酒》。

4 译作《创造亚当》,是《创世纪》的 9 幅壁画中最具盛名的一幅。

Q by Michelangelo

I saw the angel in the marble and carved until I set him free.

The greater danger for most of us lies not in setting our aim too high and falling short; but in setting our aim too low, and achieving our mark.

Genius is eternal patience.

If you knew how much work went into it, you wouldn't call it genius.

A man paints with his brains and not with his hands.

改写 | Rewrite the Story | in Your Own Words

拉斐尔
RAPHAEL[1] (1483–1520)

For centuries Raphael ***has been recognized as*** [被认为是] the ***supreme High Renaissance painter*** [文艺复兴盛期最杰出的画家], more ***versatile*** [多才多艺的] than Michelangelo and ***more prolific*** [更多产] than Leonardo. Though he died at 37, Raphael's example as a ***paragon of classicism*** [古典主义模范] dominated the academic tradition of European painting until the mid-19th century.

Italian art soared in the early 1500s ***for three major reasons*** [三个主要原因]. One of them was Raphael. During his final 12 years, spent in Rome, he ***produced a series of masterpieces*** [创作一系列杰作], including perhaps his greatest work, ***The School of Athens***[2] [《雅典学院》], ***a Vatican fresco*** [梵蒂冈壁画] showing ***Plato*** [柏拉图] and ***Aristotle*** [亚里士多德] surrounded by philosophers past and present [古今哲学家环绕] that ***perfectly embodies the Renaissance spirit*** [完美地诠释文艺复兴精神].

K now
more

Renaissance

The word "Renaissance" is the French word for "rebirth." [法语中 "新生" 的意思] The Renaissance ***refers to the rebirth of humanism***[3] [指的是人文主义的新生] during the 14th, 15th and 16th centuries in Europe. The Renaissance period was a time of new discoveries in fine arts, music, literature, philosophy, science and technology, architecture, religion and spirituality.

Renaissance began in Italy in the fourteenth century [文艺复兴发端于 14 世纪的意大利], spread to the north, including England, by the 16th century, and ended in the north in the mid-seventeenth century（earlier in Italy）.

Yet the Renaissance was more than a "rebirth." It was also an age of new discoveries, both geographical（***exploration of the New World*** [发现新世界]）and intellectual. Both kinds of discovery resulted in ***changes for Western civilization*** [给西方文明带来巨大的变革].

The ***innovative technology*** [创新科技] of the Renaissance ***was sparked by*** [被点燃] ***Johannes Gutenberg's***[4] [谷腾堡] ***reinvention of the printing press*** [印刷机的再发明] in the 1450s.

In science, for example, Copernicus（1473–1543）attempted to prove that ***the sun rather than the earth was at the center of the planetary system*** [太阳，而不是地球，是星系的

---

1 Master painter and architect of the Italian High Renaissance.

2 《雅典学院》，又译《雅典学派》，拉斐尔创作的一幅壁画，现存于罗马的梵蒂冈博物馆拉斐尔画室中。

3 人文主义，在这里特指 14 到 16 世纪间比较先进的思想。人文主义的特点是以理性推理为思想基础，以仁慈博爱为基本价值观。

4 约翰内斯•谷腾堡（1398–1468），欧洲近代活字印刷术的发明人，迅速推动了西方科学和社会的发展。

中心], thus *radically altering the cosmic world view* [彻底地变革宇宙观] that had *dominated antiquity and the Middle Ages* [统治古代和中世纪].

Italian physicist, astronomer and philosopher *Galileo Galilei* [伽利略] *improved the telescope* [改良望远镜] and made important *astronomical observations* [天文学观察]. *Christopher Columbus* [哥伦布] became the first explorer to *sail across the Atlantic Ocean to North America* [横渡大西洋到达北美].

During the Renaissance, *Martin Luther*[1] [马丁•路德] started the *Protestant Reformation* [宗教改革] in Germany. Luther *was distraught over* [悲痛欲绝] the *selling of indulgences* [销售赎罪券] by the *Roman Catholic Church* [罗马天主教], and he set up the *Ninety-Five Theses*[2] [《九十五条论纲》] *on the door of Castle Church Wittenberg* [维腾贝格宫殿教堂门口] in 1517.

Painters began to *utilize methods of realism* [使用现实主义手法] by improving skills in *three-dimensional perspective* [三维透视]. Painters began to *veer away from religious themes* [从宗教题材转移注意力] and *focused more on people and landscapes* [更关注人物和风景]. Leonardo Da Vinci, Raphael and Michelangelo were some of *the most prominent Renaissance painters* [著名的文艺复兴艺术家].
In the early Renaissance [在文艺复兴早期], particularly in Italy, writers focused mostly on *translating and studying classic Latin and Greek works* [翻译并学习古典拉丁和希腊著作]. Many writers attempted to take the styles of ancient writers like *Aristotle* [亚里士多德] or *Homer*[3] [荷马] and to apply them to their own works. *Sonnets* [十四行诗] also *became a popular style of poetry* [成为深受欢迎的诗体]. Some of the most famous Renaissance writers were *William Shakespeare* [莎士比亚], and *Giovanni Boccaccio*[4] [乔万尼•薄伽丘].

改写 | Rewrite the Story | in Your Own Words

---

1 马丁•路德（1483–1546），新教宗教改革发起人。

2 译作《九十五条论纲》。

3 荷马（约公元前 9 世纪–公元前 8 世纪），相传为古希腊游吟诗人，创作史诗《伊利亚特》(*Iliad*)和《奥德赛》(*Odyssee*)，两者统称为《荷马史诗》。

4 乔万尼•薄伽丘(1313–1375)，文艺复兴时期意大利作家、诗人，以故事集《十日谈》(*Decameron*)留名后世。

凡•高
VINCENT VAN GOGH[1] （1853–1890）

拥抱太阳的画家
Well-known post-Impressionist painter

In 1987, **_one of the sunflower paintings sold at auction for nearly forty million dollars_** [众多向日葵作品中的一幅就在拍卖会上以近四千万美元成交], but **_supremely ironic given that_** [莫大的讽刺却是] **_Van Gogh failed to sell more than a single picture in his lifetime_** [凡•高生平却仅卖出一幅作品].

Van Gogh lived his life in isolation, poverty, obscurity, and notoriety [在孤独、贫困、卑微和声名狼藉中度过了他的一生], **_feared as a madman_** [像疯子般令人恐惧]. But now, he's loved around the world. He's become **_a cultural legend_** [文化界的传奇人物], the **_stuff which Hollywood movies are made of_** [好莱坞影视作品的素材].

But **_amidst the industry that's grown up around Van Gogh_** [在围绕凡•高而涌现的各行业中], **_it's easy to lose sight of the radical expressiveness of his paintings_** [人们很容易忽略其作品狂热的表现力]—their **_edginess_** [画风锐利], their **_delicacy_** [细致], and **_precariousness_** [飘忽不安], surfaces which still **_seem fresh, radiating light and energy and feeling_** [历久如新的画面散发着光芒、力量和情感].

In the February of 1888, he arrived in **_Arles, Provence_**[2] [普罗旺斯的阿尔], where he believed **_he could find the right warmth and brightness for his work_** [他为创作找到惬意的温暖和阳光]. By the time summer arrived, Van Gogh **_was in his element_** [如鱼得水] and thought he'd **_found an artist's paradise_** [找到画家的天堂].

He started painting like a man possessed [他开始疯狂地绘画]. And the result was the many **_vivid, eye-assaulting canvases_** [色彩鲜艳、极具视觉冲击力的帆布油画] for which Van Gogh is now **_monumentally famous_** [举世闻名的].

Vincent van Gogh had **_entered his prime at the age of 35_** [在 35 岁那年，自己的事业达到巅峰]. He **_became more confident in his work_** [他对自己的作品变得更有自信] and **_his output was phenomenal_** [产量惊人]. In fact, Van Gogh's mind **_was troubled by much more than isolation_** [不仅仅受到孤独困扰].

He told Theo, "**_There are moments when I'm twisted by enthusiasm or madness or prophecy_** [有时我在热诚、疯狂或预感之中挣扎]. **_The uglier I get, the older, sicker and poorer_** [我变得越是难看、年老、体弱且贫困], **_the more I want to avenge myself by going in for brilliant, resplendent color_** [便越想以鲜艳夺目的色彩给以还击]." Because of their emblematic quality, to many people the sunflowers are Van Gogh.

His later works, including numerous **_self-portraits_** [自画像], a series of sunflower [向日葵] paintings, and **_Starry Night_** [《星夜》], are characterized by **_bold and rhythmic brush_**

---

1 Dutch painter, generally considered the greatest after Rembrandt, and one of the greatest of the Post-Impressionists. The striking colour, emphatic brushwork, and contoured forms of his work powerfully influenced the current of Expressionism in modern art. Van Gogh's art became astoundingly popular after his death, especially in the late 20th century, when his work sold for record-breaking sums at auctions around the world and was featured in blockbuster touring exhibitions.

2 普罗旺斯，古罗马的一个行省，现为法国东南部的一个地区，毗邻地中海，和意大利接壤。境内有马赛等名城，并出产优质葡萄酒。普罗旺斯的薰衣草(lavender)花田更是难得的美景。

strokes [大胆的、有节奏的笔调] and **_vivid colors_** [鲜艳颜色].

He suffered from **_recurrent bouts of mental illness_** [间歇性精神疾病]. He once cut off a part of his ear. His long **_struggle with depression_** [和忧郁症长期抗争] **_ended in suicide_** [以自杀结束生命].

Vincent van Gogh **_was a complete and utter failure_** [全然的失败] in everything that seemed important to his **_contemporaries_** [同时代的人]. He was neither able to **_start a family_** [成家], nor **_earn his own living_** [谋生], nor even keep his friends.

His great mind **_was not recognized by his peers_** [没有被同时代的人欣赏] when he was alive. His artistic talents were only recognized after his death and **_have made tremendous effect on_** [产生重大影响] the **_generation after him_** [后人].

Qby Quotes **Vincent van Gogh**

I dream my painting and I paint my dream.

I would rather die of passion than of boredom.

Great things are not done by impulse, but by a series of small things brought together.

I am seeking, I am striving, I am in it with all my heart.

改写 | **Rewrite the Story** | **in Your Own Words**

香奈尔

COCO CHANEL[1] (1883-1971)

Coco Chanel ***reached a peak of fame and popularity*** [达到名气和人气的顶峰] in the 1920s when she ***succeeded in*** [成功地做到] replacing the ***extravagant pre-war fashions*** [奢华的战前流行时尚] with simple comfortable clothes. The same ***cardigan jackets*** [开衫外套] and easy skirts that she popularized then ***were revived in her successful comeback*** [成功复出后梅开二度] in the late fifties and her famous Chanel No. 5 scent ***kept her name in the public eye*** [让她的名字紧抓公众眼球] throughout her long career.

She ***became a legend in the world of fashion*** [成为时尚界的传奇] and a ***Broadway musical*** [百老汇音乐剧], based on her career and starring ***Katharine Hepburn***[2] [凯瑟琳•赫本], was put on in 1968.

Orphaned at an early age [很小就成为孤儿], she worked with her sister in a milliner's in Deauville[3], where she finally opened a shop in 1912.

After ***a brief spell of nursing*** [短暂的护士工作] in the war, she ***founded a couture house*** [成立了高级时装店] in the ***Rue Cambon in Paris*** [巴黎康邦街]. There she worked, lived and entertained for much of the rest of her life, although she actually slept in the ***Ritz hotel***[4] [丽兹酒店] on the other side of the road.

Chanel ***sensed the profound need for change, renewal, and emancipation*** [感受到变革、复兴和解放的巨大需求] that was sweeping the world [席卷全球] in 1914 and ***set out to revolutionize women's clothing*** [开始彻底变革女装]. ***It was her talent, drive, and inspiration*** [正是她的才华、动力和灵感] that ***brought about a complete metamorphosis of fashion*** [引领时尚巨大的蜕变] ***in post-war years*** [战后的岁月里].

She began by ***liberating women from the bondage of the corset*** [把女性从束腹胸衣的禁锢中解放出来]. In 1920, she made the first ***chemise dress*** [衬裙礼服] and the "poor girl look" ***in contrast to*** [对比] the rich woman of pre-war years was born.

She succeeded in ***making women look casual*** [让女性看起来轻便] but ***at the same time elegant*** [同时又优雅] by using the then ***revolutionary combinations of jersey, tweed, and pearls*** [革命性地组合毛料、斜纹呢料和珍珠]. ***Dior***[5] [迪奥] was to say of her later: "with a black sweater and 10 rows of pearls Chanel revolutionized fashion". In 1925 she made fashion history again with the ***collarless cardigan jacket*** [无领开衫外套].

"A woman can be over-dressed, never over-elegant," Coco knew very well that style comes not only from apparel, but also from attitude.

---

1 French fashion designer who ruled over Parisian haute couture for almost six decades. Her elegantly casual designs inspired women of fashion to abandon the complicated, uncomfortable clothes—such as petticoats and corsets—that were prevalent in 19th-century dress.

2 凯瑟琳•赫本 (1907–2003)，美国电影与戏剧界的标志性人物，共获得过 4 次奥斯卡最佳女主角奖，12 次奥斯卡最佳女主角奖提名。

3 多维尔，靠近法国首都巴黎。

4 丽兹酒店，位于巴黎市中心旺多姆广场。可可•香奈尔女士曾在巴黎丽兹酒店居住超过 30 年的时间，她把巴黎丽兹酒店作为他的家。1971 年 1 月 10 日，她在巴黎•兹酒店的私人套房中被发现死于心脏病。

5 克里斯汀•迪奥 (Christian Dior, 1905–1957)，法国时装设计师，创立迪奥 (Dior) 公司。

Q by Quotes Chanel

Fashion fades, only style remains the same.

Fashion is not something that exists in dresses only. Fashion is in the sky, in the street, fashion has to do with ideas, the way we live, what is happening.

If you want to be irreplaceable, you have to be different.

The poetry of fashion lies in creating illusion.

Nature gives you your face at twenty. Life shapes your face at thirty. But the face you have at fifty is the face you have earned.

Let my legend makes its way in life. I wish it a long one.

改写 Rewrite the Story | in Your Own Words

卓别林
CHARLIE CHAPLIN[1] （1889-1977）

"The funniest man in the world?"

Perhaps it depends on who's laughing, but ***it is a fact that*** [事实是] people over the world have been ***giggling*** [咯咯地笑] or ***roaring with laughter*** [纵情大笑] for much the better part of a century at the ***antics*** [滑稽的表演] of the little man with the ***baggy pants*** [宽松的裤子], the ***bowler hat*** [圆顶礼帽], the ***cane*** [手杖], and the ***moustache*** [小胡子]. ***There can be little doubt*** [毫无疑问] that Charlie Chaplin was and is the most famous film star in the world.

He was the last ***survivor*** [幸存者] from among the ***founding fathers of the American cinema*** [美国电影界的创立者], one of the greatest comic creators in film, and achieved greater, more ***widespread fame*** [声名远扬] in his own lifetime than perhaps anyone else in the history of mankind.

He was the ***darling of the intellectuals*** [学者的挚爱] who loved to ***theorize on*** [建立理论] the ***significance of his comedy*** [喜剧的意义], and its ***social responsibility*** [社会责任]. But he also had ***to a unique degree*** [某种独特程度上的] ***the common touch*** [通俗的表演技巧] —***people of virtually any culture*** [任何文化背景的人] were able to respond with laughter to his screen antics.

Charles Spencer Chaplin was born in London, England, on April 16th 1889. His father was a ***versatile vocalist*** [多才多艺的歌手] and actor; and his mother, known under the stage name of Lily Harley, was an attractive actress and singer, who ***gained a reputation*** [赢得声誉] for her work in the ***light opera field*** [轻歌剧领域].

His childhood was an unhappy one, and when Charles was five, his mother, who was never strong, found that the problems of looking after the family ***in the face of poverty and adversity*** [面对贫穷和逆境] had become too much for her. Charles and his half-brother Sydney ***were therefore sent to an orphanage*** [被送到孤儿院].

This was a great shock to the sensitive child [对这个敏感的孩子产生了巨大的打击] and it gave him ***a sense of insecurity*** [不安全感] which was to ***haunt him throughout his life*** [萦绕他整个生命]. He emerged from the orphanage in 1896, and ***became a waif of the London slums*** [成为伦敦贫民窟的流浪儿].

Having inherited natural talents from their parents [从父母那里继承来天赋], the youngsters took to the stage as the best opportunity for a career. Charlie ***made his professional debut*** [首次专业的演出] and ***rapidly won popular favor*** [很快赢得公众喜爱].

His best films—"***Modern Times***[2] [《摩登时代》]", "***City Lights***[3] [《城市之光》]", and "***The Great Dictator***[4] [《大独裁者》]"—were all conceived during the 1930s. "The Great Dictator",

---

1 British comedian, producer, writer, director, and composer who is widely regarded as the greatest comic artist of the screen and one of the most important figures in motion-picture history.

2 《摩登时代》，1936 年查理•卓别林最著名的电影之一。本片讲述经济危机给失业工人带来痛苦的故事。

3 《城市之光》，1931 年查理•卓别林自编自导自演的一部电影。本片讲述流浪汉与盲女的悲喜故事。

4 《大独裁者》，查理•卓别林自导自演的一部电影，于 1940 年首映，它尖锐地讽刺了纳粹主义和阿道夫•希特勒（Adolf Hitler，1889–1945）。

released in 1940, was a damning satirical look at fascism and way ahead of its time.

Charlie Chaplin was not just a silent movie actor, he was **_an icon of early cinema_** [早期电影界的标志]. Chaplin was a writer, director, performer, producer, as well as composer, and the co-founder of revolutionary studio United Artists[1].

Chaplin

A day without laughter is a day wasted.

Dictators free themselves, but they enslave the people.

Failure is unimportant. It takes courage to make a fool of yourself.

Life could be wonderful if people would leave you alone.

The hate of men will pass, and dictators die, and the power they took from the people will return to the people. And so long as men die, liberty will never perish.

改写 **Rewrite the Story** **in Your Own Words**

1 联艺电影公司 (United Artists Corporation，简称 UA)，成立于 1919 年。

玛丽莲·梦露
MARILYN MONROE[1] (1926–1962)

Her career was not so much a Hollywood legend as the **_Hollywood legend_** [好莱坞的传奇]: the **_poor orphan_** [穷苦的孤儿] who became one of **_the most sought after_** [炙手可热的] and **_highly paid_** [高薪的] women in the world; the hopeful Hollywood unknown who became the **_most potent star attraction_** [最抢眼的明星] in the American cinema; the **_uneducated beauty_** [缺乏教育的美女] who married one of America's leading intellectuals.

She **_was brought up in an orphanage_** [在孤儿院长大] and a series of **_foster homes_** [寄养家庭], married first at the age of 15, obtained a **_divorce_** [离婚] four years later and began a career as photographer's model.

Studio executives [工作室主管], directors and **_photographers_** [摄影师] immediately recognized her ability to **_capture and hold the attention of anyone_** [吸人眼球] **_on the opposite end of a camera lens_** [在镜头另外一端].

Over a little more than a decade Monroe **_captivated audiences through a multitude of comedic and dramatic roles_** [通过众多的喜剧和戏剧角色令观众为之着迷].

Regardless, Marilyn Monroe's personal history, achievements and contributions have made her one of the world's greatest icons. She inspired musicians, writers and artists like Madonna and Lady Gaga **_to name just a few_** [仅举几例], with her **_timeless glamour and extraordinary character_** [永恒的魅力和非凡的个性].

More relevant today than ever [比以往任何时候] Marilyn Monroe lived a life and **_left a legacy_** [留下的遗产] that continues to excite fans all over the world.

 Monroe

What do I wear in bed? Why, Chanel No. 5, of course.

I knew I belonged to the public and to the world, not because I was talented or even beautiful, but because I had never belonged to anything or anyone else.

My work is the only ground I've ever had to stand on. I seem to have a whole superstructure with no foundation but I'm working on the foundation.

Sex is a part of nature. I go along with nature.

A career is wonderful, but you can't curl up with it on a cold night.

---

1 American actress who became a major sex symbol, starring in a number of commercially successful motion pictures during the 1950s.

I want to grow old without facelifts... I want to have the courage to be loyal to the face I've made. Sometimes I think it would be easier to avoid old age, to die young, but then you'd never complete your life, would you? You'd never wholly know you.

改写 | **Rewrite the Story** | **in Your Own Words** |

Chapter 8

音乐与演艺

MUSIC AND PERFORMING

本 章 目 录

巴赫

JOHANN SEBASTIAN BACH[1] （1685–1750）

We are now so ***accustomed to*** [习惯于] thinking of J.S. Bach as ***a composer of superstar rank*** [巨星级作曲家] that it is hard to believe that in his own lifetime his ***reputation rested on*** [声誉仰赖于] his ***virtuosity*** [精湛的技艺] as an ***organist*** [管风琴家] and teacher.

Though his works ***were admired by*** [被钦佩] ***Mozart*** [莫扎特] and ***Beethoven*** [贝多芬], for some 75 years after his death, ***his compositions were virtually unknown*** [他的作品基本上无人知晓]. They were considered too complex, too difficult.

However, one magic day in 1829 his *St. Matthew Passion*[2] was discovered by no less a composer than Felix Mendelssohn[3], also a leading ***conductor*** [指挥家] of his time. ***Thanks to his efforts*** [多亏他的努力], ***Bach's compositions quickly won the prestige*** [巴赫的作品迅速赢得声誉] they so richly deserve.

Born into a family of musicians [出生在音乐世家] in central Germany, J.S. Bach synthesized European music of his time without ever really leaving home.

The Bach family [巴赫家族] produced more than 50 ***noted musicians*** [著名音乐家] ***over several generations*** [连续几代].

His compositions ***stand unchallenged*** [地位毫不动摇] as the ***high point of the Baroque period of music*** [巴洛克风格音乐巅峰]. A man of ***inexhaustible energy and imagination*** [不竭的精力和想象力], Bach composed in every form known in the baroque era, except the ***opera*** [歌剧]. His enormous output includes works for the ***organ*** [管风琴], ***violin*** [小提琴], ***chamber orchestra*** [室内管弦乐], and voice.

Organs were central to Bach's music [管风琴在巴赫音乐中占据核心地位]. He composed many organ pieces, some of which were to be performed by ***choir*** [唱诗班], orchestra, and organ together.

Like any good 18th century composers, Bach wrote what was demanded of him. Bach was famous in his lifetime for his genius at ***improvising music at the organ*** [即兴演奏管风琴]. Early in his career, Bach ***got into trouble for*** [惹麻烦] improvising so wildly that he confused the people trying to sing along in church.

He ***was immensely gifted*** [富有天赋], but said of his gifts: "***I am obliged to work hard*** [不得不努力创作]. ***Whoever is equally industrious will achieve just as well*** [和我一样努力的人也能获得和我一样的成就]."

---

1 Composer of the Baroque era, the most celebrated member of a large family of northern German musicians.

2 马太受难曲，一部由巴赫创作的清唱剧受难曲，是一部重要的宗教音乐。内容是根据马太福音中有关耶稣的受难 (Passion of Jesus) 和耶稣被钉在十字架 (Crucifixion of Jesus)。

3 费利克斯•门德尔松 (1809–1847)，德国犹太裔作曲家，德国浪漫乐派最具代表性的人物之一。

 **Bach**

Music is an agreeable harmony for the honor of God and the permissible delights of the soul.

I play the notes as they are written, but it is God who makes the music.

The final aim and reason of all music is nothing other than the glorification of God and the refreshment of the spirit.

There's nothing remarkable about it. All one has to do is hit the right keys at the right time and the instrument plays itself.

改写 **Rewrite the Story** | **in Your Own Words**

拯救我的 SAT
写作

Saving My SAT
Essay

海顿
FRANZ JOSEPH HAYDN[1] （1732–1809）

Haydn is the composer who did more than any other to **create the Classical style of music** [创造古典主义音乐风格], which **emphasizes melody and harmony** [强调旋律与和谐] over **polyphony**[2] [复调]. It **gave rise to** [引起] new musical forms that enabled composers to tell musical "stories"—in particular, they developed the symphony to do this.

A symphony[3] is a large work with three or four sections called **movements** [乐章], and it uses some **Baroque musical forms** [巴洛克音乐形式] within it, especially dances, such as **minuets** [小步舞曲]. It took many years and many composers to create this new music.

Haydn is known as the "**Father of the Symphony** [交响乐之父]," and he wrote over 100 such works. He also wrote more than 700 pieces of **chamber music**[4] [室内乐]—music for small **ensembles** [演奏团体], or groups, like **string quartets** [弦乐四重奏].

Haydn was prolific not just because he was a **tireless** [孜孜不倦的] worker with an **inexhaustible musical imagination** [无穷无尽的音乐想象力], but also because of the **circumstances of his musical career** [音乐生涯的外界环境]: he was the last **prominent beneficiary** [突出的受益者] of the system of **noble patronage** [贵族赞助] that had **nourished European musical compositio**n [滋养欧洲音乐创作] since the **Renaissance** [文艺复兴].

Musical creativity may often, it is true, **meet a tragic end** [结局悲惨], but Haydn lived long enough to **reap the rewards** [获得回报] of his own imagination and **toil** [辛苦]. In 1790, Haydn was known all over Europe and widely considered the greatest living composer.

Chapter 8 音乐与演艺 MUSIC AND PERFORMING

Haydn

I listened more than I studied... therefore little by little my knowledge and ability were developed.

I was cut off from the world. There was no one to confuse or torment me, and I was forced to become original.

I was never a quick writer, but composed with great care and efforts.

---

1 Austrian composer who was one of the most important figures in the development of the Classical style in music during the 18th century.

2 复调音乐，一种多声部音乐，即作品中含有两条以上独立旋律，并且两者和谐地结合。卡农（Canon）便是复调音乐谱曲技法的主要形式之一。

3 交响曲，包含多个乐章的大型管弦乐曲，通常分为四个乐章。第一乐章，奏鸣曲（Sonata），快板（Allegro）。第二乐章，慢乐章（Slow movement），柔板（Adagio）。第三乐章，三段体小步舞曲乐章（A minuet with trio）。第四乐章，快板（Allegro）、回旋曲（Rondo）或奏鸣曲（Sonata）。

4 室内乐，为几件在室内演奏的乐器所作。比如常见的四重奏（Quartet）和三重奏（Trio）等。

莫扎特

WOLFGANG AMADEUS MOZART[1] （1756–1791）

音乐神童
A classical music genius

Today, people ***debate over*** [争论] whether listening to his music makes children smarter, ***dubbed*** [被称作] the "Mozart Effect".

Mozart ***was described by his father as*** [被其父亲称作] a ***"miracle which God let be born in Salzburg*** [上帝赐给萨尔茨堡的奇迹]."

Mozart had an early musical start. Mozart began ***composing*** [作曲] at the age of four. He spent much of his childhood and teenage years ***touring Europe*** [周游欧洲]. These travels ***gave the young Mozart invaluable exposure to the musical styles*** [给年轻的莫扎特弥足珍贵的机会去接触各种音乐]. Mozart was a musical "***sponge*** [海绵]", ***soaking up*** [给养] music wherever he went.

Mozart is considered one of the most brilliant and ***versatile composers*** [才华横溢的作曲家] ever. He worked in all ***musical genres*** [音乐风格] of his era and ***produced an extraordinary number of compositions*** [创作大量作品], especially ***considering his short life*** [鉴于其短暂的一生].

By the time Mozart died at age 35, he had completed 41 ***symphonies*** [交响乐], 27 piano ***concertos*** [钢琴协奏曲], 23 ***string quartets*** [弦乐四重奏], 17 ***piano sonatas*** [钢琴奏鸣曲], 7 major ***operas*** [歌剧], and numerous works for voice and other instruments.

He composed great operas such as ***The Marriage of Figaro*** [《费加罗的婚礼》], ***The Magic Flute*** [《魔笛》] and ***Don Giovanni*** [《唐璜》].

Mozart is one of the ***heavyweights of classical music*** [古典音乐的重量级人物], generally placed in the top rank of composers along with ***Beethoven*** [贝多芬] （1770–1827） and ***Bach*** [巴赫] （1685–1750）.

However his great works ***were not appreciated by his peers*** [没有被同一时代的人欣赏]. Mozart ***suffered from financial difficulties*** [为经济困难所迫] and always ***begged for loans*** [乞求借贷]. ***Ironically*** [具有讽刺意味的], Mozart's ***popularity seems to have been rising just before he died*** [刚逝世不久便声名鹊起].

 Mozart

The music is not in the notes, but in the silence between.

Neither a lofty degree of intelligence nor imagination nor both together go to the making of genius. Love, love, love, that is the soul of genius.

---

1 Austrian composer, widely recognized as one of the greatest composers in the history of Western music.

改写 **Rewrite the Story** | **in Your Own Words**

贝多芬

LUDWIG VAN BEETHOVEN[1] (1770–1827)

Beethoven's contemporaries [贝多芬同时代的人] ***were quick to note the striking contrast between the man and his music*** [很快会发现贝多芬本人和其音乐作品间的天壤之别].

"Whoever sees Beethoven for the first time and knows nothing about him." Wrote an **observer** [观察家] in 1797, "would surely take him for a ***malicious*** [恶毒的], ***ill-natured*** [性情怪僻的], ***quarrelsome*** [争吵不休的] **drunkard** [酒鬼] who ***has no feeling for music*** [没有任何音乐细胞]…on the other hand, ***he who sees him for the first time surrounded by his fame and his glory*** [当人们第一次看到他的声望和光环], will surely see ***musical talent*** [音乐天赋] in every feature of an ugly face."

Beethoven's tendency to ***isolate himself from society*** [与世隔绝] ***grew with his increasing deafness*** [耳聋日益加重]. His ***despair drove him almost to suicide*** [绝望几乎把他推向死亡的深渊]. "***It was only my art that held me back*** [是音乐把我一把拉了回来]," he concedes. "Ah, it seemed to me impossible to ***leave the world until I had brought forth all that I felt was within me*** [把我内心流淌的音乐呈献给世人]."

Born in Bonn in 1770, Beethoven ***grew up in a musical household*** [在音乐世家长大成人]. His father was a singer. But his father was ***alcoholic*** [酒鬼], and the young Beethoven had to ***take on adult responsibilities at an early age*** [在早年就开始负担家庭责任]. While still a boy, he ***supported his family as a traveling performer*** [以巡游演奏支撑家庭开支].

Beethoven is often linked with ***Austrian composers Joseph Haydn*** [奥地利作曲家海顿] (1732–1809) and Wolfgang Amadeus Mozart (1756–1791) as ***a chief figure of the Viennese classical style*** [维也纳古典音乐大师].

At the age of 17 Beethoven impressed Mozart and briefly studied with Mozart ***in his teens*** [在青少年时期], and the two might have become contemporary rivals if Mozart had not died in 1791 at the age of 35.

Beethoven ***moved permanently to Vienna, Austria*** [在奥地利维也纳永久定居下来], in 1792 to ***study with Haydn*** [师从海顿], and he remained there the rest of his life. ***The student soon surpassed the teacher*** [徒弟很快青出于蓝而胜于蓝].

The French Revolution[2] [法国大革命] of 1789 ***had a profound effect*** [产生深厚影响] on Beethoven and he came to admire ***Napoleon*** [拿破仑] as the ***embodiment of its ideas*** [理想的化身]. His ***Symphony No. 3 in E flat major*** [《降 E 大调第三交响曲》] (***The Eroica Symphony*** [《英雄交响曲》]) was an expression of his admiration for the "***Little Corporal*** [身材矮小的下士]".

However when Napoleon had himself ***crowned Emperor*** [加冕称帝] in 1803, Beethoven ***tore up*** [撕下] his dedication of the work to Napoleon and ***inscribed*** [题字] instead the words "to the memory of a great man."

---

1 German composer, the predominant musical figure in the transitional period between the Classical and Romantic eras. Widely regarded as the greatest composer who ever lived, Ludwig van Beethoven dominates a period of musical history as no one else before or since.

2 法国大革命（1789–1799），期间统治法国多个世纪的绝对君主制封建制度（Absolute Monarchy）土崩瓦解，传统观念逐渐被全新的天赋人权（Natural and legal rights）、三权分立（Trias Politica）等的民主思想所取代。

Beethoven's compositional skill was truly incomparable [贝多芬的作曲才能无与伦比]. **His composing brilliance extended to every genre of classical music** [在古典音乐各种流派，贝多芬的作曲天赋都流光溢彩], from **concertos** [协奏曲] to **symphonies** [交响乐], from **sonatas** [奏鸣曲] to **operas** [歌剧] and **string quartets** [弦乐四重奏].

Beethoven's life and career **were colored by** [增光添彩] an unusual tragedy that **gave him no choice** [没留有其他余地] but to change and adjust: He gradually lost his hearing in the early 1800s and remained deaf for the rest of his life. Although he could **no longer perform in public** [不再公开演出] and for a time even **contemplated suicide** [曾经一度要自行了断], Beethoven could still compose.

Some of his greatest works, such as his *Eroica Symphony*, were written during and after the time of his **hearing loss** [失聪]. Beethoven relied on "conversation books" to communicate with friends, but found it increasingly difficult to perform.

The opening strains [开场的紧张气氛] of his **Symphony No. 5 in C Minor** [《C 小调第五交响曲》] (1808) are instantly recognizable today, and the "**Ode to Joy** [《欢乐颂》]" **choral finale** [曲终合唱] of his **Ninth Symphony** [《第九交响曲》]（1824）is one of the most famous pieces of music ever written. *Ode to Joy* **is a monumental cry for brotherhood among people** [人类追求博爱里程碑式的呼喊].

Beethoven's **artistic achievement** [艺术成就] **cast a long shadow over** [深刻影响] the 19th century and beyond, having set a standard against which later composers would **measure** [评估] their work.

Beethoven

I shall seize fate by the throat.

Music is the one incorporeal entrance into the higher world of knowledge which comprehends mankind but which mankind cannot comprehend.

Music is the mediator between the spiritual and the sensual life.

改写 | Rewrite the Story | in Your Own Words

柴可夫斯基

PYOTR IIYICH TCHAIKOVSKY[1] (1840–1893)

Tchaikovsky's music ***expertly blends*** [技巧性地融合] the European forms of the **symphony** [交响曲], **concerto** [协奏曲], and **opera** [歌剧] with the ***vitality and flavor*** [活力与风格] of his ***native Russian music*** [俄国本土音乐].

He is the most ***emotional*** [情感丰富的] of all the ***Romantic composers*** [浪漫主义作曲家]: sometimes ***feverish*** [狂热的] and ***desperate*** [绝望的], sometimes ***ecstatic*** [狂喜的], other times ***hushed*** [沉默的] and ***secretive*** [神秘的].

His mother died when he was 14, and he suffered enormously during his life. His 1877 ***marriage was disastrous*** [婚姻是场灾难], and the effects of this nearly ***drove him mad*** [把他逼疯]. As a result, his music became his ***boldest public statement*** [最大胆的宣泄] and his ***greatest private refuge*** [最重要的避难所].

His ***Romeo and Juliet*** [《罗密欧与朱丽叶》] is an all-time favorite, and his ***concertos*** [协奏曲] for violin and piano are essential for any ***soloist's repertoire*** [独奏者保留曲目]. Tchaikovsky also wrote 11 operas, but most of all, he is known for his three famous ballets, ***Swan Lake*** [《天鹅湖》], ***The Nutcracker*** [《胡桃夹子》], and ***Sleeping Beauty*** [《睡美人》].

A far more influential woman in Tchaikovsky's life was ***a wealthy widow*** [富有的寡妇], with whom he ***corresponded*** [通信来往] from 1877 to 1890. At her insistence [坚持主张] they never met; they ***did encounter each other on two occasions*** [确实有两次邂逅对方], ***purely by chance*** [完全巧合], but did not ***converse*** [交谈].

As well as financial support of 6000 ***rubles*** [卢布] a year, she ***expressed her interest in his musical career*** [对他的音乐事业表现出兴趣] and ***admiration for his music*** [羡慕他的音乐]. However she ***abruptly cut off her support*** [突然终端支持] for the composer. ***It is widely believed*** [很多人认为] that she did so because she found out about Tchaikovsky's **sexual preference** [性取向].

Tchaikovsky

Inspiration is a guest that does not willingly visit the lazy.

The creative process is like music which takes root with extraordinary force and rapidity.

1 The most popular Russian composer of all time. His music has always had great appeal for the general public in virtue of its tuneful, open-hearted melodies, impressive harmonies, and colorful, picturesque orchestration, all of which evoke a profound emotional response.

音乐与演艺 MUSIC AND PERFORMING

Chapter 8

路易斯·阿姆斯特朗
LOUIS ARMSTRONG[1] （1901–1971）

爵士乐之父
Mr. Jazz

Armstrong defined what it was to play Jazz. His amazing ***technical abilities*** [技术能力], the joy and ***spontaneity*** [自发性], and ***amazingly quick*** [令人惊奇的速度], ***inventive musical mind*** [富有创造性的音乐天赋] still dominate Jazz to this day.

Louis ***was born into extreme poverty*** [出生于赤贫] ***in a black slum of New Orleans*** [新奥尔良的黑人贫民窟]. He ***was raised by his mother alone*** [由母亲一手抚养成人], ***a loving but rather eccentric woman*** [一位慈爱但又古怪的女人] ***with little income*** [几乎没有收入].

As a result, young Louis had to ***scramble for survival*** [为生存而奋斗], ***scavenging and trying to earn a few pennies somehow*** [在垃圾堆寻找有用之物，用各种方法试着赚钱].

He would follow some of the famous New Orleans ***brass bands*** [铜管乐队] through the streets, ***picking up nickels and dimes*** [捡拾铜板] by ***singing for spectators*** [为沿街观众表演].

Almost inevitably [几乎不可避免的], Louis ***got into trouble with the law*** [犯了法]. He was sent to the ***New Orleans Home for Colored Waifs*** [新奥尔良流浪黑人儿童收容所]. ***It turned out to be a blessing in disguise*** [结果塞翁失马焉知非福], for Louis was given a ***cornet*** [短号] and a place in the Home's band.

In no time at all [根本没多久时间] he had mastered the instrument and was soon ready to face the world as a young adult. "***Me and music got married in the Home*** [我和音乐在收容所里结合了]," ***he recalled later*** [他后来回忆].

After being released at age fourteen, he worked selling papers, ***unloading boats*** [卸船], and selling coal from a ***cart*** [手推车]. He didn't own an instrument at this time, but continued to listen to bands at clubs. Joe "King" Oliver[2] was his favorite and the older man ***acted as a father to Louis*** [像父亲一样对他], even giving him his first real cornet, and instructing him on the instrument.

In 1929 Armstrong appeared in a Broadway show, which was a great success. He now began to ***concentrate on his personal career*** [专注他的个人事业] as a popular entertainer, rather than the leader of a jazz group. He began to appear in ***feature-length films*** [标准长度电影] and ***starred in his own radio show*** [出演自己的广播剧].

Armstrong ***toured with his band extensively travelling to Africa, Asia, Europe and South America*** [和他的乐队到非洲、亚洲、欧洲和南美巡演] for the next twenty years until Louis's failing health caused them to ***disband*** [解散]. Armstrong became known as America's ***Ambassador*** [大使].

音乐与演艺 MUSIC AND PERFORMING

Chapter 8

---

1 The leading trumpeter and one of the most influential artists in jazz history.

2 乔·奥利弗（1885–1938），爵士乐先驱。

Armstrong

What we play is life.

Seems to me it ain't the world that's so bad but what we're doing to it, and all I'm saying is: see what a wonderful world it would be if only we'd give it a chance.

If you have to ask what jazz is, you'll never know.

改写 | Rewrite the Story | in Your Own Words

拯救我的 SAT 写作

Saving My SAT Essay

猫王

ELVIS PRESLEY[1] （1935–1977）

Gladys and Vernon Presley were hardly expecting twins when Gladys ***went into labor*** [分娩] in Tupelo, Mississippi, back in the middle of the ***Great Depression***[2] [大萧条], but that is what occurred. Unfortunately Elvis's brother Jesse was ***stillborn*** [生下来已经死亡的] and his parents only saved Elvis's life by putting him into an ***oven*** [烤箱] to ***keep him warm*** [保持温暖].

Elvis's ***musical career was launched*** [音乐生涯开始] ***at the tender age of eight*** [年仅八岁时], when he won $5.00 in a local song contest.

By 1956, he was ***an international sensation*** [轰动全世界的人物]. With a sound and style that uniquely combined his diverse musical influences and ***blurred and challenged the social and racial barriers of the time*** [搅动并挑战这个时代的社会和种族禁忌], he ***ushered in a whole new era of American music and popular culture*** [引导了美国音乐和流行文化的新纪元].

His private life remained largely a matter of speculation [他的私生活大部分都是些揣测]. ***There were rumors*** [有些传闻] ***concerning his erratic temper*** [关于他反复无常的性格], his ***diffidence*** [羞怯], and his ***preoccupation with his mother and religion*** [对母亲和宗教的专注].

His talent, good looks, ***sensuality*** [纵欲], ***charisma*** [魅力], and good humor ***endeared him to millions*** [受到大众的喜爱], as did the ***humility*** [谦逊] and human ***kindness*** [仁慈] he demonstrated throughout his life.

Although the influence of rock and roll appeared to ***wane*** [减弱] during the sixties, it was to provide the ***stimulus*** [刺激] for the most of the next generation of young musicians, including ***the Beatles*** [披头士].

Known over the world by his first name, he is regarded as one of the most important figures of the popular culture in the 20th century. Elvis died at his Memphis home, ***Graceland*** [雅园], on August 16, 1977.

 Presley

Don't criticize what you don't understand, son. You never walked in that man's shoes.

---

1 American popular singer widely known as the "King of Rock and Roll" and one of rock music's dominant performers from the mid-1950s until his death.

2 大萧条，是指发生于 1929 年至 1933 年间的全球性经济大衰退。

When I was a child, ladies and gentlemen, I was a dreamer. I read comic books and I was the hero of the comic book. I saw movies and I was the hero in the movie. So every dream I ever dreamed has come true a hundred times...I learned very early in life that: "Without a song, the day would never end; without a song, a man ain't got a friend; without a song, the road would never bend..." So I keep singing a song.

...the image is one thing and the human being is another...it's very hard to live up to an image.

改写 | Rewrite the Story | in Your Own Words

列侬

JOHN LENNON[1] (1940–1980)

John Lennon, ***a dominating member of the Beatles*** [披头士乐队主要成员], played an important part in a pop music success. The Beatles dominated the pop music of 1960s, creating in the "***Beatlemania*** [披头士狂热]" which struck their audiences and young followers wherever they went, ***paroxysms of enthusiasm*** [狂热的发作] which ***rivaled and even surpassed*** [匹敌甚至超过] anything that had gone before them in the short history of rock and roll.

While in the Beatles, Lennon ***displayed an outspokenness*** [表现出的坦率] that ***immersed the band in controversy*** [让乐队深陷争论的漩涡] and helped redefine the rules of acceptable behavior for rock stars.

He famously remarked in 1965 that the Beatles were "more popular than Jesus"—a statement that was more an observation than a ***boast*** [吹嘘], but that resulted in the ***band's records being burned*** [乐队唱片被焚毁] and removed from radio station playlists in the U.S.

In 1969 the Beatles had started to ***split up*** [解散]; it was John Lennon who was the main factor behind this. After 1970, John Lennon created a very successful solo career, often with the help of his second wife, ***Yoko Ono*** [小野洋子].

In the early 1970s John Lennon also ***became a figurehead for the anti-war Movement*** [成为反战的代表人物]. His song "Give Peace a Chance" became an ***anthem*** [颂歌] for the anti-war movement.

John Lennon was shot dead in 1980, by David Chapman—***an obsessed fan*** [疯狂的乐迷]. The death ***shocked the world*** [震惊世界], both musical and non-musical.

Q_{uotes} ^{by} Lennon

A dream you dream alone is only a dream. A dream you dream together is reality.

All we are saying is give peace a chance.

Part of me suspects that I'm a loser, and the other part of me thinks I'm God Almighty.

---

1 Leader or co-leader of British rock group the Beatles, author and graphic artist, solo recording artist, and collaborator with Yoko Ono on recordings and other art projects.

音乐与演艺 MUSIC AND PERFORMING

Chapter 8

迈克尔·杰克逊

MICHAEL JACKSON[1] (1958–2009)

Known as "the King of Pop," Michael Jackson ***became an instant star*** [瞬间成为明星] at age 11 as the youngest member of the family group, the Jackson Five [杰克逊五人组]. His ***solo musical career*** [单飞的音乐生涯] ***dominated the pop charts and airwaves*** [主导流行乐排行榜和电台广播] around the world throughout the 1980s and 1990s, before ending in controversy.

He has ***enthralled his worldwide audience*** [让全世界观众为之痴狂] with dancing skills that put him in a tradition of great entertainers. Jackson is a singer, songwriter, ***record producer*** [唱片制作人], actor, and ***choreographer*** [编舞]. He is one of the best-selling artists of all time and has donated millions of dollars to charity.

Jackson's career is a catalog of achievement: he has received 13 ***Grammy Awards*** [格莱美] and has had 13 ***number-one chart singles*** [排行榜冠军的单曲] in the US. He has been named the "Most Successful Entertainer of All Time" by ***Guinness World Records*** [吉尼斯世界纪录].

Through stage performances and music videos, Jackson ***popularized a number of dance techniques*** [推广一系列舞蹈技巧], such as the robot and the moonwalk. His ***distinctive*** [独特的] musical sound and vocal style have influenced numerous hip hop, pop, contemporary ***R&B*** [节奏布鲁斯] (Rhythm and Blues) and rock artists. Jackson's 1982 album ***Thriller*** [《战栗》] is ***the best-selling album of all time*** [史上最畅销唱片].

Jackson

In a world filled with hate, we must still dare to hope. In a world filled with anger, we must still dare to comfort. In a world filled with despair, we must still dare to dream. And in a world filled with distrust, we must still dare to believe.

Hope is such a beautiful word, but it often seems very fragile. Life is still being needlessly hurt and destroyed.

We have to heal our wounded world. The chaos, despair, and senseless destruction we see today are a result of the alienation that people feel from each other and their environment.

All of us are products of our childhood.

---

1 American singer, songwriter, and dancer who was the most popular entertainer in the world in the early and mid-1980s.

Chapter 9

挑战与竞技

CHALLENGE AND COMPETITION

本 章 目 录

哥伦布

CHRISTOPHER COLUMBUS[1] (1451–1506)

发现新大陆
The man who discovered America

Hero or villain [英雄，还是恶棍]?

Five hundred years after his first voyage to the Americas, ***these questions still arouse passions*** [这些问题仍然唤起激情] in both Europe and the western hemisphere.

Europeans, especially in Italy（where he was born）and Spain, tend to ***regard him as a heroic figure*** [将哥伦布看成是英雄式的人物]—***a courageous mariner*** [勇敢的航海家] who ***opened up a new world*** [开启新大陆] with his "discovery" of America.

Native peoples of both North and South America, ***as well as many historians*** [还有很多历史学家], argue that the ***arrival of Columbus*** [哥伦布的到来] and his ***Spanish crews*** [西班牙船员] was an ***unmitigated disaster for the native civilizations*** [对当地文明来说是十足的灾难] they encountered, bringing in their oppression, disease and slavery.

Known as "the man who discovered America", Columbus was in fact trying to ***find a westward sea passage to the Orient*** [找到一条向西到达东方的海上航路] when he landed in the New World in 1492. This ***unintentional discovery was to change the course of world history*** [这偶然发现却改变了世界历史的走向].

Imagine ***Italy*** [意大利] without tomatoes, ***Ireland*** [爱尔兰] or Russia without potatoes, and ***Switzerland*** [瑞士] without ***cocoa*** [可可豆]. Until Columbus returned to Europe with these ***crops*** [作物], they were unknown outside of the Americas.

Today ***it is generally recognized that*** [人们公认] Italian-Spanish navigator Christopher Columbus did not "discover" the Americas, which ***were already inhabited by native peoples*** [居住着土著人]. However, he did ***instigate the European exploration of these lands*** [激起了欧洲人探索新大陆的热情] at the end of the 15th century.

Columbus was ***an Italian explorer*** [意大利探险家] ***in the service of Spain*** [效力西班牙] who ***determined that the earth was round*** [认定地球是圆的] and attempted to reach Asia by sailing west from Europe, thereby discovering America（in 1492）.

Columbus and his sailors brought with them ***diphtheria*** [白喉], ***measles*** [麻疹], ***smallpox*** [天花], ***malaria*** [疟疾], and other diseases unknown in the Americas. Within little more than a decade of Columbus's first arrival, an ***estimated*** [约有] three million ***indigenous American population*** [美洲土著居民] had perished.

Columbus died in 1506, just a few years after his last voyage. He ***never set foot on the North American mainland*** [没有踏上北美大陆]. The many explorers who followed him ***opened up the continent for European colonization*** [在这片土地上开启了欧洲殖民运动], ***reshaping humanity's view of the world*** [改造了人类的世界观].

挑战与竞技 CHALLENGE AND COMPETITION

Chapter 9

---

1 Master navigator and admiral whose four transatlantic voyages opened the way for European exploration, exploitation, and colonization of the Americas.

Columbus's achievements were key in the transition from the **_Middle Ages_**[1] [中世纪] (about AD 476 to about 1450) to the **_modern age_** [现代]. More than 500 years later, Columbus's name **_still looms large_** [仍然显得举足轻重].

Columbus

By prevailing over all obstacles and distractions, one may unfailingly arrive at his chosen goal or destination.

Following the light of the sun, we left the Old World.

These people have no religion, neither are they idolaters, but are a very gentle race, without the knowledge of any iniquity; they neither kill, nor steal, nor carry weapons...they have a knowledge that there is a God above, and are firmly persuaded that we have come from heaven.

改写 | Rewrite the Story | in Your Own Words

1 中世纪(约476–1453)，又称中古时代，由西罗马帝国灭亡开始计算，直到东罗马帝国灭亡。中世纪或者中世纪早期在欧美普遍称作"黑暗时代 (Dark Ages)"，传统上认为这是欧洲文明史上发展较缓慢的时期。

230

达·伽马
VASCO DA GAMA[1] （1460–1524）

Vasco da Gama was one of the most successful **Portuguese explorers** [葡萄牙探险家] in the **Age of Discovery**[2] [大航海时代]. He **achieved a tremendous popularity** [大受欢迎] when he **explored the first water trade route between Europe and India** [找到欧洲和印度之间的第一条航线].

In this **epic voyage** [史诗般的航程], he **sailed around Africa's Cape of Good Hope** [驶过非洲的好望角]. He **was successful in breaking** [成功地打破] **the monopoly of the Arab and Venetian spice traders** [阿拉伯和威尼斯商人对香料贸易的垄断].

Vasco da Gama's pioneering sea voyage to India is **one of the defining moments in the history of exploration** [人类探索史上标志性的时刻之一]. Apart from being one the greatest pieces of European seamanship of that time—a far greater achievement than Christopher Columbus's **crossing of the Atlantic** [横跨大西洋]—his journey **acted as a catalyst** [起到催化剂作用] for **a series of events that changed the world** [改变世界的一系列事件].

K now more

Age of Discovery

The Age of Discovery [大航海时代] is an age in which European sailors and ships left the coastal waters of the Old World and **embarked on their adventure** [开始他们的探险] on the vast "green sea of darkness".

For mariners it **was an age of adventure** [探险的时代], risk, hardship, disease, and death; for nations it **was an age of struggle** [奋起的时代], defeat, or conquest and an age for acquiring new, **near-primitive lands** [近乎原始的土地] and colonizing and **gaining dominion over foreign territories** [占领外国领地].

For **European commercial interests** [欧洲商业利益] it was an age of rewarding success, which **broke the monopoly of Venice** [打破威尼斯商人的垄断], **overcame the Muslim domination of the spice trade** [战胜穆斯林对香料贸易的统治], **created trade routes** [开辟商路] between Europe and the Far East, and opened up a New World.

First, **Portuguese** [葡萄牙的] ships, then Spanish and finally, in the late 15th and early 16th centuries, British, French and **Dutch** [荷兰的] ships **set out to discover a world** [开

---

1 Portuguese navigator whose voyages to India opened up the sea route from western Europe to the East by way of the Cape of Good Hope.

2 地理大发现，又名"探索时代"或"大航海时代"，从 15 世纪持续到 17 世纪。该时期内，欧洲的船队出现在世界各处的海洋上，寻找着新的贸易路线和贸易伙伴，以发展欧洲新生的资本主义。伴随新航路的开辟，东西方文化、贸易交流开始激增，殖民主义（Colonialism）和自由贸易（Free trade）开始出现。其中著名的航海家包括哥伦布（Christopher Columbus，1451–1506）、达伽马（Vasco da Gama，1469–1524）、麦哲伦（Ferdinand Magellan，1480–1521）等。

始探索新世界], a world they originally called the Other World[1], but eventually called the Mundus Novus[2] —the New World[3].

The New World is one of the names used for the ***Western Hemisphere*** [西半球], specifically the Americas and sometimes ***Oceania*** [大洋洲]. ***The term originated in*** [这个词起源于] the early 16th century, shortly after America was discovered by European explorers, ***expanding the geographical horizon*** [扩展地理视野] of the people of the European middle Ages, who had thought of the world as consisting of Europe, Asia, and Africa only: ***collectively now referred to as the Old World*** [统称为"旧世界"].

Cinnamon [肉桂], ***cardamom*** [小豆蔻], ginger, pepper and ***turmeric*** [姜黄], known to Eastern peoples thousands of years ago, were important ***spices of commerce*** [贸易香料] early in the evolution of trade.

Arabians were ***making direct sailings*** [直航] before the Christian era[4]. ***From time immemorial*** [从远古时期], southern Arabia had been ***a trading centre*** [贸易中心] for these items. ***Arab traders artfully withheld the true source of these spices*** [阿拉伯商人狡猾地保密香料的真正货源]. To ***satisfy their curiosity*** [满足好奇心], to protect their market, and to ***discourage competitors*** [阻止竞争者], they ***spread fantastic tales*** [散播奇异的故事] that cassia grew in shallow lakes ***guarded by winged animals*** [被长着羽翼的动物保护着] and that cinnamon ***grew in deep glens*** [长在深谷中] ***infested with poisonous snakes*** [遍布着毒蟒].

By the 10th century Venice was beginning to prosper in trading in the spices of the East; by the early part of the 13th century it ***enjoyed a monopoly of the spice trade of the Middle East*** [独霸中东的香料贸易]. They obtained the spices in ***Alexandria***[5] [亚历山大港] and sold to northern and western European buyers ***at exorbitant prices*** [极高的价格]. By the 15th century it was ***a formidable power in Europe*** [欧洲强国].

The Europeans knew the origin of the spices reaching Alexandria and, ***unable to break the hold of Venice*** [无法打破威尼斯控制], determined in the last third of the 15th century to build ships and venture abroad in search of a route to the ***spice-producing countries*** [香料产地国]. So began the famed voyages of discovery.

The Portuguese, led by Prince Henry the Navigator[6], ***were first in the race*** [在航海竞赛中冲锋在先] and the first to bring spices from India to Europe by way of the Cape of Good Hope in 1501. In 1492 Christopher Columbus sailed under the flag of Spain, and in 1497 John Cabot[7] sailed for England, but they both ***failed to find the fabulous spice lands*** [没有找到传说中的香料产地].

拯救我的SAT 写作
Saving My SAT Essay

---

1 旧大陆，或称"旧世界"，指新大陆发现之前，欧洲所认识的世界，其中包括欧洲、非洲和亚洲。

2 拉丁文的"新世界"或"新大陆"。Mundus Novus（New World）据称是意大利航海家亚美利哥•韦斯普奇（Amerigo Vespucci，1454–1512）公开发表的信件之一。

3 新大陆，或"新世界"，是欧洲人于15世纪末发现美洲大陆后对其称呼，有时这个名称也包括大洋洲。

4 公元，即"公历纪元"，英文为Common Era, Current Era, 或Christian Era, 起源于西方基督教国家，简写作C.E.。A.D.是拉丁文"Anno Domini"的缩写，B.C.E.（Before the Common Era）是"公元前"，或简称B.C.（Before Christ）。

5 亚历山大港，现为埃及第二大城市，地中海港口，非洲的重要海港。

6 亨利王子（1394–1460），葡萄牙航海家，建立了世界首间航海学校。

7 乔瓦尼•卡博托（Giovanni Caboto，1450–1498），意大利航海家。

罗伯特·皮尔里

ROBERT E. PEARY[1] (1856–1920)

The discovery of the North Pole [发现北极] is one of the noblest stories in the history of exploration. It is a story of the battle of **_two invincible Americans_** [两个无畏的美国人] against the terrible elements of the Arctic; a battle which lasted eighteen years and left one of the Americans, **_a steel-willed man_** [钢铁般意志的人], a **_cripple for life_** [身体残疾].

It is a human story **_filled with_** [充满着] **_tragic suffering_** [悲惨遭遇], **_pathos_** [痛苦] and **_humiliation_** [羞辱]. And it is noble, because these two Americans, who made the last great discovery in the Northern Hemisphere, were a white man and a **_Negro_** [黑人].

Why it was that Peary chose to take Henson, the **_Negro_** [黑人], with him to the Pole is best answered in the simple statement that **_there was no one better qualified_** [没有人更有资格]. Without Henson, Peary might never have reached the Pole.

No man in the expedition, except Peary himself, had as much **_Arctic experience_** [极地经验] as Henson. **_Peary spoke Eskimo falteringly_** [讲爱斯基摩语时支支吾吾], while **_Henson spoke as fluently as a native_** [说话像本地人一样流利].

Peary, **_his toes amputated_** [脚趾锯断], **_had difficulty walking on snowshoes_** [穿雪鞋走路困难], **_not to mention_** [更别提] **_driving a dog sledge_** [驾驶狗拉的雪橇], and Henson could handle a team of dogs and sledge more competently than many of the Eskimos.

Peary was **_a battle-scarred man_** [身经百战的人] of fifty-three, while Henson, ten years his junior, **_had an unlimited amount of endurance_** [有不竭的耐力].

When two men have faced the same hardships, the same **_threat of starvation and death_** [饥饿与死亡的威胁], together for so many years, **_a deep bond of trust and understanding_** [信任与理解的深厚情谊] **_is bound to grow_** [势必增长] between them.

Mr. Peary, the hero of eight polar expeditions, covering a period of twenty-three years, at last **_realized his ambition_** [实现了他的抱负].

In 1908, Peary **_set out on his last quest for the North Pole_** [踏上了最后一次探索北极的征程]. From Ellesmere Island[2], accompanied by Matthew Henson and four Eskimos, he **_made a final dash_** [做最后冲刺] for the pole, which he claimed to have reached on April 6, 1909.

Congress recognized Peary's achievement [美国国会承认了皮尔里的成就] and **_offered him its thanks_** [向他致谢] in 1911, the year in which he **_retired from the navy_** [从海军退役] with **_the rank of rear admiral_** [海军少将军衔]. Nevertheless, **_it remains questionable_** [至今仍有疑问] as to whether Peary reached the exact location of the North Pole.

---

1 U.S. Arctic explorer usually credited with leading the first expedition to reach the North Pole (1909).

2 埃尔斯米尔岛(Ellesmere Island)，加拿大北极群岛中最北的岛屿，世界第十大岛。

Peary

Find a way, or make one.

I have nailed the stars and stripes to the North Pole.

改写 | Rewrite the Story | in Your Own Words

莱特兄弟

ORVILLE（1871–1948），WILBUR（1867–1912）

人类飞行之父
A flying legend

Ever since the dawn of history [从有历史记录以来]，***humans dreamed of flying*** [人类就梦想飞行]. Over the centuries, ***many schemes were evolved*** [各种方法不断地被改进], most of them ***hopelessly impractical*** [令人绝望地不切实际]. ***Yet the dream never faded*** [然而这个梦想从未褪色].

Even Leonardo da Vinci ***sketched out a design for a flying machine*** [绘制了一幅飞行器设计草图], but it was not until the development of the lightweight gasoline engine in the 19th century that human flight ***became a practical possibility*** [变得具有实际的可能性].

Hot air balloons [热气球] were first developed in the 18th century, but ***progress toward heavier-than-air flying machines was slow and difficult*** [密度重于空气的飞行器方面的研究进展缓慢而艰难]. A considerable step forward was the development of the glider, but ***this still a far cry from the airplane*** [和飞机相距甚远].

Yet to brothers in Dayton[1], Ohio, who ***had not even graduated from high school*** [甚至没有高中毕业], ***resolved the difficulties in a matter of a half-dozen years*** [用了六年的时间解决这一难题].

The Wright brothers[2], who ***designed and made bicycles for a living*** [以设计制作自行车为生], were so distressed after hearing that the German scientist Otto Lilienthal[3] ***had died in a gliding experiment*** [在一次滑翔机实验中丧命], that they ***determined to pursue his dream of flight*** [决心追寻他的飞行梦].

Stimulated by the work of engineer Otto Lilienthal, they ***began to experiment with kites and gliders*** [开始用风筝和滑翔机实验]. They ***went so far as to construct their own wind tunnel*** [竟然建造自己的风洞] to test their ideas, conducting experiments with over 200 ***wing designs*** [机翼设计].

For eight years the brothers ***studied flying buzzards*** [研究飞翔的秃鹰], tested wing models in the homemade wind tunnel, built engines, and launched gliders, but ***most of them doomed*** [大多数以失败告终].

Finally, on December 17, 1903, Orville Wright ***took off in their primitive airplane*** [驾驶着原始的飞机腾空而起], and flew 120 feet in 12 seconds. They made three more test runs on the same day; in the last one Orville covered 852 feet in 59 seconds.

The Wright brothers had proved that ***gravity could be overcome*** [重力可以被克服], that human beings could fly. Obviously, ***there were still many problems to resolve*** [仍有很多问题需要解决], and the brothers did not rest on their achievements. They made over 200 flights

---

1 代顿，美国俄亥俄州西南部城市。

2 American brothers, inventors, and aviation pioneers who achieved the first powered, sustained, and controlled airplane flight（1903）. Wilbur Wright and his brother Orville Wright also built and flew the first fully practical airplane（1905）.

3 奥托•李林塔尔（Otto Lilienthal，1848–1896），德国航空先驱，以"德国滑翔机之王"闻名于世。传世名言之一是"要想学会飞行，就要做出牺牲（Sacrifices must be made!）"。

拯救我的 SAT 写作
Saving My SAT Essay

in the next two years, and ***pushed up the flying time of their aircraft*** [提高飞机飞行时间] to 5 minutes.

Aircraft had p***layed a significant role in World War I*** [在一战中扮演了重要角色], and industry and the public alike were ***looking forward to*** [期待着] the ***development of passenger aircraft*** [开发民用客机].

The Wright brothers ***saga came to an end*** [传奇画上句号] with Orville's death in 1948, but ***their contribution to science and engineering changed the course of human history*** [他们对科学和工程学的贡献已经改变了人类历史].

Wright Brothers

The desire to fly is an idea handed down to us by our ancestors who, in their grueling travels across trackless lands in prehistoric times, looked enviously on the birds soaring freely through space, at full speed, above all obstacles, on the infinite highway of the air.

If we worked on the assumption that what is accepted as true really is true, then there would be little hope for advance.

If birds can glide for long periods of time, then... why can't I?

We were lucky enough to grow up in an environment where there was always much encouragement to children to pursue intellectual interests; to investigate what ever aroused curiosity.

改写 | Rewrite the Story | in Your Own Words

Chapter 9 挑战与竞技 CHALLENGE AND COMPETITION

杰西·欧文斯

JESSE OWENS[1] （1913-1980）

Not only did Owens win four medals in athletics events in Berlin, ***an individual medal haul*** [个人金牌数的大幅提高] that was to ***stand as a record*** [保持纪录] for many years, but his performance will ***be remembered as*** [被铭记] being particularly ***galling to Hitler*** [激怒希特勒] who ***had intended the games as a showpiece for Nazi Germany*** [本打算把奥运会作为纳粹德国的一场秀] and as ***a propaganda exercise for his philosophy of Aryan supremacy***[2] [一场宣传"雅利安人种至上"理论的宣传].

Jesse Owens was born in Alabama on September 12, 1913, one of 11 children of a ***poor cropper*** [穷苦农民]. Later, when ***pests and diseases struck local cotton crops*** [虫害打击当地的棉花作物], his family was forced to move north to Cleveland, Ohio.

At school he ***became a shoeshine boy in his spare time*** [业余时间做擦鞋匠] and his ambitions might well have ***been circumscribed by*** [仅限] the ***aim of having a shoe shop of his own*** [目的是有家自己的鞋店] when he grew up, if he had not ***attracted the attention*** [吸引注意力] of ***a sports school coach*** [体育学校教练] named Charles Riley, who persuaded him to ***take training seriously*** [认真地对待训练].

This move soon ***bears fruit*** [结出果实] when in 1933 he equaled the world record [平了世界纪录] （9.4 seconds for the 100 yards） at ***an interschool athletics meeting*** [校际体育比赛] in Chicago. Owens ***attended Ohio State University*** [入读俄亥俄州立大学] and ***broke his first world record*** [第一次打破了世界纪录] in 1935 when, while ***representing the university*** [代表大学], he ran the 220 yards low hurdles in 22.9 seconds.

In the following week at the ***college championships*** [大学锦标赛] in ***Ann Arbor*** [安娜堡], ***Michigan*** [密歇根], he ***performed the astonishing feat*** [上演惊人的壮举] that first ***signaled his immense potential to the athletics world*** [向体育界展示了他的巨大潜力] when he ***broke five world records*** [打破了五个世界纪录] and equaled a sixth.

These performances ***assured him a place in the United States Olympic team*** [在美国奥运会代表队赢得一个席位] of 1936 where he won gold medals in the 100 meters, 200 meters, long jump, and the 4×100 meters relay. This success enraged [惹怒] Hitler, who ***snubbed*** [冷落] Owens by ***refusing to shake hands with him*** [拒绝和他握手].

1 American track-and-field athlete, who set a world record in the running broad jump （also called long jump） that stood for 25 years and who won four gold medals at the 1936 Olympic Games in Berlin. His four Olympic victories were a blow to Adolf Hitler's intention to use the Games to demonstrate Aryan superiority.

2 纳粹分子用"雅利安"这个字眼指"高尚的纯种"，认为以德意志人为代表的日耳曼人是雅利安人的典范。

Jesse Owens

We all have dreams. In order to make dreams come into reality, it takes an awful lot of determination, dedication, self-discipline and effort.

For a time, at least, I was the most famous person in the entire world.

One chance is all you need.

改写 | Rewrite the Story | in Your Own Words

挑战与竞技 CHALLENGE AND COMPETITION

Chapter 9

加加林

YURI GAGARIN[1] (1934–1968)

One hundred and eight minutes on April 12, 1961, in the front of the **_Soviet multi-stage rocket_** [苏联多级火箭], Vostok 1[2], turned an unknown 27-year-old Soviet Air Force officer into **_"The Columbus of the Interplanetary Age"_** [星际时代的哥伦布]. **_Manned space travel_** [载人太空旅行] **_escaped the pages of fanciful fiction_** [逃离了科幻小说的书页].

The first space flight was a triumph for the Soviet Union [首次太空旅行是苏联的胜利] and **_a political and diplomatic setback for the US_** [是美国政治和外交的挫败]. But Yuri Gagarin **_was an instant history-maker_** [瞬间书写了历史] whose **_achievement transcended the politics of the time_** [成就超越了当时的政治].

He **_was born in the village outside Moscow_** [生在俄罗斯郊外的村庄]; his father was a **_carpenter_** [木匠], while his mother worked as a **_milkmaid_** [挤奶女工]. His family, like many others, had **_suffered at the hands of the Nazis in World War II_** [在二战时饱受纳粹的折磨].

The story goes that Gagarin **_yelled_** [大喊一声] "**_poyekhali_** [出发]" ("here we go") as his **_rocket blasted off from Earth_** [火箭从地球发射升空]. For many, **_the line drew by the rocket in the air embodied the impatience of all_** [火箭在空中划出的轨迹内含很多人的焦躁] those who had **_for decades dreamed of exploring space_** [数十年来梦想着探索太空].

During the historic 108-minute orbital flight [在这历史性的绕地球飞行的 108 分钟里], Gagarin was able to **_consume food through squeeze tubes_** [从挤压管里吃东西] and **_kept mission control updated on his condition_** [向地面控制中心报告他的最新情况] **_using a high-frequency radio and a telegraph_** [通过高频无线电和电报].

The mission **_came perilously close to disaster_** [几乎成为一场灾难]. During **_re-entry_** [返回阶段], cables linking the **_spacecraft's descent module to the service module failed to separate_** [飞船的推进舱没有与返回舱分离]. **_This caused violent shaking_** [导致巨大的震动] during the re-entry **_through the Earth's atmosphere_** [穿过大气层].

Gagarin **_baled out_** [跳伞] **_before his capsule hit the ground_** [在返回舱着陆之前] and **_parachuted to a safe landing_** [跳伞安全着陆] near the Volga River[3].

---

1 Soviet cosmonaut, the first man to travel into space in 1961.

2 东方一号，前苏联的太空计划，也是人类首次载人太空飞行任务，1961 年 4 月 12 日发射升空，尤里•加加林成为第一个进入外层空间的人，也是第一个进入地球轨道的人。

3 伏尔加河，位于俄罗斯西南部，全长 3,692 公里，世界最长的内流河，流入里海。

Gagarin

I could have gone on flying through space forever.

What beauty. I saw clouds and their light shadows on the distant dear Earth...The water looked like darkish, slightly gleaming spots...When I watched the horizon, I saw the abrupt, contrasting transition from the Earth's light-colored surface to the absolutely black sky. I enjoyed the rich color spectrum of the earth. It is surrounded by a light blue aureole that gradually darkens, becoming turquoise, dark blue, violet, and finally coal black.

When I orbited the Earth in a spaceship, I saw for the first time how beautiful our planet is. Mankind, let us preserve and increase this beauty, and not destroy it.

改写 | Rewrite the Story | in Your Own Words

挑战与竞技 CHALLENGE AND COMPETITION

Chapter 9

阿姆斯特朗

NEIL ARMSTRONG[1] （1930–）

For thousands of years [几千年来], man had ***looked to the heavens*** [仰望苍穹] and ***dreamed of walking on the moon*** [梦想着在月球上行走]. In 1969, as part of the Apollo 11[2] mission, Neil Armstrong became the very first to ***accomplish that dream*** [实现这个梦想], followed only minutes later by Buzz Aldrin[3]. Their accomplishment ***placed the United States ahead of the Soviets*** [让美国领先苏联] in the Space Race[4] and gave people around the world the hope of future space exploration [未来太空探索的希望].

Armstrong ***will always be remembered for*** [被铭记] the words he spoke ***as his boot touched the lunar surface*** [当他的靴子踏上月球表面] in July of 1969: "***That's one small step for man, one giant leap for mankind*** [我的一小步，人类一大步]."

The two astronauts ***set up an American flag*** [竖起美国国旗], ***collected rock samples*** [采集岩石样本], and ***set up several scientific experiments and instruments on the lunar surface*** [在月球表面架设一些实验仪器]. They stayed out for about two and a half hours. The next day, they left the Moon and rejoined Collins[5] in the ***command module*** [指令舱]. The three astronauts returned home on July 24 and ***were hailed as heroes*** [被称赞为英雄].

拯救我的 SAT 写作

Saving My SAT Essay

Armstrong

This is one small step for a man, one giant leap for mankind.

The Eagle has landed.

改写 | Rewrite the Story | in Your Own Words

---

1 U.S. astronaut, the first person to set foot on the Moon.

2 阿波罗 11 号，美国国家航空航天局（National Aeronautics and Space Administration，简称 NASA）的阿波罗计划（Project Apollo）中的第五次载人任务，是人类第一次登月任务。

3 巴兹•奥尔德林（Buzz Aldrin，1930–），阿波罗 11 号登月舱驾驶员。

4 太空竞赛（1957–1975），美国和苏联在开发人造卫星、载人航天和人类登月等空间探索领域的竞争。

5 迈克尔•科林斯（Michael Collins），指令舱驾驶员。

Chapter 10

附录

APPENDIX

SAVING
MY SAT
ESSAY

本 章 目 录

人名字母排序

ABRAHAM LINCOLN 林肯	*1809–1865*	*The 16th US president*
ADOLF HITLER 希特勒	*1889–1945*	*Dictator of Germany*
ALBERT EINSTEIN 爱因斯坦	*1879–1955*	*The most famous scientist of the 20th century*
ALEXANDER FLEMING 弗莱明	*1881–1955*	*Discoverer of penicillin*
ALEXANDER GRAHAM BELL 贝尔	*1847–1922*	*Inventor of the modern telephone*
ALEXANDER THE GREAT 亚历山大大帝	*356–323 BC*	*Greatest military commander*
ALFRED BERNHARD NOBEL 诺贝尔	*1833–1896*	*Founded the Nobel Prizes*
ANDREW CARNEGIE 卡内基	*1835–1919*	*The King of Steel*
ANNE FRANK 安妮	*1929–1945*	*A courageous young girl*
ARCHIMEDES 阿基米德	*287–212 BC*	*Father experimental science*
ARISTOTLE 亚里士多德	*384–322 BC*	*One of three great ancient Greek philosophers*
BENJAMIN FRANKLIN 本杰明·富兰克林	*1706–1790*	*A leader in the American struggle for independence*
BILL GATES 比尔·盖茨	*1955–*	*Founder of Microsoft*
CHARLES DARWIN 达尔文	*1809–1882*	*Laid the foundations of the theory of evolution*
CHARLES DICKENS 狄更斯	*1812–1870*	*Greatest novelist of the Victorian period*
CHARLIE CHAPLIN 卓别林	*1889–1977*	*Comic genius of the cinema screen*
CHRISTOPHER COLUMBUS 哥伦布	*1451–1506*	*The man who discovered America*
COCO CHANEL 香奈尔	*1883–1971*	*A pioneering French fashion designer*
CONFUCIUS 孔子	*551–479 BC*	*A highly influential thinker and educator*
EDWARD JENNER 爱德华·詹纳	*1749–1823*	*Father of immunology*
ELVIS PRESLEY 猫王	*1935–1977*	*The king of rock of roll music*
EMPRESS WU 武则天	*624–705*	*The Only Empress in the history of ancient China*
ERNEST HEMINGWAY 海明威	*1899–1961*	*An outstanding creative writer*
FLORENCE NIGHTINGALE 南丁格尔	*1820–1910*	*The lady with the lamp*
FRANCIS BACON 培根	*1561–1626*	*A pioneer of modern scientific thought*
FRANCIS CRICK 克里克	*1916–2004*	*Biologist unlocked the 'secret of life'*
FRANKLIN D. ROOSEVELT 罗斯福	*1882–1945*	*Four times President of US*
FRANZ JOSEPH HAYDN 海顿	*1732–1809*	*Father of the Symphony*
FRIEDRICH NIETZSCHE 尼采	*1844–1900*	*Famous for the quote "God is dead"*
GALILEO GALILEI 伽利略	*1564–1642*	*Father of modern science*
GENGHIS KHAN 成吉思汗	*1162?–1227*	*Famous conqueror*
GEORGE BERNARD SHAW 萧伯纳	*1856–1950*	*Famous dramatist*

GEORGE WASHINGTON 华盛顿 *1732–1799*   *The first President of US*

GIORDANO BRUNO 布鲁诺 *1548–1600*   *A precursor of modern civilization*

GREGOR MENDEL 孟德尔 *1822–1884*   *Father of Genetics*

HELEN KELLER 海伦•凯勒 *1880–1968*   *An inspiration for people with disabilities*

HENRY FORD 福特 *1863–1947*   *Changed the face of automobile manufacture*

HIPPOCRATES 希波克拉底 *460–377 BC*   *Father of modern medicine*

JAMES WATT 瓦特 *1736–1819*   *Renowned for his improvements in steam engine*

JESSE OWENS 杰西•欧文斯 *1913–1980*   *Memorable performance at the Berlin Olympics*

JOAN OF ARC 圣女贞德 *1412–1431*   *A national heroine*

JOHANN SEBASTIAN BACH 巴赫 *1685–1750*   *Greatest Musician in the Baroque era*

JOHN DAVISON ROCKEFELLER 洛克菲勒 *1839–1937*   *Founder of the Standard Oil*

JOHN F. KENNEDY 肯尼迪 *1917–1963*   *The 35th president of the United States*

JOHN LENNON 列侬 *1940–1980*   *Dominant role in a pop music revolution*

JULIUS CAESAR 恺撒大帝 *100–44 BC*   *Imperator*

LEO TOLSTOY 列夫•托尔斯泰 *1828–1910*   *One of the world's greatest novelists*

LEONARDO DA VINCI 达•芬奇 *1452–1519*   *A true Renaissance man*

LOUIS ARMSTRONG 路易斯•阿姆斯特朗 *1901–1971*   *Mr. Jazz*

LOUIS PASTEUR 巴斯德 *1822–1895*   *Father of microbiology*

LUDWIG VAN BEETHOVEN 贝多芬 *1770–1827*   *Greatest composer*

MAHATMA GANDHI 甘地 *1869–1948*   *The leader of the Indian nationalist movement*

MARIE CURIE 居里夫人 *1867–1934*   *The discoverer of radium*

MARILYN MONROE 玛丽莲•梦露 *1926–1962*   *Hollywood Legend*

MARTIN LUTHER KING 马丁•路德•金 *1929–1968*   *Civil Rights Movement Leader*

MARTIN LUTHER 马丁•路德 *1483–1546*   *Initiator of Protestant Reformation*

MICHAEL JACKSON 迈克尔•杰克逊 *1958–2009*   *King of Pop*

MICHELANGELO 米开朗基罗 *1475–1564*   *One of the great artists of the Renaissance*

MOTHER TERESA 德雷莎修女 *1910–1997*   *A living saint*

NAPOLEON BONAPARTE 拿破仑 *1769–1821*   *A brilliant military commander*

NEIL ARMSTRONG 阿姆斯特朗 *1930–*   *The first man to walk on the Moon*

NELSON MANDELA 曼德拉 *1918–*   *First President of new South Africa*

NICCOLÒ MACHIAVELLI 马基雅维利 *1469–1527*   *Author of The Prince*

NICOLAUS COPERNICUS 哥白尼 *1473–1543*   *Proposed a sun-centered model*

NIELS BOHR 波尔 *1885–1962*   *Known for investigating atomic structure*

NORMAN BETHUNE 白求恩 *1890–1939*   *An international soldier*

OPRAH WINFREY 奥普拉 *1954–*   *Great media leader*

PLATO 柏拉图 *428?–347 BC*   *One of the most important Western philosophers*

PYOTR IIYICH TCHAIKOVSKY 柴可夫斯基	*1840–1893*	*A significant composer of his time*
RAPHAEL 拉斐尔	*1483–1520*	*Greatest High Renaissance painter*
RAYMOND ALBERT KROC 雷蒙德•克罗克	*1902–1984*	*Founder of McDonald's Corporation*
RENÉ DESCARTES 笛卡儿	*1596–1650*	*Father of modern philosophy*
RICHARD NIXON 尼克松	*1913–1994*	*The 37th US President*
ROBERT E. PEARY 罗伯特•皮尔里	*1856–1920*	*Leading the first expedition to reach the North Pole*
RONALD REAGAN 里根	*1911–2004*	*President who ended the Cold War*
SAM WALTON 山姆•沃尔顿	*1918–1992*	*Founder of Wal-Mart*
SIR ISAAC NEWTON 牛顿	*1642–1727*	*The greatest scientist of his era*
SIR WINSTON CHURCHILL 丘吉尔	*1874–1965*	*World leader in war and peace*
SOCRATES 苏格拉底	*469–399 BC*	*Lay the foundation for Western philosophy*
STEPHEN HAWKING 霍金	*1942–*	*Greatest physicist on a wheel chair*
STEVE JOBS 乔布斯	*1955–2011*	*The spirit of Apple*
THOMAS EDISON 爱迪生	*1847–1931*	*The Wizard of Menlo Park*
VASCO DA GAMA 达•伽马	*1460–1524*	*Opened a sea-based trade route to India*
VINCENT VAN GOGH 凡•高	*1853–1890*	*Well-known post-Impressionist painter*
VOLTAIRE 伏尔泰	*1694–1778*	*Planted the seed of French Revolution*
WALT DISNEY 迪士尼	*1901–1966*	*Creator of Disney Empire*
WARREN BUFFETT 巴菲特	*1930–*	*Successful investor*
WILLIAM HARVEY 哈维	*1578–1657*	*Discoverer of blood circulation*
WILLIAM SHAKESPEARE 莎士比亚	*1564–1616*	*Greatest playwright of all time*
WOLFGANG AMADEUS MOZART 莫扎特	*1756–1791*	*A classical music genius*
WRIGHT BROTHERS 莱特兄弟	*1871–1948,* *1867–1912*	*A flying legend*
YURI GAGARIN 加加林	*1934–1968*	*First man to fly in space*

Chapter 10 附录 APPENDIX

人名时间排序
CHRONOLOGICAL NAME LIST

CONFUCIUS 孔子 *551–479 BC*   *A highly influential thinker and educator*

SOCRATES 苏格拉底 *469–399 BC*   *Lay the foundation for Western philosophy*

HIPPOCRATES 希波克拉底 *460–377 BC*   *Father of modern medicine*

PLATO 柏拉图 *428?–347 BC*   *One of the most important Western philosophers*

ARISTOTLE 亚里士多德 *384–322 BC*   *One of three great ancient Greek philosophers*

ALEXANDER THE GREAT 亚历山大大帝 *356–323 BC*   *Greatest military commander*

ARCHIMEDES 阿基米德 *287–212 BC*   *Father experimental science*

JULIUS CAESAR 恺撒大帝 *100–44 BC*   *Imperator*

EMPRESS WU 武则天 *624–705*   *The Only Empress in the history of ancient China*

GENGHIS KHAN 成吉思汗 *1162?–1227*   *Famous conqueror*

JOAN OF ARC 圣女贞德 *1412–1431*   *A national heroine*

CHRISTOPHER COLUMBUS 哥伦布 *1451–1506*   *The man who discovered America*

LEONARDO DA VINCI 达•芬奇 *1452–1519*   *A true Renaissance man*

VASCO DA GAMA 达•伽马 *1460–1524*   *Opened a sea-based trade route to India*

NICCOLÒ MACHIAVELLI 马基雅维利 *1469–1527*   *Author of The Prince*

NICOLAUS COPERNICUS 哥白尼 *1473–1543*   *Proposed a sun-centered model*

MICHELANGELO 米开朗基罗 *1475–1564*   *One of the great artists of the Renaissance*

RAPHAEL 拉斐尔 *1483–1520*   *Greatest High Renaissance painter*

MARTIN LUTHER 马丁•路德 *1483–1546*   *Initiator of Protestant Reformation*

GIORDANO BRUNO 布鲁诺 *1548–1600*   *A precursor of modern civilization*

FRANCIS BACON 培根 *1561–1626*   *A pioneer of modern scientific thought*

WILLIAM SHAKESPEARE 莎士比亚 *1564–1616*   *Greatest playwright of all time*

GALILEO GALILEI 伽利略 *1564–1642*   *Father of modern science*

WILLIAM HARVEY 哈维 *1578–1657*   *Discoverer of blood circulation*

RENÉ DESCARTES 笛卡儿 *1596–1650*   *Father of modern philosophy*

SIR ISAAC NEWTON 牛顿 *1642–1727*   *The greatest scientist of his era*

JOHANN SEBASTIAN BACH 巴赫 *1685–1750*   *Greatest Musician in the Baroque era*

VOLTAIRE 伏尔泰 *1694–1778*   *Planted the seed of French Revolution*

BENJAMIN FRANKLIN 本杰明•富兰克林 *1706–1790*   *A leader in the American struggle for independence*

GEORGE WASHINGTON 华盛顿 *1732–1799*   *The first President of US*

FRANZ JOSEPH HAYDN 海顿 *1732–1809*   *Father of the Symphony*

JAMES WATT 瓦特 *1736–1819*   *Renowned for his improvements in steam engine*

EDWARD JENNER 爱德华•詹纳	*1749–1823*	*Father of immunology*
WOLFGANG AMADEUS MOZART 莫扎特	*1756–1791*	*A classical music genius*
NAPOLEON BONAPARTE 拿破仑	*1769–1821*	*A brilliant military commander*
LUDWIG VAN BEETHOVEN 贝多芬	*1770–1827*	*Greatest composer*
ABRAHAM LINCOLN 林肯	*1809–1865*	*The 16th US president*
CHARLES DARWIN 达尔文	*1809–1882*	*Laid the foundations of the theory of evolution*
CHARLES DICKENS 狄更斯	*1812–1870*	*Greatest novelist of the Victorian period*
FLORENCE NIGHTINGALE 南丁格尔	*1820–1910*	*The lady with the lamp*
GREGOR MENDEL 孟德尔	*1822–1884*	*Father of Genetics*
LOUIS PASTEUR 巴斯德	*1822–1895*	*Father of microbiology*
LEO TOLSTOY 列夫•托尔斯泰	*1828–1910*	*One of the world's greatest novelists*
ALFRED BERNHARD NOBEL 诺贝尔	*1833–1896*	*Founded the Nobel Prizes*
ANDREW CARNEGIE 卡内基	*1835–1919*	*The King of Steel*
JOHN DAVISON ROCKEFELLER 洛克菲勒	*1839–1937*	*Founder of the Standard Oil*
PYOTR IIYICH TCHAIKOVSKY 柴可夫斯基	*1840–1893*	*A significant composer of his time*
FRIEDRICH NIETZSCHE 尼采	*1844–1900*	*Famous for the quote "God is dead"*
ALEXANDER GRAHAM BELL 贝尔	*1847–1922*	*Inventor of the modern telephone*
THOMAS EDISON 爱迪生	*1847–1931*	*The Wizard of Menlo Park*
VINCENT VAN GOGH 梵高	*1853–1890*	*Well-known post-Impressionist painter*
ROBERT E. PEARY 罗伯特•皮尔里	*1856–1920*	*Leading the first expedition to reach the North Pole*
GEORGE BERNARD SHAW 萧伯纳	*1856–1950*	*Famous dramatist*
HENRY FORD 福特	*1863–1947*	*Changed the face of automobile manufacture*
MARIE CURIE 居里夫人	*1867–1934*	*The discoverer of radium*
MAHATMA GANDHI 甘地	*1869–1948*	*The leader of the Indian nationalist movement*
Wright Brothers 莱特兄弟	*1871–1948* *1867–1912*	*A flying legend*
SIR WINSTON CHURCHILL 丘吉尔	*1874–1965*	*World leader in war and peace*
ALBERT EINSTEIN 爱因斯坦	*1879–1955*	*The most famous scientist of the 20th century*
HELEN KELLER 海伦•凯勒	*1880–1968*	*An inspiration for people with disabilities*
ALEXANDER FLEMING 弗莱明	*1881–1955*	*Discoverer of penicillin*
FRANKLIN D. ROOSEVELT 罗斯福	*1882–1945*	*Four times President of US*
COCO CHANEL 香奈尔	*1883–1971*	*A pioneering French fashion designer*
JESSE OWENS 杰西•欧文斯	*1913–1980*	*Memorable performance at the Berlin Olympics*
YURI GAGARIN 加加林	*1934–1968*	*First man to fly in space*
NIELS BOHR 波尔	*1885–1962*	*Known for investigating atomic structure*
ADOLF HITLER 希特勒	*1889–1945*	*Dictator of Germany*

CHARLIE CHAPLIN 卓别林 *1889–1977*   *Comic genius of the cinema screen*

NORMAN BETHUNE 白求恩 *1890–1939*   *An international soldier*

LOUIS ARMSTRONG 路易斯•阿姆斯特朗 *1901–1971*   *Mr. Jazz*

ERNEST HEMINGWAY 海明威 *1899–1961*   *An outstanding creative writer*

WALT DISNEY 迪士尼 *1901–1966*   *Creator of Disney Empire*

RAYMOND ALBERT KROC 雷蒙德•克罗克 *1902–1984*   *Founder of McDonald's Corporation*

MOTHER TERESA 德雷莎修女 *1910–1997*   *A living saint*

RONALD REAGAN 里根 *1911–2004*   *President who ended the Cold War*

RICHARD NIXON 尼克松 *1913–1994*   *The 37th US President*

FRANCIS CRICK 克里克 *1916–2004*   *Biologist unlocked the 'secret of life'*

JOHN F. KENNEDY 肯尼迪 *1917–1963*   *The 35th president of the United States*

NELSON MANDELA 曼德拉 *1918–*   *First President of new South Africa*

SAM WALTON 山姆•沃尔顿 *1918–1992*   *Founder of Wal-Mart*

MARILYN MONROE 玛丽莲•梦露 *1926–1962*   *Hollywood Legend*

ANNE FRANK 安妮 *1929–1945*   *A courageous young girl*

MARTIN LUTHER KING 马丁•路德•金 *1929–1968*   *Civil Rights Movement Leader*

NEIL ARMSTRONG 阿姆斯特朗 *1930–*   *The first man to walk on the Moon*

WARREN BUFFETT 巴菲特 *1930–*   *Successful investor*

ELVIS PRESLEY 猫王 *1935–1977*   *The king of rock of roll music*

JOHN LENNON 列侬 *1940–1980*   *Dominant role in a pop music revolution*

STEPHEN HAWKING 霍金 *1942–*   *Greatest physicist on a wheel chair*

OPRAH WINFREY 奥普拉 *1954–*   *Great media leader*

BILL GATES 比尔•盖茨 *1955–*   *Founder of Microsoft*

STEVE JOBS 乔布斯 *1955–2011*   *The spirit of Apple*

MICHAEL JACKSON 迈克尔•杰克逊 *1958–2009*   *King of Pop*

重要历史事件表

INFLUENTIAL HISTORICAL EVENTS

BC−1 AD

4400 BC【驯化野马】Domestication of horses provided an important new power of transportation and a new means of conducting warfare

3250 BC【纸草发明】Paper made from papyrus reed was first produced in Egypt.

3200 BC【象形文字】The Egyptians developed a system of writing known as Hieroglyphics.

3000 BC【埃及王朝】King Menes founded the first dynasty of Egypt.

2900 BC【胡夫金字塔】The Great Pyramid of Cheops at Giza was built.

2900 BC【印度文明】Indian Civilization began in the Indus Valley.

2000 BC【六十进制】The Babylonians developed a mathematical system based on units of 60.

1772 BC【《汉谟拉比法典》】 **The Code of Hammurabi** was enacted.

1766 BC【商朝】The Shang dynasty was established.

1400 BC【铁器】The production of iron was invented in Armenia.

800 BC《伊利亚特》和《奥德赛》】Homeric Hymns, *Iliad* and *Odyssey*, were written by Homer.

753 BC【罗马】Rome was founded.

638 BC【梭伦改革】Solon's Reform, the Athenian economic system so poor inhabitants of Attica no longer had to go into bondage over debt, started.

521 BC【大流士一世】Cyrus was succeeded by Darius I.

509 BC【罗马共和国】The Roman Republic was founded.

499 BC【大运河】The Chinese began work on the Grand Canal.

490 BC【马拉松战役】The complete Greek victory at the Battle of Marathon ended the immediate Persian threat.

483 BC【释迦牟尼】Gautama Buddha, the founder of Buddhism, died.

479 BC【孔子】Confucius, the founder of Confucianism, died.

460 BC【希波克拉底】Hippocrates, the father of Western medicine, was born.

447 BC【帕提农神庙】The Parthenon, a temple on the Athenian Acropolis, Greece, began its construction.

431 BC【伯罗奔尼撒战争】Peloponnesian War was fought between Athens and Sparta.

399 BC【苏格拉底】Socrates was sentenced to death by drinking a mixture containing poison hemlock.

385 BC【学院】Academy was founded by Plato.

384 BC【亚里士多德】Aristotle was born.

370 BC【公路】The Romans built their first road.

326 BC【亚历山大大帝】Alexander the Great created one of the largest empires of the ancient world.

300 BC【《几何原本》】*Elements*, a mathematical and geometric treaties, was written by the Greek mathematician Euclid in Alexandria.

280 BC【亚历山大灯塔】The Lighthouse of Alexandria was built.

240 BC【阿基米德】Archimedes, the Greek mathematician, was the first to determine the value of pi.

221 BC 【始皇帝】 Qin Shihuang became the first emperor of a unified China in 221 BC.

221 BC 【长城】 The Great Wall of China was begun to build.

206 BC 【汉代】 Han dynasty, a golden age in Chinese history, was established.

44 BC 【恺撒】 Caesar was assassinated, with his last words "Et Tu, Brutus（You too, Brutus）?"

1 AD-1000

1 AD 【耶稣】 Jesus Christ was born.

14 【奥古斯都】 Augustus, the first emperor of the Roman Empire, died on August.

64 【罗马城】 The city of Rome was nearly destroyed in a catastrophic fire.

72 【罗马大剧场】 The construction of Colosseum started.

105 【蔡伦造纸术】 Cai Lun invented the composition for paper along with the papermaking process.

132 【地动仪】 Zhang Heng developed the first seismograph.

170 【《沉思录》】 Marcus Aurelius Started to write *Meditations*.

303 【迫害基督徒】 Diocletian began a general persecution of Christians.

330 【君士坦丁大帝】 Constantine the Great established his new capital at Byzantium.

363 【罗马分裂】 Emperor Julian the Apostate was killed in the Battle of Samarra. After his death, The Roman Empire was divided into the Eastern Roman Empire and Western Roman Empire.

410 【洗劫罗马】 Rome was sacked by Visigoths.

476 【西罗马】 Western Roman Empire ended.

529 【《查士丁尼法典》】 *Code of Justinian* was issued.

537 【圣索菲亚大教堂】 The Hagia Sophia Cathedral, which represented the culmination of Byzantine architecture, in Constantinople was completed

581 【隋朝】 Sui Dynasty reunited China.

604 【《十七条宪法》】 Shotoku issued a seventeen-article. "Constitution", which called for a strong central government in Japan.

618 【唐朝】 Tang Dynasty was Founded.

630 【穆罕穆德】 Mecca was conquered by Muhanm and his followers.

642 【阿拉伯占领埃及】 Arabs conquered Egypt.

700 【火药】 The Chinese invented gun power, a mixture of saltpeter, sulpher, and carbon.

705 【武后】 Empress Wu became the first woman to rule China.

711 【查理曼大帝】 Charlemagne became the Frankish ruler in the east.

960 【宋朝】 Song Dynasty was founded. It was period known for progressive social policies, as well as a productive period for art, poetry and philosophy.

1000-1500

1066 【伦敦塔】 William the Conqueror began building the Tower of London.

1088 【博罗尼亚大学】 University of Bologna was founded in Italy.

1096 【十字远征军】 The First Cruse began with a call by Alexius I.

1140 【吴哥窟】 Angkor Wat, a symbol of Cambodia, began its construction.

1163 【巴黎圣母院】 Work began on Notre Dame.

1168 【牛津】 The school of Oxford was founded.

1173【比萨斜塔始建】The Leaning Tower of Pisa began its construction.

1184【罗浮宫】The streets in front of the Louvre were paved.

1206【铁木真】Temujin was proclaimed Genghis Khan.

1215【《大宪章》】A group of determined barons forced King John of England to sign the *Magna Carta*.

1239【采煤许可】A royal charter was issued in 1239 for the development of the coal fields in New Castle. This began the rapid development of coal as a source of energy.

1250【复活节岛石像】Moai, monolithic human figures carved from rock on the Chilean Polynesian island of Easter Island, were carved.

1271【马可波罗】Marco Polo, accompanied by his father, set off for China.

1298【火炮】The Chinese developed the first prototype canon. However, it was the Europeans who soon developed pistols and other guns that gave them a decisive military vantage.

1321【《神曲》】*Divine Comedy*, an epic poem written by Dante Alighieri, was finished.

1326【土耳其帝国】The Ottoman Empire was established.

1337【英法百年战争】The Hundred Years War began.

1347【黑死病】The Black Death, bubonic plague, started. Jews were accused of causing the plague. Over 60 Jewish communities were entirely wiped out in Germany alone.

1420【明朝】The Second Ming Emperor moved the capital of China from Nanking to Peking.

1429【圣女贞德】Joan of Arc, a peasant girl, led a small army and freed Orleans.

1450【古藤堡】Johannes Guttenberg invented the printing press.

1492【哥伦布】Columbus set sails for New World and discovered America.

1498【达·芬奇】Leonardo Da Vinci painted the *Last Supper*.

1498【达伽马】Vasco De Gama reached India.

1500-1800

1504【《大卫》】*David*, a masterpiece of Renaissance sculpture, was completed by Michelangelo.

1506【《蒙娜丽莎》】*Mona Lisa* was completed by Leonardo da Vinci.

1508【米开朗基罗】Michelangelo began painting the Ceiling of the Sistine Chapel.

1517【宗教改革】The Protestant Reformation was launched when Martin Luther nailed his criticism of the. Catholic Church on the door of the Wittenberg Cathedral.

1519【麦哲伦】Portuguese navigator Magellan set off around the world.

1543【哥白尼】Nicolaus Copernicus claimed Earth circles Sun.

1600【东印度公司】The English East India Company was granted a Royal Charter.

1602【《哈姆雷特》】*Hamlet* was completed by William Shakespeare.

1609【开普勒】Kepler published his laws of planetary motion.

1611【《钦定圣经》】*King James Bible* was completed.

1616【莎士比亚】William Shakespeare died.

1628【血液循环】William Harvey described completely and in detail the blood circulation.

1628【《权利典章》】The English Parliament passed the *Petition of Rights*.

1631【泰姬陵】The Taj Mahal, built by Mughal emperor Shah Jahan in memory of his third wife, Mumtaz Mahal. started its construction.

1637【《方法论》】Descartes published "*Discours De la Methode*".

1638【伽利略】Galileo explained the principles of falling bodies.

1661【欧洲使用纸币】The first European banknotes were issued by Stockholm Banco, a predecessor of the Bank of Sweden.

1667【输血】The first fully documented human blood transfusion.

1673【显微镜】Antonie van Leeuwenhoek's earliest observations were published.

1687【牛顿】Newton founded the study of mechanics（Newton's three laws of motion and the principal of universal gravitation）.

1764【珍妮纺纱机】The spinning jenny was invented by James Hargreaves.

1786【《费加罗的婚礼》】*The Marriage of Figaro* was completed by Wolfgang Amadeus Mozart.

1776【蒸汽机】James Watt developed a steam engine.

1770【澳大利亚】James Cook claimed Australia for Britain.

1776【《独立宣言》】The United States *Declaration of Independence* was issued.

1789【华盛顿】George Washington was elected as the first president of US.

1789【法国大革命】French Revolution started.

1792【纽交所前身】Traders formalized their association with the Buttonwood Agreement which was the origin of the New York Stock Exchange.

1793【罗浮宫博物馆】The Louvre Museum，one of the world's largest museums, the most visited art museum in the world and a historic monument，opened to public.

1796【天花疫苗】Edward Jenner demonstrated the effectiveness of cowpox to protect humans from smallpox.

1800–1900

1804 【《拿破仑法典》】*Napoleonic Code* was established under Napoleon I.

1808【《命运交响曲》】*Symphony No. 5* was completed by Ludwig van Beethoven.

1813【《傲慢与偏见》】*Pride and Prejudice*, authored by Jane Austen, was first published.

1815【滑铁卢战役】Napoleon's forces were defeated at the Battle of Waterloo.

1819【蒸汽机轮船】Savannah, the first steam-powered ship crossed the Pacific.

1821【电磁感应】Michael Faraday discovered electromagnetic induction.

1824【《欢乐颂》】Beethoven completed *Symphony No. 9: Ode To Joy.*

1830【《自由引导人民》】*Liberty Leading the People* was completed by Eugène Delacroix.

1831【《巴黎圣母院》】*The Hunchback of Notre-Dame* by Victor Hugo was published.

1836【凯旋门】The Arc de Triomphe, which honors those who fought and died for France in the French Revolutionary and the Napoleonic Wars, was completed.

1839【鸦片战争】The Opium War started. The British won and demanded an opening of five Chinese cities to trade.

1842【《婚礼进行曲》】Mendelssohn completed *Midsummer Night's Dream: Wedding March.*

1844【电报】The first inter-city telegraph was demonstrated by Samuel Morse.

1848【《共产党宣言》】*The Communist Manifesto* was published.

1852【《汤姆叔叔的小屋》】*Uncle Tom's Cabin* was published， which helped lay the groundwork for the Civil War.

1855【维多利亚瀑布】David Livingstone discovered the Victorian falls.

1859【《物种起源》】Darwin published *Origins of Species*.

1859【油井】First oil well started.

1860【伦敦地铁】Work on London's underground railroad was begun.

1861【美国内战】The American Civil War was started.

1863【《解放奴隶宣言》】*The Emancipation Proclamation* was issued by Abraham Lincoln

1865【林肯遇刺】Abraham Lincoln was assassinated.

1866【《蓝色多瑙河》】Strauss completed the *Blue Danube*.

1867【混凝土】Reinforced concrete was invented by Joseph Monier who received a patent in 1867.

1868【明治维新】Meiji Restoration started.

1869【苏伊士运河】The Suez Canal opened to traffic.

1869【《战争与和平》】*War and Peace* by the Russian author Leo Tolstoy, first published.

1869【《匈牙利舞曲第五号》】Brahms completed the *Hungarian Dance No. 5*.

1869【元素周期表】Mendeleev's periodic table was published.

1871【德国统一】Germany was politically and administratively integrated.

1872【《印象·日出》】*Impression, Sunrise* was completed by Claude Monet.

1876【电话】Alexander Graham Bell successfully tested the first telephone.

1877【巴斯德】Louis Pasteur proposed the Germ

Theory of disease.

1879【灯泡】Thomas Edison overcame the obstacle to finding a light bulb that would burn long enough to become commercially viable. The invention of the light bulb began the electrical revolution that soon swept the country and the world.

1880【《1812序曲》】Tchaikovsky completed the *1812 Overture*.

1884【华盛顿纪念碑落成】Washington Monument was completed. It was built to commemorate the first U.S. president, General George Washington.

1886【自由女神】The Statue of Liberty, an icon of freedom, was dedicated.

1887【自动步枪】The world's first automatic rifle was patented.

1888【汽车】Bertha Benz, the wife of Karl Benz, undertook the first road trip by car.

1888【《向日葵》】*Sunflowers* was completed by Vincent van Gogh.

1890【梵高自杀】Vincent Van Gogh committed suicide.

1890【埃菲尔铁塔】The Eiffel Tower was completed.

1893【《自新大陆》】*The Symphony No. 9 in E Minor "From the New World"* was composed by Antonín Dvořák.

1895【X射线】Wilhelm Röntgen discovered X-rays.

1897【无线电报】Marconi sent the first ever wireless communication over open sea.

1900–1950

1900【量子力学】Quantum Theory was published.

1903【太平洋海底电缆】First message was sent over Pacific cable.

1903【飞行】Wright Brothers started man's first flight in a heavier-than-air vehicle.

1904【纽约地铁】The first section of the New York Subway system was opened.

1905【相对论】Theory of Relativity was published.

1906【妇女选举权】Finland became the first country in Europe to give its woman the right to vote. Within a year there were women members of the Finnish Parliament.

1908【飞跃英吉利海峡】Louis Bleriot became the first person to fly across the English Channel.

1911【辛亥革命】Chinese Revolution started and the Republic of China was established.

1912【泰坦尼克号】Titanic sank in the North Atlantic Ocean.

1913【福特】The Ford Motor Company began the first moving assembly line in the world.

1914【德国对法国宣战】Germany declared war against France.

1916【《童工法》】*The Child Labor Law*, the first child labor law, was passed.

1917【俄国十月革命】Russian Revolution started.

1918【流行性感冒】Flu pandemic spread across the world

1919【《凡尔赛条约》】*The Treaty of Versailles* was signed thereby officially ending World War I.

1920【印度独立运动】Gandhi became the leer of Indian Independence Movement.

1922【墨索里尼】Mussolini came into power.

1927【电视机】Television was invented by Philo Farnsworth.

1930【大萧条】The Great Depression started.

1931【帝国大厦】The Empire State building in New York, the largest building in the world, opened for the public.

1934【长征】Mao set off on Long March.

1936【图灵计算机】A Turing machine was described by Alan Turing.

1937【金门大桥】Golden Gate Bridge was completed.

1941【青霉素】Penicillin was used to treat infections.

1941【偷袭珍珠港】Imperial Japanese Navy attacked the United States naval base at Pearl Harbor.

1942【斯大林格勒战役】The Battle of Stalingrad, a major and decisive battle of World War II, started.

1944【诺曼底登陆】The Normandy landings.

1945【广岛长崎】Atomic bombings of Hiroshima and Nagasaki.

1945【联合国】The United Nations was founded.

1946【电子计算机】The first all-electronic computer, the ENIAC（Electronic Numerical Integrator And Computer）, was designed by John William Mauchly.

1946【原子弹】The United States began a series of atomic bomb tests at Bikini Islands in the Pacific.

1948【以色列】The State of Israel was established.

1949【新中国】The People's Republic of China was officially proclaimed, with Peking as its capital.

1950–Now

1951【彩色电机节目】CBS（Columbia Broadcasting System）introduced the first color television broadcast.

1952【小儿麻痹症】A vaccine that prevented polio was developed by Jonas Salk.

1952【伦敦烟雾事件】Great Smog, a severe air pollution event, affected London.

1954 【波音公司】 Boeing unveiled the "707."

1954 【肾脏移植】 A team from Harvard Medical School successfully completed the first kidney transplant operation.

1961 【太空旅行】 Gagarin became both the first human to travel into space, and the first to orbit the earth.

1962 【古巴导弹危机】 The Cuban Missile Crisis.

1963 【麻疹疫苗】 A vaccine against measles was proved.

1963 【肯尼迪遇刺】 John F. Kennedy was assassinated.

1967 【切•格瓦拉】 Che Guevera was killed in Bolivia.

1968 【百米突破】 Jim Hines was the first man to break the 10-second barrier in the 100 m.

1969 【登月】 Apollo 11, with Neil Armstrong, Michael Collins and Edwin Aldrin, Jr., landed on Moon.

1972 【奥运会恐怖】 Arab terrorists murdered 11 athletes at the Olympic Games.

1972 【尼克松访华】 President Nixon arrived in Peking for a seven-day stay.

1973 【悉尼歌剧院】 Sydney Opera House, one of the great iconic buildings of the 20th century, an image of great beauty and a symbol for a continent, opened.

1978 【天花】 The smallpox disease was completely eradicated from the Earth, thanks to a worldwide prevention program, combined with wide distribution of a vaccine.

1978 【试管婴儿】 Louise Joy Brown, world's first test tube baby, was born.

1984 【艾滋病大爆发】 AIDS broke out.

1986 【挑战者号】 The Space Shuttle Challenger disaster.

1989 【柏林墙】 Tearing down of Berlin Wall.

1990 【哈勃望远镜】 The space shuttle Discovery launched the Hubble Telescope.

1990 【海湾战争】 Gulf War started.

1990 【万维网】 World Wide Web was proposed.

1991 【苏联解体】 USSR came to a formal end.

1996 【克隆羊】 The cloning of Dolly.

1997 【登陆火星】 The US spacecraft Pathfinder landed on Mars.

1998 【欧盟】 The Eurozone came into existence.

1999 【伦敦眼开幕】 The London Eye opened to public.

2000 【同性婚姻】 Queen Beatrix of the Netherlands signs into law the first same-sex marriage bill in the world.

2001 【9•11】 Four groups of terrorists from al-Qaeda, hijacked four aircraft and attacked World Trade Center and Pentagon.

参考文献
REFERENCES

Curley, R. 2010. *The Britannica Guide to Inventions That Changed the Modern World*. Britannica Educational Publishing.

Duignan, B. 2010. *The 100 Most Influential Philosophers of All Time*. Britannica Educational Publishing.

Encyclopedia Britannica 2009 Ultimate Reference Suite. 2009. Chicago: Encyclopedia Britannica.

Garyling, A. 2008. *The Britannica Guide to the Ideas That Made the Modern World: The People, Philosophy, and History of the Enlightenment*. Encyclopedia Britannica, Inc.

Gribbin, J. 2008. *The Britannica Guide to the 100 Most Influential Scientists*. Encyclopedia Britannica, Inc.

Kuiper, K. 2010. *The Britannica Guide to Theories and Ideas That Changed the Modern World*. Britannica Educational Publishing.

Kuiper, K. 2010. *The 100 Most Influential Painters & Sculptors of the Renaissance*. Britannica Educational Publishing.

Kuiper, K. 2010. *The 100 Most Influential Women of All Time*. Britannica Educational Publishing.

Kuiper, K. 2011. *Ancient Egypt From Prehistory to Islamic Conquest*. Britannica Educational Publishing.

Luebering, J. 2010. *The 100 Most Influential Writers of All Time*. Britannica Educational Publishing.

McKenna, A. 2010. *The 100 Most Influential World Leaders of All Time*. Britannica Educational Publishing.

Microsoft® Student 2009 [DVD]. 2008. WA: Microsoft Corporation.

Pletcher, K. 2010. *The Britannica Guide to Explorers and Explorations That Changed the Modern World*. Britannica Educational Publishing.

Shane, G. 1999. *It Could Have Happened: How Things Might Have Turned out if History Had a Sense of Humour*. Editions Soleil Publishing Inc.

Shapiro, F. 2006. *The Yale Book of Quotations*. Yale University Press.

拯救我的 SAT
写作

Saving My SAT
Essay